Contents

INTRODUCTION: More Language on Language?   v

PART ONE: PRODUCTIVE LEADERSHIP   1

CHAPTER ONE   Working Towards Working Together   1
CHAPTER TWO   Language Leadership Across the   30
                 Curriculum and Beyond the School

PART TWO: LEADERSHIP AND EXPERTISE   61

CHAPTER THREE   Producing Talk Together   63
CHAPTER FOUR   Producing Readings Together   81
CHAPTER FIVE   Producing Writing Together   103

PART THREE: REFLECTING ON LANGUAGE
AND EQUALITY   137

CHAPTER SIX   Flagging Issues   137

PART FOUR: SCAFFOLDING: PRODUCTIVE SUPPORT   155

CHAPTER SEVEN   Subject Expertise: Knowledge about 155
                 Language
CHAPTER EIGHT   Performance: Media Education,
                 Writers and Performers in School   167
CHAPTER NINE   Recording and Assessment   177
CHAPTER TEN   Resources   184

Reference Section   193
1. Useful Addresses   193
2. Glossary   195
3. Bibliography   198

INDEX   207

ACKNOWLEDGEMENTS

Our thanks to Alison Tucker, Jennifer Nias, Andy Hannan, Mike Newby, Bill Howitt, Alison Neely, Jan Savage, Sarah Payne, Catherine Lawes, Anthony Browne, Greta Telford, Kathryn Falkner, Pat Ashford, the late Howard Crosland and many others whose advice and support has made this book possible. Any faults it contains, however, are our own.

INTRODUCTION

More Language on Language?

This is not the first book for primary language leaders, but it is a new book for the Revised English Order nineties. It has its own model, which combines theory with practice, and it is written with the stressful demands made on primary- and middle-school teachers very much in mind. We have used the term language leader, but you may prefer the term language co-ordinator, language consultant, language arts leader, or even curriculum leader for language. Ultimately, the role is the same.

Unless this book has been recommended and you have bought it already you are probably browsing and glancing at this opening section, in library or bookshop, wondering if it can be of any use to you. If you are a nearly or newly-qualified teacher, then we hope that all of it will be of some use. For among other things it is meant to be a checklist of all the things that you as a potential or practising language leader will be thinking about at one time or another during your period of leadership. If you are an experienced teacher some of these chapters may appear to tell you things that you already know, and are already practising. If so, remember that what may seem obvious to you as, say, an early years' teacher, may be a source of great mystery to a language leader who has a Year Six class, or vice versa. For you these 'obvious chapters', and perhaps the whole book, will come as a reassurance. Even so, all the chapters are intended for all teachers, however experienced. For example, we would want you to use the practical activities in staff development sessions. We all need to be reminded what it is that others find difficult, particularly when they are things we take for granted. And it is likely that there are some chapters that deal with issues that you do want to think some more about. In fact we would be very surprised if any language leader was advancing on all these fronts at once: to do so would be superhuman!

Most teachers worry about how well they are doing their job. If they did not worry, they probably would not be so good. For many there is the additional worry of Key Stage assessments, of winning the approval of either Head, Inspectors and advisers, parents, or, not least, the children themselves. Ours is a profession of worriers.

What we have tried to do, to assuage some of those worries, is to address every possible aspect of the work that the perfect language leader would be doing. We know that no one will be an expert in all of the chapter headings listed on the contents page. The best thing to do is to choose one and make this your speciality. It will happen naturally in most cases. Person A will have a special interest in drama, person B in media education, person C in the provision of exciting and stimulating books across the school. All the other things must be addressed and not neglected, and it is the purpose of this book to show that although there are one or two chapters that might make you want to start out in a completely new direction, most nights, having glanced at the pages of this book, you will be able to go to bed, thinking 'Yes, I've done that, that and that − so there's not so much to worry about as I thought!'

Models of English

This book was written in England against the background of one of those titanic struggles between conflicting models of English. The fact that, because of the National Curriculum, we shall be using the term 'English' in the context of the primary school, where 'language' has been the term in use, suggests which model is in the ascendant. 'English' is a subject that fought its way onto the university curriculum in the late nineteenth century as a synonym for 'literature in English'. It is associated with a special series of activities, and one might have expected tremendous resistance from both secondary teachers who were questioning the appropriateness of this term for studies which increasingly included media texts, and primary teachers who are more comfortable with the notion of 'language' or 'language arts' which is something that permeates the curriculum. In Australia, where the discussion about a national curriculum is still at the planning stage, teachers are free from the burden of Key Stage assessments or a model of language imposed by central government. But in England the picture is complex and full of ironies. Two recent models of English − that proposed by the Kingman Committee and that recommended by the Cox Committee − attempted a consensus, drawing on what they saw as the best of traditional and so-called progressive practice. The Cox Report, *English 5-16*, was welcomed by most teachers who were relieved that it was not more rigid. It is true that it was subject to a rigorous critique by those who detected − and identified − what they saw as the politicisation of 'English' by a liberal hegemony, which, for example, took a patronising attitude to the 'self-expression' strand of primary education, separating it from the social needs which become the hallmark of education post 11, according to the Committee. Some of these ideas are developed in the essays in *English in the National Curriculum* (Ken Jones (ed.), 1992), and *English at the Core: Dialogue and Power in English Teaching* (Peter

Griffith, 1992), the latter a more theoretical analysis in the light of the work of Michel Foucault and Mikhail Bakhtin. Despite such murmurings of discontent, the general reaction to Kingman, and more significantly Cox, seemed to be a sigh of relief. For a brief period in 1990 and 1991 a mood of optimism was enjoyed by language and English teachers.

Meanwhile, the storm clouds had been gathering. As Kelly noted in 1990 (A. V. Kelly, 1990) the systematisation of subject knowledge in the National Curriculum represented 'a version of curriculum sharply at variance with that espoused in the primary mainstream during the last three decades' (Alexander, 1993, p. 27). At the same time, the model proposed by *English 5-16* was sharply attacked from the right by those who found fault with it on three fundamental grounds – it did not give enough prominence to Standard English, it was not specific about how children should be taught to read, and it did not subscribe clearly enough to the notion of a canon of great literature. In September 1992 the National Curriculum Council (as it then was) recommended to the Secretary of State for Education that the Order for English be rewritten, and followed this up with a series of recommendations in the Spring of 1993. Many of these recommendations, particularly those concerning the role of spoken Standard English, provoked a hostile response, and in September 1993 the NCC, now chaired by Sir Ron Dearing, produced a consultation report written in the light of some of these criticisms (NCC, 1993a). The Dearing Report (*The National Curriculum and its Assessment*, December 1993) recommends that the 1995 revised English Order should be based on this document. Meanwhile, teachers were advised to continue working from the existing Cox version of *English in the National Curriculum*. The actual model with which the UK will end up is anyone's guess. While the political argument continues to rage we shall now consider our own model.

Language and pedagogy: one model

When we started writing this book we had to make a decision. Did we want to describe the ideal world and the ideal school, or did we want to address the realities of school life which are often far from ideal, and have to take into account the sometimes acrimonious debate about what and how children should be taught. The key quesiton was 'Which approach would the language leader find most helpful?'

We decided that teachers would find it most helpful if all our discussions of curriculum and teaching methods took place with due regard to current experience and practice. We concluded that it would be reductive, cynical, unprofessional and most of all unhelpful to dwell on the many problems that beset education as we approach the millenium. On the other hand, to ignore the realities is to devalue the classroom teacher's experience, and to erect barriers between theory and practice that should never be there. We have compromised, therefore. Occasionally you will find us referring to inadequate buildings, overcrowded classes, inefficient Heads and less than enthusiastic colleagues. Since you have taken the trouble to buy this book, we know you are neither of the last two! Most of the time we shall be emphasising what can be done and what has been done. We always need to remind ourselves that what really matters is our enthusiasm or *enthousiasmos (Gk)*, the inspiration that comes from the god inside us. Education has to work through us: legislation can never by-pass teachers.

We have tried to express this in our own model, which combines three main ideological assumptions:

1. That learning takes place through the social medium of language when there is an emphasis on individuals or groups as *producers* of texts, rather than as consumers. This is our model for both childhood and adulthood.

2. That learning takes place in structured contexts, for which we shall use the term 'scaffolding', though going beyond the sense in which Bruner (1985) uses it. The word is now generally used to mean the supports and structures which allow building development to take place. In the school, scaffolding may be manifest in terms of classroom management, structured activities, or adults acting as practitioners and thus models. The scaffolding is thus formed from a combination of what we shall call 'texts', introduced by producer-learners, and involves an interactive process. Put simply, this means that children interrogate the texts which form the scaffolding, whether they are books, directions or performances given by fellow children or adults, or the demands of a task or assignment. In many cases the precise form of scaffolding will be chosen by the children themselves through their selection of texts, form and audience. In all cases, the selection process itself will be the subject of discussion and, like the builder, the more the child builds the higher he or she gets.

3. That the human element is acknowledged best by the model of the 'reflective teacher', who will be actively involved in the production of texts, and constantly assessing and evaluating the products

themselves in the light of the response of a critical audience. As we indicate above, the texts can range from lesson plans to the teacher's own creative and research writing.

These three activities — production, scaffolding, reflection — clearly interact with one another, and are frequently simultaneous. Running through them all is the common thread of language, and at the heart of these activities is the learning process itself — in which children, teachers and other adults are engaged. This can be represented diagrammatically:

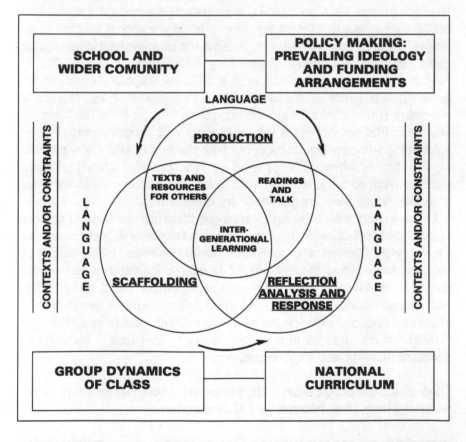

Proposed model for language leaders: children and teachers as producers and learners

In arriving at this model we have clearly drawn on a number of theories of learning. The emphasis on production has its roots in Piaget's cognitive theory, which sees children as active makers of the world, applying their intelligence to problems in ways that reflect both their development and an acquired ability to modify their understanding in the light of experience (Paiget, 1953). By identifying language with the circumferences of the intersecting circles we mean to suggest its transforming nature, which is recognised in Vygotsky's linguistic model (Vygotsky, 1962). For until language is acquired, and form given to the world through it, intellectual development and control over the world remains extremely limited. Language not only permeates the three zones, it offers boundaries or concepts which allow interaction to take place. This interaction suggests the pedagogical model proposed by Bruner (Bruner 1986 and 1987), with its emphasis on the social and collaborative nature of learning. Not only do we accept that the child learns by interacting with others, but that the inter-generational contact should be seen as a mutually enriching experience, with the adult to be seen as a learner and producer at a different stage of development. In other words, the model of the teacher as producer and learner is necessary if the child is to get the maximum benefit from the learning situation. For not only is it the adult who will produce much of the scaffolding within which learning can take place, it is adults who provide models for children. The productive teacher who clearly derives pleasure from reading, writing, and talking and listening validates those activities when they are practised by children.

Other writers who have influenced our thinking are Donald Graves and James Moffett, with their emphasis on language as a process, and Courtney B. Cazden who in *Whole Language Plus* (1992) offers us ways of reconciling the concept of language immersion and whole language experience with the occasional need for scaffolding, skills and textual models. Finally, our model incorporates some of the elements contained in the 'learning cycle' of Kolb, Rubin and McIntyre (1979), with its emphasis on active learning, reflection, conceptualisation and experimentation.

Towards production: classroom management and managing the National Curriculum

In emphasising the importance of language, we would not go so far as those who seem to argue that we *are* language! This is a philosophical issue which we address later, but for now we will concentrate on the empirical aspects of language, and more specifically, the paralinguistic aspects of learning. As Macnamara (1972) points out, there are such things as non-linguistic cues which children respond to when they learn, whether it is pictures in a picture book or the gestures of the teacher. The very way we manage the classroom is a powerful agent of learning. Whether you are an experienced teacher, or just about to start your first year of teaching, you will have quickly come to see the value of advertising your own classroom as a place in which language is celebrated through displays, the prominence given to books, and the plentiful evidence of children's writing and book-making. Similarly, you will know that the success with which you manage your own class

---

Practical activity: discussing classroom management.

In pairs, and then groups, discuss your response to the following questionnaire. Tick the box which matches your opinion.

In classroom management each of the following is essential:

Sense of humour

| Strongly agree | Agree | Neutral | Disagree | Strongly disagree |

Giving praise for good behaviour

| Strongly agree | Agree | Neutral | Disagree | Strongly disagree |

Prevention of noisy chatter

| Strongly agree | Agree | Neutral | Disagree | Strongly disagree |

Prevention of movement without permission

| Strongly agree | Agree | Neutral | Disagree | Strongly disagree |

Scanning to ensure children are on task

| Strongly agree | Agree | Neutral | Disagree | Strongly disagree |

Clarity and consistency of classroom rules

| Strongly agree | Agree | Neutral | Disagree | Strongly disagree |

In groups, discuss what you would add to this list.

In pairs, consider the following:
What are the strengths of your partner's teaching and classroom management?
What do you think of the following conclusions reached by the discussion paper written and published in England by Alexander, Rose and Woodhead (1992), the so-called 'Three Wise Men':

1. Group work may be too difficult for trainee teachers to organise.
2. There are many occasions when whole-class teaching is desirable.
3. Tasks should be appropriately demanding.
4. There should be regular checks that children are actually learning what they are supposed to be learning.
5. In future, to cope with the subject demands of the National Curriculum, all teachers should be proficient in the three core subject areas.
6. Non-teaching Heads and Deputies should each take on two subject specialist leadership responsibilities.

will have a great bearing on your effectiveness as a language leader in the school.

Even if it was desirable, no book can tell anyone how to teach, any more than a book can tell you how to ride a bicycle (both perilous, but ultimately liberating activities). A book such as *Teaching in the Primary School* (Galton, 1989) offers, in its own words, 'a review of current teaching methods and curriculum practice against the reality of classroom practice and recent educational objectives and policies'. It does not prescribe, but in quoting from teachers who are effective in classroom management it demonstrates what can be done. In *Organizing for Learning in the Primary Classroom* (1991) Janet Moyles describes, among other things, how a successful classroom can be organised, offering clear advice based on experience, and management about straightforward but important things, such as making sure that the children can see the teacher, adult assistance in the classroom, the need for things to be tidied away with the children knowing exactly where they are kept, and children's independence and autonomy.

Managing the National Curriculum

This section is clearly not about teaching to the National Curriculum across the board — you have either been doing that for several years or are just about to start. The problem of fitting it all in, described in *Breadth and Balance in the National Curriculum* (Campbell (ed.), 1993) will be familiar to you, whether you have had one year's experience or ten. This is more specifically about how to make sure that all the National Curriculum English targets are being covered, and that when it comes to assessment your colleagues are as well informed as you about the structure of the Order for 'English in the National Curriculum'. The original Order has five strands:

1. Speaking and listening
2. Reading
3. Writing
4. Spelling
5. Handwriting

The NCC Consultation Report of September 1993 proposes that these are reduced to three:

1. Speaking and listening

2. Reading
3. Writing (including spelling, grammar and handwriting)

The original Order separates Writing from Spelling (Attainment Target 4) and Handwriting (Attainment Target 5) and that remains in force at least until 1995.

One simple way of promoting awareness of the scope of the National Curriculum for English would be to run a staff development session on a non-pupil day, comparing the May 1989 document with that of September 1993, highlighting a relatively straightforward issue like the number of strands.

The reflective language leader

It is all to easy to get bogged down in the mire of administrative detail. We find we are spending all our time responding and reacting, and there is no time at all for reflection and an overview. Teacher initiative is depressed, and educational change is driven by a bureaucracy, rather than educational experiment. Yet why do we assume that a primary-school language leader needs to be reflective and analytical, as well as productive and well organised?

We have come a long way since John Dewey (1933) first related reflective thinking to the education process but now, as we approach the end of the century, the models of the reflective practitioner (Schon, 1983) and the reflective teacher (Pollard and Tann, 1987) are the ones that have found increasing acceptance among teachers, though we must be careful not to imply that being reflective is something new, or that reflection without action is of any use at all. In the intervening years since Dewey there was, firstly, a move towards the child-centred model of education associated with Piaget and celebrated in the Plowden Report of 1967, and more recently a loudly voiced reaction to the notion of child centredness. One consequence of this has been to give more prominence to the idea of whole class management, and another to focus attention on assessment. In some ways the movement in primary education parallels the movement in secondary English, in that a challenge to an orthodoxy led to a consensus, which was in turn challenged and made problematical from within and from without − by the forces of light and the forces of darkness. In England the two movements have not been synchronised: the assumptions behind F. R. Leavis's emphasis on a close reading of the text and the importance of the teacher as transmitter of culture (Leavis and Thompson, 1933), was being quietly challenged in France (Barthes, 1953) long before the Plowden Report's vision of a modern child-centred primary school (Central Advisory Council on Education, 1967) was endorsing the findings of child psychologists such as Piaget (1926). Yet in the way that a former 'broad consensus on the characteristics of "good practice". . . has now been shattered' (Pollard and Tann, 1987, p. 6), there are similarities between the pendulum swings in both primary and secondary English, not least in the feeling that we are in the middle of a very long earthquake.

It is in the context of such seismic movements that primary and middle school teachers with a curriculum responsibility for what the National Curriculum calls English have to make their way. It is not easy to journey through a landscape in which the signposts have either disappeared or are pointing the wrong way, or are so numerous that they obscure one another. That is why the model of the reflective teacher is such an important one, because it assumes a practitioner who has reflected, developed strategies, and subjected these strategies to further reflection to assess exactly how successful they have been in achieving what was intended. It acknowledges the intelligence, independence and professional expertise of the teacher. Although this seems to call for a considerable degree of autonomy and self-reliance, the reflective teacher is not alone, as she or he works in what should be the supportive and collegial environment of the school; in the case of the English Curriculum Leader, there may be access to advisers, associations such as NATE, Academic Councils or Pyramids, higher education institutions and networks of language specialists from other schools who may meet under a variety of umbrellas. Unfortunately, many of these extramural supports are themselves under threat, either through under-funding or because teachers just do not have the time to attend out-of-school meetings on a regular basis. It is partly in recognition of the reduction in these support services that we have written this book, which is offered as a kind of map to help you negotiate your way across this confusing landscape. We hope that at times you will find it reassuring, at other times challenging, but at all times useful.

An important footnote

Finally, a note on how the book is organised and how it is to be used. The book is informed by the model of learning we have just described, in that each of the three parts includes the three elements of production, reflection and scaffolding, but with a particular emphasis on one of them. Similarly, each chapter acts as a scaffold, begins with an emphasis on understanding through reflection and analysis, and then moves on 'towards production'. In addition, each chapter contains one or more practical activities. Some of these are ideas to be tried out with children in or out of school, but the majority are ideas for non-pupil-day staff development sessions that you may wish to lead in your school.

PART ONE: PRODUCTIVE LEADERSHIP

CHAPTER ONE
Working Towards Working Together

1.1. Reflection and analysis

As the pace of administrative and curricular change in education continues unabated, and as more and more is demanded of primary-school staff, it is the exceptional teacher who does not at times feel overburdened, and in need of encouragement and recognition. To take on a leadership role at such a time would seem to many an act of masochism, and yet curriculum leaders have a crucial role to play in the new model of primary education which is currently unfolding. In this chapter we shall consider how powerful and pivotal language is, with a view to devising ways in which the widespread public and political concern about standards can be used to the primary school's advantage. After a brief historical sketch chronicling the emergence of the language co-ordinator in the primary school we shall consider what is meant by the term 'leadership', and what is expected of the leader under an approach to primary education which gives great emphasis to the idea of a subject leader. We shall try to demythologise the concept of leadership by breaking it down into a number of characteristics, many of which will already be in your repertoire. If you think 'But I am doing that already', that is the precise point of this book: to validate and endorse practices already in place. We all know that these professional practices *are* in place, that teachers do not need to be told how to do their jobs, but it is sometimes necessary to state this with reference to relevant research as a strategy to support the practices that have been devised and developed in schools. At the same time we shall be addressing the concerns, expressed by many newly appointed language leaders, about taking on the role of teaching adults through staff development sessions, and we shall explore briefly some of the strategies that facilitate adult learning. Finally we shall focus on the crucial importance of the kind of school that you are working in, the network of relationships that characterise the ideal of the 'whole-school' approach, and the very real obstacles that often stand in the way of realising the collegial ideal.

The language volcano

We get an insight into the political and economic importance of language only occasionally. But as with a volcano, when language issues do surface and enter the public domain, they do so with a force that is devastating. Over the past few years we need only to look at the polarisation caused by the debate in England over the LINC project materials, the confrontational reporting of the issues of reading methods and political correctness, the furore over spelling and grammar following Prince Charles's comments about his staff, and the tabloid coverage given to the appearance of the Frederick Forsyth novel on an A-level syllabus to see the violent emotions that can be stirred. In 1993 all these issues erupted over, firstly, the issue of assessment in English at Key Stage 3, and then, even more spectacularly, over the revision to the Order for English. The treatment of the issues has often be trivial and distorted, which is a serious and difficult problem. But looked at another way, this struggle over what it is that constitutes an appropriate agenda for English is very revealing. What all this demonstrates is that politicians, newspaper editors, members of the Royal Family and Prime Ministers all seem to be much more concerned about language, than say, science, which seems to attract much less public criticism. Instead of feeling threatened by this we should feel flattered — for these controversies show how access to, and the ownership of, language is clearly and demonstrably linked to power, otherwise it would not move the passions so. In developing a whole-school approach to language we are therefore very much in the business of empowering children. And as a language leader, over the next few years, you will be instrumental in shaping the destiny of at least a thousand people who will be the adults of the twenty-first century. It is such a powerful job that some would see the under-funding of education and attempts to erode the teacher's status as unconscious attempts to limit this power. Whether or not that is the case, we should never forget that the job of shaping of society. Hence the pyrotechnics.

1.2 A short history: what is language for?

Before the era of mass education, terms like language and literature were less familiar than terms like rhetoric and the classics, which formed the proper study of the young gentleman. Educating girls and the poor was not thought to be necessary, and many regarded education as a dangerous thing if it got into the wrong hands. The rise of capitalism modified this view. Since the middle of the Industrial Revolution there has been a specific anxiety about literacy. In the years leading up to 1870 it was feared that if Britain did not have a literate population she would be economically disadvantaged. Such utilitarian concerns have continued to this day, but, in the twentieth century, the idea of reading and writing for pleasure is encouraged by the availability of cheap books, and the recognition of the importance of leisure and personal development. At the same time, with the expansion of education, particularly further and higher education, literacy becomes the key to advancement, and the first step on the route to tertiary colleges, polytechnics or universities.

Although we can trace these developments in Britain in such reports as the Newbolt Report (1921) and the Plowden Report (1967), it was the Bullock Report (DES, 1975) which finally recognised the central place of language in schools, and advanced the concept of language across the curriculum. This proposal led to the establishment of language co-ordinators in both primary and secondary schools, and these co-ordinators were charged with raising awareness of the importance of language teaching, encouraging every teacher to see him or herself as a teacher of language, whether by interest and specialism they were scientists, mathematicians or historians. In other countries, such co-ordinators have been called language consultants, or, less simply, curriculum leaders in the language arts. Their roles have become increasingly demanding. In England, the dual importance of cross-school collaboration and a greater degree of role specialisation, has been reinforced by the need to implement the National Curriculum, as a major study in Leeds has recently shown (Primary Education in Leeds: Primary Needs Independent Evaluation Project, 1991).

Another reason why it became essential to have a language co-ordinator was the enormous expansion in the provision of children's books. In the sixties and seventies there was a sudden flowering of well-written, attractively illustrated books for children, which were cheap enough for schools to buy in considerable numbers. Book corners and school libraries flourished, and became a feature of every primary-school classroom.

In the eighties, with a greater awareness of multicultural education and bilingualism, publishers and schools responded, and this has meant another responsibility for the language co-ordinator: not just *language* across the curriculum, but *languages* and *literatures* across the curriculum. At the same time another movement has gained a great deal of publicity. This movement, which favours a return to an earlier model of teaching and learning, has had an exceptionally strong influence on the way that the curriculum is to be assessed, and in some cases on the way that the National Curriculum Orders have been revised. For it is the introduction of the National Curriculum, following the Education Act of 1988, and the modification of the English Order, only three years after the original document, that has had a much greater impact on the role of language leaders than might at first have been imagined. Far from removing the need for curriculum leaders, the National Curriculum has given them more responsibilities. With the emphasis on subject knowledge, accountability and assessment the curriculum leader has to have subject expertise, be prepared to report to parents and governors, and work with the staff on issues such as the assessment of curriculum performance. All this on top of keeping abreast of current developments in your specialist field, and evaluating what is good and bad about what is being done in the school currently. As the person with responsibility for language you will be subject to conflicting pressures which frequently push you in entirely different directions. In these circumstances, even to stay on your feet calls for considerable skills and inner resources!

First term as language leader: consolidating your own interests

We have probably made the position of language leader sound much more intimidating than is intended. If you are not experienced, and feel overwhelmed by the sheer range of messages about language in education, begin by setting yourself modest, reliable targets. If at times you just don't know what these might be, or where to begin, take heart from the following. If there is one idea that underpins this book it is this: always start from what interests *you* and use this interest as the foundation of your professional development — hence the model of the productive, reflective teacher. Maybe you are a great lover of fiction, in which case you could start with some fiction-based topic work, built around a shared text such as *The Very Hungry Caterpillar, Piggybook, Carrie's War* or *The Machine Gunners*. It may be that you like playing around and experimenting with language, and enjoy working with children on poems in some of the ways suggested by Michael Rosen in *Did I Hear Your Write?* Perhaps, like the Year 4 teacher in the case study below, your consuming interest is not specific to language at all, but is cross-curricular.

Case study: the Earth Summit

I am particularly interested in the environment, and the summer term was a particularly good time to develop this theme because the Earth Summit was taking place in Brazil. I belong to Friends of the Earth and in their magazine they printed leaf sillhouettes which they invited readers to cut out and fill in, and send off to the Summit. This gave me an idea, so I used the leaf in a template and the children wrote two leaf letters which they then cut out. One was sent to the Prime Minister and the other to Brazil. On one side they wrote what they wanted Governments to do to help the environment, and one thing they as children were prepared to do (such as saving newspapers, turning off unnecessary lights, and so on).

This led to a whole series of activities – in technology the children designed and made receptacles for recycling items ranging from cans to toilet rolls, in maths they produced graphs showing how many cans were sold each day in local shops, and in history we looked at health, smoking, and the introduction of tobacco to England.

What this teacher is too modest to say is that it led to some marvellous displays of original language work, and the letter-writing project, with its real audience and real purpose, seized the imagination of the whole school. Soon every class was involved, and a massive 'Tree of Life', with hundreds of letter leaves on it, was displayed in the foyer. The teacher's own class had a reply from the Prime Minister's office, and this was put on display and discussed. In this one example we have the teacher as producer generating ideas and structures, the children as producers generating letters, ideas and their own structures, and the two generations meeting as reflective learners in the way that we have indicated in our model.

It clearly makes sense to start from your own interests, and then to draw on the strengths of others once you have got things under way. It should come as no surprise that in writing this book we have drawn on the help of others, particularly for the chapter on I.T., and drama, as these are areas in which we know others are more experienced. No one is going to be good at everything, and part of the mission of a successful school is to build up a team which is able to offer something in every department. As language leader you will play to your strengths, like the teacher quoted above. It is only then, when you have constructed a programme of work for the term or year, that you will want to reflect on the extent to which it has offered children opportunities to explore the aspects of language work considered in the separate chapters of this book. In reflecting on your own 'scaffolding' programme, you will not want to lose sight of the theoretical issues that arise from the questions 'What am I trying to achieve?' and 'Does this programme give children the scope to achieve objectives?'

1.3 An aerial reconnaissance: flying over the language volcano

Let us assume that the first term is over, you have a fairly good relationship with your class, and you are beginning to get to know one or two of your colleagues quite well. It is time for a breather, and so we shall indulge in a little imaginative excursion to view the topography, including the language volcano.

If we chartered a plane and took a brief flight over the metaphorical landscape of the curriculum, we might feel we had no use for any maps. We already possess a set of files which describe the terrain, and we could indeed use the National Curriculum document for English to help us identify some of the more salient features to those of us with a special interest in language. These features include the twin peaks of reading and writing, the mighty rivers called speaking and listening, the graceful synclinal folds of handwriting and presentation, and the small, idiosyncratic but much commented upon surface deposit called spelling. But this would allow a map which has been designed to concentrate on discrete aspects of the landscape to dictate the way that we see what lies before us. In so doing we may miss many other features, not least the beautiful wholeness of the scene, or the way that the dominant Mount Writing leaves unexplored valleys in its shadow. And what about all the rich minerals that are hidden beneath the surface? Let us for the moment leave the National Curriculum in the locker.

A more reflective approach to our flight might be to take off in our light aircraft equipped with a set of questions — questions about exactly what can be expected of a curriculum leader who can act as a guide as we make our way across this landscape. These questions take the language leader well beyond her or his first term when the priority was simply to develop personal interests and get to know the staff. They help us to start thinking in years rather than months, long-term ambitions as well as short-term goals.

Having focussed our minds, we shall land this plane and ground this metaphor, carrying these questions with us and keeping them in the front of our minds. Aware now of the terrain we shall be crossing, we must turn our attention to the team we shall be working with, and the kind of leadership role that will be necessary to make a successful journey. In plain, unmetaphorical language, we shall now take a serious look at the meaning of leadership, for which some may wish to read the word 'consultancy'.

1.4 Working together: the issue of leadership

In their fifth report on the implementation of the Leeds Primary Needs Programme (Alexander *et al.*, 1989) the authors identified four distinct ways in which co-ordinators undertook their curriculum responsibilities. These were:

  − as *Curriculum Managers* involved in overall school curriculum policy as part of a senior management team
  − as *Curriculum Consultants* responsible for the school-wide review and development of a specific subject or subjects (so called 'specialists')
  − as *Curriculum Enhancers* working collaboratively with other staff in a class or year group to support development, inject new ideas and serve as a catalyst for change
  − as *Curriculum Facilitators* having no direct engagement in curriculum development processes themselves but releasing other staff to undertake this work

In attempting to define the specific demands made of the language leader, it may be helpful to look at ways in which management theory has attempted to characterise the role of curriculum leaders in general. In *Management in Education* (Clark, 1993) the following distinction is made:

MANAGING YOURSELF _____ MANAGING OTHERS

Jim Campbell (1991) makes another distinction:

CURRICULUM SKILLS _____ INTERPERSONAL SKILLS

Under curriculum skills Campbell lists the following:

  i) Knowledge of subject: how up to date are you on current developments in language teaching?

ii) Professional skills: devising, introducing, maintaining and assessing a programme of work.

iii) Professional judgement: matching the programme to children's development and abilities.

Under interpersonal skills the following are listed:

i) Social skills: ability to work with colleagues, inspire confidence through leadership, advise probationers, and so on.

ii) External representation: this involves talking (to parents, governors, advisers and so on) about the subject on which he or she has expertise.

The two pairs of skills identified jointly by Clark and Campbell can be combined in the following model:

```
                    MANAGING YOURSELF
                           ∧
                           ∧
                           ∧
CURRICULUM<<<<<<<<<<<<<<<<<>>>>>>>>>>>INTERPERSONAL
SKILLS                     ∨                  SKILLS
                           ∨
                           ∨
                    MANAGING OTHERS
```

These four elements clearly interact. Self-management will impinge on interpersonal skills, and will in turn be supported by your curriculum and teaching skills. All three elements will contribute to your ability to manage others, and if you see them as a series of stepping stones the idea of managing others will not seem so intimidating. Nevertheless, the teaching of adults − colleagues, parents and governors − is the one aspect of the curriculum leader's role that is seen as a particular source of anxiety, and so we shall complete this section by touching on the subject of adult learning, even though this is only one aspect of team leadership.

Self-management

Managing the self involves such issues as the following:

EFFECTIVE CONTROL OF TIME

SETTING ATTAINABLE OBJECTIVES: short, medium and long term

BEING ORGANISED

PLANNING

Some teachers have suggested that it is also useful to keep a stress log, and to give yourself a personal reward as a means of sustaining motivation and re-inforcing a sense of achievement. Planning has an equally fundamental role. All teachers are experienced in the art of curriculum planning and the production of schemes of work for English is an automatic part of overall class preparation. But language leaders need to plan on another level, to ensure effective time management and the identification of realistic goals. Time management simply involves drawing up a short-term and medium-term timetable to which you then stick. If you are working on a reading policy, for example, your week-by-week targets may involve talking to a different member of staff each week, your term's target may involve drawing up a short discussion paper following these conversations, and your target for the year may be to produce an agreed reading policy. Some people find it helpful to draw diagrams of their week, of the weeks of the term and of the year to show when they intend to set aside time for the targets they have set themselves, when they intend to have 'free time', and when all the demands of class teaching will have to occupy them. Targets can be ticked off to show that tasks have been completed — something which can be very gratifying!

Many teachers think that much depends on the ability to be well organised. This aspect of leadership may easily be forgotten, but it is crucial. Good self-management is informed by curriculum expertise, which for the language leader simply means being conversant with the issues and approaches that we explore in the chapters. In those chapters we offer a survey of theory and practice of talking, listening, reading and writing, and the cross-curricular language implications of drama and Information Technology.

Managing others: interpersonal skills

As we discuss in the second part of this chapter, it is the relationships within the school that determine the degree to which curriculum leaders make an impact. Some schools have an outlook which is receptive to change, and if you are working in a school where there is a culture of collaboration, innovation and mutual support, then your job will probably be less demanding. Whatever the kind of school, the curriculum leader's interpersonal skills — the way we approach, treat and respond to other adults — will contribute to her or his success. These skills come into operation in the following leadership situations:

PROBLEM SOLVING	RUNNING MEETINGS
INITIATING PROJECTS	CONSULTANCY
PERSUADING SCEPTICAL MEMBERS OF STAFF	REPORTING TO GOVERNORS
REPORTING TO PARENTS	DISCUSSIONS WITH HEAD/DEPUTY
TEACHING ALONGSIDE COLLEAGUES	RUNNING STAFF DEVELOPMENT SESSIONS

In all these situations it is clearly helpful if our self-image is reasonably good, and if we successfully convey the impression that we are interested in other people and what they have to say, but at the same time sincerely hold the beliefs which justify our suggestions for change.

Problems and obstacles

In the mid 1980s, as Alexander's commentary on his Leeds report (1992) shows, one of the main obstacles to the effectiveness of the curriculum leaders was his or her exclusion from the decision-making process, including curriculum policy. With the arrival of the National Curriculum, following the 1988 Education Reform Act, schools inevitably found themselves automatically developing a more collective policy-making approach and this particular obstacle receded. Another major difficulty is that of time, or rather the lack of it. The report *Curriculum Organisation and Classroom Practice in Primary Schools* (Ofsted, 1993) acknowledged this:

> Most of the schools had curriculum co-ordinators with clearly defined roles. In a significant number of the schools, their influence on teachers' planning was evident. However, due to a lack, or poor use, of non-contact time they were able to take little part in the monitoring of work in the classrooms. (paragraph 17, p. 11)

Alexander (1992) notes that in Leeds one of the most powerful devices for monitoring curriculum improvement was the practice of collaborative teaching (what the report called 'Team Teaching Together'), but in reality most language leaders will be unable to introduce team teaching to schools where it is not already the practice. Alexander notes the worrying tendency for clear links to be observable between particular curriculum leadership posts, and status and gender. In the Leeds study a disproportionate number of female language leaders were not in senior management positions, although the post had more status than art and music where postholders were largely MPGs. Another problem is LEA support, which, where it is not fast diminishing for reasons of funding (the 'funding arrangements' context for learning shown in our model), tends to be more generous for mathematics than language.

Similar problems are described by Campbell (1991) who carried out a number of case studies and summed up the difficulties faced by curriculum co-ordinators as follows:

1. Ambiguity in relationships with other classteachers, whose view of classroom autonomy clashed with the whole-school responsibility of the co-ordinator;
2. Conflicting priorities, mainly arising out of inadequate time and facilities for carring out the co-ordination action role as well as more normal classroom teaching duties;
3. Uncertainty in performing the role of 'educationalist', that is, in articulating the reasons, justifications and 'theory' of a subject in workshop setting, or in representing the rationale of the subject to colleagues, teachers in other schools and to governors.

It is this last problem which we shall now address.

Adult Learning

As well as teaching children, language leaders have to continue their own learning, and extend their teaching repertoire to include adults. Such teaching takes place in hardly the most propitious circumstances: staff development sessions often take place straight after a hard day in school, with colleagues who are all too aware of the marking and preparation that still awaits them that evening. Presentations to governors or parents may well take place in tiny staffrooms or draughty halls. Perhaps the first practical step to take is to ensure that tea and biscuits are available on arrival. Many teachers use overhead projector transparencies to help structure their presentations, and this is a way of overcoming the anxiety of speaking in front of those who have a great deal of influence over the development of one's career! Running a meeting is a difficult skill, and in the Leeds study Alexander (1992) observed the following characteristics of successful meetings:

- a clearly understood and stated purpose
- an agreed focus and/or agenda
- a clear structure, moving from analysis of a problem or need through to a conclusion and decision
- support from the Head, though the meeting was not necessarily led by him/her
- on complex issues, some kind of prepared oral or written input – if the latter, then preferably in advance
- someone, not necessarily the Head, taking a chairing or leading role
- genuine rather than token involvement of all those attending, with particular attention paid to staff reluctant to press their case and those inclined to view the proceeding with suspicion or disdain
- individual preparedness to submit to the disciplines of
(a) sticking to the point
(b) decentring from one's own particular preoccupations and situation to the wider issue at hand
(c) resisting the urge to hog the proceedings
- a recognisable outcome in the form of decisions or documentation.
(Alexander, 1992, p.36)

Now that we have reminded ourselves – if any reminder were needed – of the problems and obstacles that the language leader will inevitably encounter at one time or another, let us consider in a little more detail what exactly the language leader can be expected to do.

What language leaders do

In the same article cited above, R. J. Campbell includes the table which appears opposite indicating the range and frequency of language leader roles in ten school-based curriculum initiatives.

Many teachers find the ordering and auditing of resources one of the most time-consuming aspects of the job, but have found it possible to enlist the help of the classroom assistant. There is more about this in Chapter 10.

Reflection: your own vision of your role

An important preliminary to active leadership is the articulation of your own beliefs. Let us approach this through a practical activity which invites you to reflect on what you consider to be the aims and methods of language work in the primary and/or middle school.

Skills involved in school-based curriculum development	Case Study									
	1	2	3	4	5	6	7	8	9	10
I. CURRICULUM SKILLS										
a. Subject Knowledge										
1. updating subject knowledge	/	/		/		/	/	/		/
2. identifying conceptual structure of subject(s)	/		/			/	/	/		
3. identifying skills in subject(s)	/		/	/		/	/	/	/	/
b. Professional skills										
4. reviewing existing practice	/	/	/	/	/	/	/	/	/	/
5. constructing scheme/programme	/	/	/	/	/	/	/	/	/	/
6. implementing scheme/programme		/	/	/	/	/	/	/	/	/
7. assessing scheme/programme	/	/	/	/	/	/			/	
c. Professional judgements										
8. deciding between available resources	/	/	/	/	/	/	/	/	/	/
9. deciding about methods	/	/	/	/	/	/	/	/	/	/
10. identifying links between subjects	/	/	/			/	/	/		
11. ordering, maintaining resources	/	/	/			/	/	/	/	/
12. relating subject to its form in other schools	/		/	/		/			/	
II. INTERPERSONAL SKILLS										
d. Working with colleagues										
13. leading workshops/discussions	/	/	/	/	/	/	/	/		
14. translating material into comprehensible form	/	/	/	/	/	/	/	/		
15. liaising with Head and/or senior staff	/	/	/	/	/	/	/	/	/	/
16. advising colleagues informally	/	/	/	/	/	/	/	/	/	/
17. teaching alongside colleagues	/					/	/	/	/	
18. visiting colleagues' classes to see work in progress	/	/							/	
19. maintaining colleagues' morale, reducing anxiety, etc	/		/			/	/			
20. dealing with professional disagreement	/	/	/	/		/				
e. External representation										
21. consulting advisers, university staff, etc	/	/		/	/	/				/
22. consulting teachers in other schools	/			/		/				/

Range of skills expected of the curriculum co-ordinators in 10 school-based curriculum developments

---

Practical Activity 1.1

Concentrating on the realm of language, what are the needs of children, and what are the needs of teachers, as we enter the twenty-first century?

Children	*You*
Specific skills?	Specific skills?
Specific knowledge?	Specific knowledge?
Opportunities for creativity?	Opportunities for creativity?
Specific strategies?	Specific strategies?
Pleasure and enjoyment?	Pleasure and enjoyment?
Specific resources?	Specific resources?

It would be useful to complete your own checklist, reflecting on the world in which we live and the world of the twenty-first century for which we are preparing children. Note down under each heading what you think primary phase children need, and what you as a teacher and language leader need to be properly prepared for autonomous and independent adulthood in the twenty-first century. In some cases it may be easier to identify children's needs before your own. For example, under 'opportunities for creativity' it may be quite easy to list the opportunities for story-making, drama and what Michael Rosen calls 'memorable speech' (Rosen, 1989) that children are entitled to, whereas your own role as a writer, performer and reader may be more problematic. How important is it that you as a teacher *experiment* with language as well as ask the children to do so? Most important of all, there are the twin issues of leadership and expertise, issues that were signalled in the title of this section. To what extent do the staff in your school look to you for leadership, and to what extent do you see yourself as a leader? To what extent do the staff look to you for expert advice when it comes to language diagnoses, and to what extent do you see this as part of your role? Answers to these questions amount to a statement of beliefs and the articulation of an agenda. There will be plenty of points here to reflect on, or discuss with your colleagues in a pre-season non-teaching-day language session. This could be the subject of the first meeting of that year in which you act as curriculum co-ordinator, and could be brief and exploratory.

1.5. The role and purpose of the language leader

Let us explore in a little more detail that crucially important first step: deciding in your own mind what the role and purpose of the language leader really is.

As one of the school's curriculum leaders you will be working in the context of what Alexander (1992) calls the repertoire of curriculum development strategies. These include:

- Defining school and teacher needs:
  staff meetings
  guidelines for internal review and development in schools (GRIDS), McMahon *et al.* (1984)
  appraisal interviews

- Delegating responsibility:
  establishing co-ordinating teams or working parties
  drafting of guidelines or policy statement by staff members

- Extending expertise
  attending courses
  requesting support from the advisory service
  visiting other schools
  inviting outside experts to talk to/work with staff

- Staff discussion
  staff meetings
  workshops
  training days
  informal discussion
  structural small group discussion
  collective formulation of guidelines or policy statements

- Classroom activity
  collaborative teaching (TTT)
  year-group planning

(Alexander, 1992, pp. 35–6)

The evolution of the curriculum leader in the primary school is well documented, and well summarised by R. J. Campbell in *Developing the Primary School Curriculum* (1985). As Campbell points out, curriculum post-holders are assumed to have a degree of 'specialist knowledge' or 'subject expertise' in primary schools which have been traditionally 'generalist' in organisation and ideology. The implied tension that this creates, is exacerbated for the language curriculum post-holder, who, in Michael Rosen's words, is operating in 'the eye of the storm' over language. Because there is such a furious debate about such issues as reading methods, spelling, grammar, and so on, the curriculum post-holder must have a very clear idea about her or his role and purpose, and so this is a subject we should address very early on.

Practical Activity 1.2

List all the things you have to do, or expect to have to do, as Curriculum Leader for Language, in the context of your school.

Then compare your notes with what follows.

As language leader you will want to be constantly reminding your Headteacher and visiting advisers and inspectors of your many, many roles, which probably include the following:

1. Encouragement
Supported by the National Curriculum document for English, you will be encouraging colleagues in your schools to implement your examples of good practice.

2. Consistency
You will be wanting to ensure that there is a consistent approach across the school in terms of such things as a reading and writing policy, and a method of record keeping.

3. Initiatives
You will be the one proposing and encouraging school-based curriculum initiatives in the area of language, trying out new ideas, setting up book clubs and arranging book weeks, introducing whole school events so that the staff work together as a language team.

4. Briefing
You will want to brief your colleagues on things you have picked up from conferences, inset sessions, NATE meetings and correspondence you have received. You will also want to brief your Head on all the proposals and developments that are taking place, so that she or he is fully aware of just how much is going on!

5. Resourcing
You obviously have a major role to play in the ordering of books, radio and television programme booklets, tape recorders, computers, video cameras and language record cards right across the school.

6. Library liaison
You will have an important link with the schools section of your nearest

town library, and will negotiate with them over the circulation of book packs, Good Books Roadshows, and library visits — both of children to the schools section and librarians to the school. You will also wish to ensure that provision to maintain these resources is continued as the 'library' resource capitation devolves from county to school.

7. Representation
You will be attending meetings, representing the school in local consortia of language leaders. You will also liaise with any primary language advisers who may be assigned to your area, although such creatures are an endangered species.

8. Parent liaison
This will be on both an informal basis, and a more formal basis, for example a meeting may be called to explain to new parents the partnership approach to reading, and what it means for them and their children.

9. Policy writing
Policy documents need to be revised regularly, and you will be working with governors and staff to ensure this happens.

10. Gender and Multicultural Issues
Arising from this you will want to discuss with colleagues their thoughts on gender and multicultural issues in relation to their approach to language.

11. Knowledge about language
You will need to have some knowledge of the way that the language is structured and organised: did you receive a good grounding during your initial teacher education course, or does your knowledge need to be extended and updated?

12. Awareness — having it and spreading it
Finally, and more fundamentally, you will want to have an awareness of what approach your colleagues adopt, and if that approach is one which you consider ready for re-examination; an awareness of sensitive ways in which you can discuss changes; and be a positive influence.

1.6 Leadership: a checklist

The word 'leader' can sound very threatening, until we start to talk about what kinds of activities count as leadership. So what does count as curriculum leadership? We have already considered some of the

18

attributes of the leader: let us now consider some more. There are some descriptions of leadership which seem to apply more to senior management than curriculum leadership. For example, the distinction, in *Managing Primary Schools* (Day, Johnston and Whitaker, 1990), between authoritarian, democratic and laissez-faire styles of leadership is redolent of post-war management theory, when authoritarian, not to say autocratic leaders could be found in both industry and schools. For the language leader, an authoritarian or laissez-faire approach is hardly likely to work, and the democratic model, involving all the staff, is the only feasible one. Yet leadership, even at the curriculum co-ordinator level, is a complex matter, in which certain useful distinctions can be made. We would suggest the following checklist, distinguishing between the *exemplary* and *proactive* aspect of leadership, between what you do now and what you suggest for the future:

Exemplary leadership

LEADERSHIP BY EXAMPLE: MODELLING
This includes the way you teach, the displays in the classroom, the use made of visiting performers, the resources you have built up in your classroom, the posters and books you have placed in the staffroom, and your classroom teaching which should support the school policy on reading, marking, computers, writing, drama and media education. Finally, there is your involvement in out-of-school activities which support language work in the school.

THE CONSULTATIVE ASPECT OF LEADERSHIP: EXPERTISE
Expertise includes the knowledge and skills you have acquired through a combination of your teacher education course and one or more of the following: a subject specialism, your own experience as a teacher, your own reading and research, and your own subsequent staff development.

Proactive Leadership

The word 'proactive' reeks of management jargon, but actually conveys a useful concept which emphasises the process of initiating rather than reacting.

INDIVIDUAL INITIATIVES: COLLABORATIVE APPROACHES
This includes developing good relationships with other members of

staff, and working with them on collaborative projects. In some schools
this may be institutionalised through the practice of team teaching, but
in schools where teachers work more on their own it constitutes any
joint project with another classroom teacher. It also includes those
frequent, informal, snatched breaktime conversations in which language
issues are raised, and future planning envisaged, with remarks such
as 'Perhaps we need to look at our books and throw away a lot of the
old stuff!' or 'I've been trying to think of ways in which we could update
the leaflet about reading we send home to parents. Do you think we
need to change it?'

INDIVIDUAL INITIATIVES: RUNNING STAFF-DEVELOPMENT SESSIONS

This is what the newly-appointed leader may find most challenging:
running sessions after school or non-teaching days. It is the most public
and obvious sign of leadership, but it is only one aspect of the term.
You will find that the bulk of this book is largely a validation of the
knowledge and approaches that exist already in the majority of primary
schools, but which sometimes seems to receive scant recognition.

1.7 Advertising your own classroom

The starting point for all of your cross-school work is obviously going
to be your own classroom. You will have that organised and running
smoothly by now, but some may want to consider a number of strategies
which could make your work more effective and widely known.

Practical Activity 1.3
First strategy

The first of these involves reflecting on the extent to which your own
classroom advertises the importance you attach to language work. At the
beginning of each week try to look at your room through a colleague's eyes
– are there on display, with explanations, examples of the kind of interesting
work that you do with children, or are these hidden away in folders? Do you
have a writing corner as well as a reading corner? In the reading corner are
there examples of the books children have made themselves?

The subject of displayed work is yet another of those areas of
controversy that flare up from time to time. For some years it has been
considered good practice for the teacher to spend a considerable amount
of time in preparing classroom displays, but recently voices have been

heard questioning whether this is the best use that should be made of precious teacher time. More time, it is suggested, should be spent on planning and discussing with colleagues. What do you think?

Practical Activity I.4

Second strategy

Before you begin this activity it may be useful to read the section called 'Whole Language' at the beginning of Chapter 4. There we summarise the theory of the wholeness of language, and the way that it is desirable to see speaking, listening, reading and writing as integrated elements of communication permeating the curriculum. At the same time for classroom management purposes, which take into account the particular needs of specific groups of children who may need help with punctuation or spelling, it is often necessary to plan activities with a particular focus. This kind of focussing is discussed in some detail by Cazden in essays 7 and 8 in Cazden's *Whole Language Plus* (Cazden, 1992). So, to get staffroom discussion going in a supportive and unhectoring way, how about listing the range of focussed language activities you do with children during a week, and asking colleagues whether there is anything they might add? This could have the dual effect of letting colleagues know what you do, and increasing your own knowledge of what they do. Here is an example taken from a Year 5/6 class in a fairly traditional urban school: how different is it from your own practice? What issues do some of these practices raise? Encourage everyone to be frank about their approach, and the reasons for it!

This list could be photocopied, and used by teachers working in pairs.

Language in the classroom: a week's planned language work

The activities listed integrate naturally with others, while the matter of record keeping is dealt with at greater length in Chapter 9. In England teachers use their records to inform the teacher assessment they must make at the end of Year 2 and Year 6 at the time of the Key Stage tests.

Activity	Recorded?
1. In the News (radio prog.) — discussion	No written record
Decision making/discussion arising from geography, history, etc (one hour)	Comment on lang. record.
2. Reading: free choice 4-5 sessions of 20-25 mins	possibly + children's record as reading log
3. Story-telling in a circle	Comment on language rec.
4. Read to class 20 mins (3 times a week)	No
5. a) Key words from books (5 children) b) Tricky words (6 children) Spelling c) Words from work (24 children)	yes
6. TV or radio tapes	No

7. Handwriting (6 children: Nelson)	yes

8. Diary writing
Story writing or
Poetry writing MAKING BOOKS 40 mins
or Autobiography
     – arises from topic
     (e.g. OURSELVES) in
       integrated day.
	No – but children's
	work is itself a record

9. Drama and role-play from topic	Notes in 1. record.
10. Prepared reading from chosen text	yes

Sometimes the above will be replaced by one or other of the following:

11. Occasional book reviews for local library	No
12. Language work arising from visits.	Possibly

It is worth noting, and perhaps discussing the issues that this will raise in the context of the following observations made in the Leeds study:

The priority according to English in the school was frequently reflected in the classroom layout, with reading and/or language bays common, though less so for the 7-11 age group than for the 5-7. Pupils spent a lower proportion of time working and a higher proportion distracted than in most other subjects: English had the highest time allocation of all subjects, but the time was not always economically used. Girls spent more time on task than did boys. Older children spent more time on task than did younger. Pupils rated as above average by their teachers worked less hard and were much more likely to be distracted than those rated average or below.

Classroom activities were dominated by writing (56 percent) and reading (39 percent) and very little time devoted to the systematic fostering of children's speaking and listening The quality of teacher-initiated classroom talk was not, in general, high. (Alexander, 1992, p. 47)

How surprising are these findings?

Some newly-appointed language-leaders have said that they would feel uneasy about exposing their first term's language work to the criticism of their more experienced colleagues, in case the work was shot down in flames! Although the idea would be to open up discussion, rather than find fault with particular details of a programme of study, to adopt this strategy does call for a degree of confidence and easy relationship with colleagues that the newly-appointed person may not have. In this case, a more collaborative exercise may be more successful and productive.

Practical Activity 1.5

Third strategy

This strategy involves the production of a booklet for student teachers and teachers who are new to the school. The booklet would include the school's language policy (about which more later) and sections which address different issues. What advice would you want to make available to student teachers and first appointment teachers who come to your school? Consider what you would include in a booklet that contained the following headings:

CLASSROOM LAYOUT

LANGUAGE WORK IN YOUR OWN CLASSROOM

RESOURCES

FICTION-BASED TOPICS AND THE NATIONAL CURRICULUM

RECOMMENDED BOOKS

SUCCESSFUL STRATEGIES AND PROJECTS.

Another in-house publication could be a book for parents, and discussion of the contents, audience, illustrations and language could form the focus for another staff development session.

Let us now consider the extent to which the kind of school in which you are working will have an important, not to say determining, influence on the success or otherwise of all the roles we have so far considered.

1.8 Working together: the whole-school context

When student teachers say 'I have been working in a really good school' they often mean that they have been working in a classroom with a really good teacher. Even on a long school placement of eight or ten weeks, the student is unlikely to have the time or the inclination to have an overview of the school as a team working on the whole curriculum. As a full-time member of staff, with a leadership responsibility, the position is very different. As Nias *et al.* show in *Staff Relationships in the Primary School* (1989), from the 1980s onwards teachers have been exhorted to engage in school-wide curricular planning. Whether there is team teaching or individuals teaching in their own classroom a team approach is still possible, with writers from Campbell (1985) onwards favouring a 'collegial model'. This model envisages a school in which the corporate body, children and staff, experience a sense of belonging and commitment, with teachers commenting freely and constructively on each other's work. There is an atmosphere of purpose, reflection and analysis of the kind we suggest in our model, and each post-holder is seen as making a significant contribution to the work of the school. Suddenly, as language leader, you are plunged into this world of leadership and management, and you wish to avoid the fate of one teacher quoted by Campbell, who had been in and out of the next-door classroom on a regular basis, but having taken on a responsibility for a particular policy was now viewed as a visitor with an inspectorial role. For the more experienced teacher such pitfalls as this will be more easily skirted, and the brief review of organisational resarch that follows will be covering familiar ground.

Until recently there was little published research into the way staff relationships either facilitated or hindered the collegial approach. Anybody teaching in a school will be able to tell you whether the staff meet regularly to plan as a team, and whether policies are prepared and implemented by the whole school. What this doesn't tell us is why some schools develop this ethos, while others do not. In both *Staff Relationships in the Primary School* (Nias, Southworth, Yeomans, 1989) and *Whole School Development in the Primary School* (Nias, Southworth, Campbell, 1992) the writers identify some of the features which characterise the successful school, one in which there is a feeling of 'working together'. Not surprisingly, although rather ironically given the non-hierarchical ring to the word 'collegial', it is the Headteacher who has a crucial role in establishing the tone and ethos of the school. Campbell (1985) suggest that collegiality will survive the departure of the Head, but the initiative to turn a non-collegial school into a collegial one has to come from the person in the primary school who exercises most power, and that is the Headteacher. The Headteacher offers leadership by introducing ideas, regularly touring the school, negotiating with staff who are unhappy about a particular policy or development, observing the staff in action and reviewing the implementation of policies. From their observations in a number of schools Nias, Southman and Yeomans (1989) considered the Heads to be the 'founders' (Schein, 1985) of their school cultures, the word culture being taken to mean a set of beliefs, attitudes and norms, and the rituals and symbols by which these are represented. In fact the word 'culture' is being used in a way which is virtually synonymous with the term 'ideology' which we have used in our model, except that we have chosen to emphasise the prevailing ideology within which the school operates. Despite the apparent independence that springs from the delegated budget, no school is an island. Even so, it is important to consider the culture created by the relationships in the school, as manifest in staffroom and assembly, Head's office and school outings.

Belief is the key element which informs all relationships, although it is over simplistic to assume that belief always determines behaviour – peer pressure, or the desire not to alienate people may be just as powerful an influence. Yet it is clear, as Nias *et al.* argues (1989), that where beliefs and values are shared the likelihood is that co-operation, collaboration and collegiality will follow. This may appear obvious, but often the conflicting values which prevent collegiality remain hidden, simply because staff do not meet to share ideas or talk frankly to each other. This is where the school documents, including the language policy and the equal opportunities policy become important, because in drawing up these statements teachers are forced to confront the issue of their own beliefs and enter into a dialogue with their colleagues.

The newly-appointed teacher is inducted into the culture of the school, and the sensitive Head will oversee and monitor this process. Most of us hope that we will be working as part of a group, but also respects the need for the independence that comes from working on one's own. In such a culture leadership is more likely to be valued and effective.

United we stand (and make progress)

During the period of the early nineties even experienced staff were reeling as expectations from the DfE were added to the expectations of children, parents, Headteacher and advisers. So much energy is required to cope with all the changes that are imposed from without, so why introduce more changes from within? In such circumstances, where there is resistance, or scepticism, the language leader begins by treading cautiously.

This is not easy to do. One of the exciting things about taking on a new responsibility such as language leader is that you begin to see things from a whole-school perspective, and you realise that you are going to be the person who turns the dark dingy corridor corner into a bright area for listening to story tapes. The temptation is to call a meeting, or even worse send a memo, informing the staff of all the things you want to do. This is not a good strategy. Instead, concentrate on establishing or extending the range of language work done in your own classroom, and establishing links with colleagues through working together on specific small projects you have set up. In the supportive, collegial school the language leader will serve a period of apprenticeship during which the confident development of interpersonal skills will be nurtured. Some language leaders will find themselves working in schools with a more difficult culture. Even if this is the case, the language leader can have considerable influence if he or she makes approaches to colleagues in a tactful and deliberate way. Here are some examples of ways in which the language leader can take the initiative in working collaboratively with colleagues.

Practical Activity 1.6

Invite a retired person who went to the school as a child. (It may be useful to read the chapter on resources at this point.)

Ask another teacher if she would like to bring her class in to listen. If she agrees, meet beforehand to discuss how you are going to lead in to it, and what follow-up work there might be.

Ask a colleague if she would like to pair her class with yours so that her children can listen to the stories written by yours in the books they have made.

Prepare the groundwork for an integrated project which involves a visit. As it involves a topic-associated visit see if you can interest another teacher in going with her class as well.

Get to know parents by inviting them in to the school to look at a special display or performance the children have put on. Invite another teacher to do the same thing at the same time, so that you can help each other with the arrangements.

Ask a colleague with a particular curriculum expertise (for example, the science leader) to look over some work you have planned. Talk about the language work you plan to get out of it when she or he makes suggestions about how it could be improved.

In each case the strategy is obvious — you are approaching colleagues in a non-threatening way, calling on their experience and expertise, and making friendly professional contact. What you have to offer is the groundwork that you will have done, so you can give collaborating teachers work and ideas for sessions, which may release some of their time for them to do other pressing things. But the real hope is that if the shared activity works, they may wish to take it further themselves. This is practical, unformalised staff development, and is the essential preparation for the building of good relations, so that if you arranged a non-teaching day session on 'language and science' later in the year, you would have already worked with the science leader, and could refer to practical examples of work in any discussion that occurs.

Fine, you may say. It's all very well giving advice which says 'work on the personal relationships before doing anything else' — but what about the immediate pressure on me from the Head, or Advisors, or Governors to show that I am taking my responsibility seriously? Don't I need to have something to show at the end of my first term? Or — yes, I've made overtures to my colleagues but they are just not interested. So what do I do?

These are fair points and not lightly dismissed. But instead of loftily exhorting you to persist, here instead is a field study to show how a newly-appointed language leader coped − and succeeded − in a school where there was not a great deal of enthusiasm for change.

Field example: The Unresponsive School

The language leader had plenty of ideas, but the majority of the staff had been at the school for quite a long time and worked out strategies and routines which they were relatively happy with, and in conversation it became clear that they were not going to be persuaded very easily of the need for change. Yet the language leader was not happy with the old books being used in some of the classrooms, the separate nature of the class libraries, the reading schemes and the outdated language policy.

During the difficult first year she kept in touch with the local language co-ordinating group (the primary adviser had put her on to this) and established a partnership with a language leader from another school. The two of them met regularly to discuss progress, and to share ideas and work together on such thorny issues as a primary language record. This collaborative work was an essential antidote to the initial feeling of isolation that the language leader had experienced. It also avoided unnecessary duplication of work, and led to awareness of the Good Books Group, organised by the children's section of the local library, through which she met other language leaders.

She decided that the first thing to be done in her school was to establish something where change would be obvious. She identified a space where a good library and reading area, available as a central resource, could be located, and persuaded the Head to set aside some money for it. Earlier she had helped at the Christmas and Summer Fayres, so when she went to the PTA and asked for additional funding she met with a sympathetic response. With money available she ordered new stock and shelving, but also began the major task of reclassifying books, persuading colleagues to put certain books into the central stock and to throw away others, and setting up a workable borrowing system. It was at this point, when the benefits of the enormous amount of work that had been done became obvious, that her colleagues started to ask about ways in which they could help, and a small but significant shift in the ethos of the school had occurred.

The culture and ethos of the school in which you are working is of crucial importance, which is why we have emphasised the need for co-operation and bridge building. It is unrealistic to think that the world can be changed overnight, but if you demonstrate, by your actions as language leader, that you are prepared to invest quite a lot of effort to achieve the things you believe in, it is sometimes surprising how even the most sceptical of colleagues can be won over. It is our aim to suggest that the idea of collaborative learning applies to staff just as much as it does to children.

1.9 The changing role of the language leader

In the heady days of Bullock the newly-created language co-ordinator had a high profile, and a recognised mission. Those in both primary and secondary schools appointed to implement a policy which recognised the centrality of language to learning often encountered resistance from teachers who felt either that they were addressing this issue already, or, in the case of secondary colleagues, that it was the shifting of responsibility from the English Department which increased the already considerable burdens on an already overloaded science curriculum, for example. On the whole, however, language co-ordinators had the support of Heads, the Government, parents and LEAs, and there was a consensus that the initiative was a good thing.

In the nineties the situation has become more complex, and more demanding for the language leader. The natural alliance between informed critical opinion, parents and Government seems to have broken down, and the current educational climate seems to be one of polarities rather than consensus. As Mike Bottery observes (Bottery, 1990) the teaching profession has not been consulted in many of the radical changes that are now being introduced to education. It would be an unusual language leader who did not experience a certain sense of confusion and anxiety in the face of the pressure for change dictated by shared beliefs in the 'ethics of participation', and the pressure for change created by the form of assessment, especially where they seem to directly conflict with each other. This makes it extremely difficult for the newly-appointed language leader. But beyond this the role and influence of the language leader may vary enormously from school to school, not just because of the character and interests of the person concerned, but because of the group dynamics and power structures within the teaching community. There may be a return to hierarchy, with a clear division between the small senior management team and a more junior group of newly-appointed teachers with largely curricular responsibilities. This may be an inevitable reaction to rapid change: Tim Packwood (1989) argues that bureaucratic hierarchies are not necessarily the monsters that they sound, for as Tony Bush (1989) explains, they have the stabilising quality of the clearly defined positions identified by Weber in his classic study of 1947. The collegial model may be our aim, but we need to remind ourselves that unless we are Headteachers it may be an extremely difficult one to bring about, particularly at a time of low morale.

Now let us consider some of the kinds of schools in which you may take up the role of language leader.

Practical Activity 1.7:

Which of the following descriptions comes closest to matching the situation in your school?

School A
The language leader is a recently appointed teacher, new to the profession. The responsibility is not recognised by a salary allowance, but it is assumed that language matters will be looked after by this person who expressed a special interest in language at interview and on the application form. Staff tend to work separately rather than as teams.

School B
There is some confusion about who exactly has the responsibility for language across the school. The Head of Infants, a very experienced teacher, has traditionally held that post, but in the past two years an experienced Year 4 teacher has accepted responsibility for getting a reading policy off the ground. Again, there is no salary allowance available, and staff have traditionally worked individually with their own classes.

School C
The language leader is a fairly experienced member of staff who has been given two incremental points for two terms to develop a reading policy. When that job has been completed the allowance will be available for another initiative.
   There is a collegial ethos in this school.

School D
The Head has taken on responsibility for language co-ordination believing it is very important and needs the impetus that senior management can give it. There are experienced, and new members of staff who tend to work separately, but are being encouraged by a supportive Head and deputy to teach in teams.

School E
The post-holder is on the senior management team and holds an allowance, or is a deputy head. The Head is supportive, but there has not been a tradition of collaborative work creating a collegial ethos in the school.

School F
The language leader has an allowance which is permanent. The school is traditional, but open to change. Progress has been made, but it is not eye catching.

Activity: Consider the modifications you would have to make to one of the above descriptions to make it a reflection of the situation in your school. Then, taking each of the descriptions in turn, consider the advantages and disadvantages of each from the point of view of
a) the language leader
b) the school as a whole
c) senior management

There are clearly elements of School C and School E which you would wish to work towards, unless they exist already in your school. In order to implement and manage any kind of change you must carry the staff with you, something which is confirmed by both common sense and research

Summary

In this chapter we have considered the following:

- The origins of the post of language co-ordinator
- The first term as language leader
- What it is that constitutes leadership
- Skills required of the language leader
- What language leaders do
- Forms of leadership
- Starting out: advertising your own classroom
- Working with colleagues
- The unresponsive school
- Reflecting on your own school context

In the next chapter we shall consider what it is that makes the post of language leader a unique curriculum leadership post, by reminding ourselves of the way that language informs almost every activity in and out of school.

CHAPTER TWO

Language Leadership Across the Curriculum and Beyond the School

In this chapter we begin by exploring the meaning of the expression 'language across the curriculum', the way that our approach to the teaching of language has been influenced by theories of language and the implications this has for the role of the language leader. We go on to consider two specific instances of cross-curricular activities that develop and enhance language expertise: Information Technology and drama. We conclude by extending the horizon beyond the school, for as we tried to indicate in our model, the learning that takes place in school may be enhanced or constrained by such external factors as the prevailing ideology and funding arrangements, a national curriculum, and the relationships with parents and secondary schools.

This chapter completes the initial general survey of the role of the language leader, and the extra-curricular leadership implications of the post, which we identified earlier as the proactive aspect of leadership and the management of change. In the following chapters we shall discuss and reaffirm the way that leadership also resides in the expertise that all language leaders have by virtue of their knowledge of the way that reading, writing, talking and listening are managed and understood across the school, and the way that these practices have been informed by research and public discussion.

2.1 Planning language across the curriculum and language across the phases

Theoretical models of language

John Dewey said that there is nothing more practical than a good theory. Every practical thing we do in education is based on some kind of theory, even if it is that 'common sense' is *better* than theory! That's still a theory!

It's not a theory that lends itself to scrutiny, however, because what may be common sense to person A (children always need to be told what to do) conflicts with person B's idea of common sense (children who are always told what to do will never develop any initiative). As reflective teachers who want to encourage reflective children (otherwise what is the point of education: why not just call it training?) we will want to justify our methodologies in terms of the evidence that careful studies have produced. The more valuable theories in education have arisen out of research that has been conducted with children in schools or in their homes, and it is perfectly true that they may simply appear to confirm what everyone regards as 'common sense'. But sometimes they don't, and that should make us think afresh.

So what are the theories about language that the language leader needs to know? At this point your heart may sink as you think about the thirty-six children you are going to teach on Monday who need a properly prepared programme of work. If only you had a sabbatical you would have time to consider theory! But don't close the book! Instead, let us assume — so, yes, it is part of another theory — that theory automatically feeds into, and can lead to a better kind of, practice. So to help us teach we'll remind ourselves what language is, and then consider some of the assumptions about language that inform current approaches. In so doing, we will develop a rationale for talking about language across the phases and across the curriculum.

The word 'language' is usually taken to mean a set of signals or symbols that encode meaning. So we talk about animal language (birds displaying, for example) and human body language (the shaking fist, the welcoming smile). 'Language' and 'literacy' in the classroom have a more specific meaning which relates to the uniquely human capacity to speak, listen, read and write with understanding. This complex system of sounds and written symbols is what constitutes language, and the child's ability to become proficient at it is the goal of every teacher and, unconsciously, every child.

The question, then, is how do children acquire and develop language? How do they learn to speak, to read and to write? Early approaches to language saw children as empty vessels who had to have language imprinted on their minds. This could be called the 'top-down' model, which we discuss in more detail with the issue of phonics and the various approaches to reading. Other theories suggested that language is innate, and that we are pre-programmed with the capacity for language. Piaget claimed that there are various conceptual stages through which a child passes and that these are paralleled in the development of language.

This led to the now discredited theory of 'reading readiness', which proposed that children should not be introduced to certain language experiences before they were 'ready'. This model of language development was replaced when language development specialists such as Frank Smith, Kenneth Goodman and Donald Graves gave emphasis to the literacy environment, suggesting that if you surround children with a rich resource of books, conversation and opportunities for active approaches to learning their language ability will grow automatically. This is the 'bottom-up' model. The work of socio-linguists like Vygotsky and Halliday emphasised an interactionist model in which it is the relationship between the child and the surrounding language environment that is important. This stresses the importance of the child, the environment, and the appropriate 'scaffolding' to induct children into the structures and forms of language. Most teachers are eclectic, and have intuitively felt that a variety of approaches, some emphasising one model and some another, were helpful to the varied needs of a class of children.

Let us examine some of the assumptions about language which informed the Language in the National Curriculum project which completed its report in 1992. As is well known, the LINC project arose out of the Kingman Report (DES, 1988) and in the introductory section of the unpublished training materials the writers are quite explicit about the theoretical assumptions which underpin their work. We shall consider these through a practical activity.

Practical Activity 2.1

How many of the following assumptions about language would a) you support, b) you and a partner from the group of local co-ordinators support, c) the staff in your school collectively support?

1. As humans we use language primarily for social reasons and for a multiplicity of purposes

2. Language is dynamic. It varies from one context to another and from one set of users to another. Language also changes over time.

3. Language embodies social and cultural values and also carries meanings related to each user's technique and identity.

4. Language reveals and conceals much about human relationships. There are intimate connections, for example, between language and social power, language and culture, and language and gender.

5. Language is a system and systematically organised.

6. Meanings created in and through language can constrain as well as liberate us. Language users must constantly negotiate and renegotiate

> meanings.
>
> (LINC (unpublished), *Language in the National Curriculum*, p. 2)

As the authors of the LINC materials acknowledge, there are two strands interwoven in these six assumptions: a linguistic strand and an educational strand. The linguistic strand has been influenced by the functional theories of language which were proposed by Michael Halliday and the holistic approach of discourse analysis, with an emphasis on whole texts rather than individual units of language. Educationally the assumptions owe most to the theories of language development constructed by James Britton, theories which influenced the Bullock report and were influential in shaping the National Curriculum for English document. The model developed by Britton *et al.* (1975) identified different categories of writing, such as expressive and transactional, according to the function or purpose of the model. Let us now consider the implications of these theories.

Assumptions implicit in the expression 'language across the curriculum'

As a language leader you will amost certainly share the belief that language is central to learning: it is not simply instrumental to learning, it *is* learning. Some critical theorists such as Jacques Derrida go much further than this, suggesting that we *are* language, that the world is constructed from language, and that all values are rooted in and determined by language. This is an interesting thesis and as a language leader you will probably want to accept the idea that language informs everything we do, but be reluctant to accept the cultural relativism of a theory which seems to regard enthusiasm for books with scepticism. As we shall see in chapter 6 the relationship between language, and power, class, race and gender is an important one. Differing theories about what it means to be a reader will alter the way we read books – anyone who has encountered even a smattering of feminist theory will see a story like 'Cinderella' in a new light, and want to use Babette Cole's Prince Cinders alongside the traditional tale. But we would not want to reduce everything to a relativism which threatens to diminish the pleasure children get from picture books.

What do we mean by language or literacy across the curriculum?

What we understand this to mean is this: since the majority of learning takes place in a context of language, then the centrality of language to the learning process should be recognised by every teacher in every aspect of the curriculum, whether the focus is science, mathematics or art. This is widely accepted across the world: in *Language Policy Across the Curriculum* David Corson (1990) writes from an internationalist perspective in New Zealand about the challenges of constructing language policies in pluralist societies, and the way that the construction of school language policies should themselves be seen as language activities. The pervasiveness of language, whether oral, reading or writing, is inescapable.

This means that teachers have to consider the language implications of all their sessions, not just in terms of what language work will be covered but also in terms of:

i The language with which the activity will be introduced and presented to the children.

ii The language skills that the children will need to have in order to carry out the activity effectively.

iii The language and literacy skills that the teacher will formally address or draw attention to in offering guidelines for the activity.

iv The literacy and language factors which will feature in the criteria for the formative assessment.

This does not mean that the matter can be addressed simply by assessing spelling and punctuation in all written assignments.

What it does mean is that children should be encouraged to think in terms of purpose and audience, drafting and revising, editing and displaying, when using language in geography, science, and so on. It also means that the kind of activities used in language sessions — for example, cloze, sequencing and prediction exercises — can be used across the curriculum. There are examples of such activities in the final section of this chapter.

Practical Activity 2.2

Language across the curriculum

In England the non-statutory guidance section of the National Curriculum for English contains a section entitled 'Planning schemes of work for English in the National Curriculum'. The opening section begins like this:

1.0 Planning for English

1.1 Plans will need to be within the framework of the whole curriculum of the school, recognising the existence of:
 – the core and other foundation subjects of the National Curriculum;
 – cross-curricular elements;
 – the school's National Curriculum Development Plan;
 – the school's curriculum policy, within the context of the local authority's curriculum policy, where relevant;
 – the importance of equal opportunities for all pupils.
We shall consider the last of these in more detail in chapter 6, but the following exercise will relate to all five items in the above list, particularly the first two.
Working with a colleague who teaches children of a similar year group to your own, choose a book which will be shared by the whole class next term. Here are a few examples, moving from early years towards Years Six and Seven:
The Tale of Mucky Mabel by Jeanne Willis and Margaret Chamberlain
Dear Milie by Wilhelm Grimm with pictures by Maurice Sendak
Mike and Tony: Best Friends by Harriet Ziefert
Frog and Toad Together by Arnold Lobel
Huxley Pig in the Haunted House by Rodney Peppé
Piggybook by Anthony Browne
The Tunnel by Anthony Browne
Father Christmas by Raymond Briggs
The Witches by Roald Dahl
Martin's Mice by Dick King-Smith
The Wolves of Willoughby Chase by Joan Aiken
Mrs Frisby and the Rats of Nimh by Robert C. O'Brien
Goggle Eyes by Anne Fine
Grinny by Nicholas Fisk.
Now construct a programme of work, in diagram form, showing how language work arising from these texts can be extended to include all of the above five categories.

2.2 Cross-curricular language in practice: using I.T.

It is clear that Information Technology pervades not only all language work, but the whole curriculum. In schools which are well equipped and have adopted a high I.T. profile such a statement will sound extraordinarily banal. It is obvious that language is the medium of learning in schools all across the curriculum, and the use of the computer in activities with science, geography or history focus is simply a more concrete sign that language is the medium of instruction across all subjects. Yet there are problems which mean that, in some schools, Information Technology is significantly less developed than in others. Although it is a common technology, many primary and middle schools still find it expensive. Many made the initial plunge and bought a set of BBCs, Archimedes or Nimbus, but now hesitate. Even if funds become available, what is the right system to buy? Will it not become out of date soon after it is bought? All organisations have this problem, but with their small budgets schools are particularly inhibited. Sometimes the county or borough may be able to provide support through special funding, but this is becoming increasingly rare. Many schools are forced to rely on their PTAs for capital expenditure on computers.

Yet there are many exciting developments taking place in the world of new technology, many of them in schools. Living books on CD Rom discs not only show the story, with sound effects and movement, but allow children to interact with the text. The benefits of the new technology are not limited to reading. Research at Bedwell School in Stevenage, where every child in a class was given a Z88 to take home and effectively have ownership of for a period of weeks, showed that children's writing improved dramatically, both in the field of creativity and the range of vocabulary used. Some schools — and these are not exclusively those from leafy suburbs — have given I.T. a high priority. Shakespeare Junior School in Eastleigh, Hampshire, transformed its stock within a year, moving from four ageing BBCs to 22 computers, including 17 new A 3000 Archimedes, some from Hampshire LEA, some from the PTA and some from the Tesco voucher scheme then in operation. Many would argue, however, that a new technology initiative of the kind introduced in the 1980s by the Secretary of State for Education, Kenneth Baker, is long overdue.

This is all very well, some of you will say, but we do not have electronic mail, CD Roms, Hypercard or Applemacs, and we are not sure we would know them if we saw them. So let us come down to earth and start with the successor to the typewriter: the word processor. On trains we see people bringing out their lap-top word processors, opening them and typing away. A new generation of lap-tops, called Notebook computers, are even lighter, smaller and more portable. But let us address the suspicion that some teachers may still harbour: is the word processor just a more sophisticated version of the typewriter?

The simple answer is that it is much more than that. Information Technology and the word processor in particular should be seen not simply as productive tools, but creative tools. The word processor allows for ease of drafting, editing and reading. Text can be edited by copying, moving or deleting words, by manipulating page layout in terms of columns and by modifying the format in terms of character-style (bold, italic or standard), size (measured in points), and line spacing. This control motivates children. It allows them to express themselves without getting tired, or without getting their work dirty. Spell checkers can improve accuracy. In Somerset one I.T. initiative seems to have had a dramatic impact on the performance of children who were experiencing difficulties with the mechanics of writing. As they type in a word the computer sounds it out exactly as they have written it, and so they know if they are making sense or not. Children report that their confidence is boosted because they don't mind being corrected by a computer — it doesn't dent their self-esteem in the way that correction from adults does.

Desktop publishing differs from word processing because it deals mainly with the layout of blocks of text on the page. Text is 'poured' into frames which can then be moved around, headlines and pictures can be added, and the shapes of boxes can be altered easily: the text inside the box automatically adjusts itself to the new shape. Desktop publishing packages can be quite expensive, which partly explains why only 6.8 per cent of primary schools were using them in 1992, according to DfE figures. As technology advances, however, and personal computers become more sophisticated, the distinction between word processing and desktop publishing seems likely to disappear.

The National Curriculum recommends introducing children to the computer from the early years. For example, this is Level 3 of Attainment Target 5 in the National Curriculum document for Technology:

> Pupils should be able to use Information Technology to make, amend and present information. Example: Use a word processor to draft a class diary.

The Programme of Study for Key Stage 2 says that pupils should be taught to 'use information technology to organise ideas in written, pictorial and aural form' (p. 54). So I.T. is something to be used across the curriculum from the earliest years, and its language potential is enormous. In this chapter we shall be considering the following, as uses of Information Technology:

word processing
the best language programs
simulation games
newspaper simulations
collecting and recording real data to form a database
gender and bilingualism
special needs

We were originally going to call this section Talking, Writing and I.T. to show how these three activities are integrated, because children will be working on the computer in twos and threes, and discussing as they write or make decisions about what information to enter. As long as the decisions to be made are genuine ones, and not ones requiring random guesses about what is in the computer's memory, then the computer can be a creative force generating informed decisions and responses made to open questions. As Anita Straker (1989) has noted:

> One of the most impressive aspects of the use of the computer in the primary classroom is the amount of talk which is generated. When three or four children are sitting around a computer they have a natural focus for their talk, which encourages listening, reflection and participation. This feature is common to many different programs although the kind of talk, and its quality, varies from one piece of software to another. In the best programs — those that require collective decision making — the children must think clearly, express themselves effectively, listen to each other and take into account alternative viewpoints. This generation of talk may be one of the greatest advantages of having computers in primary schools, but only if the computer is used by groups of children rather than by individuals, and occasionally by the teacher to promote whole class discussion. (p. 192).

Many of you will be quite happy with this, but some, and it may well be the majority, will blink at the reference to the 'best' programs because they just haven't had the time, opportunity or expert advice to help them discover what the best programs actually are, let alone how they work. It would be foolish to pretend that all teachers feel comfortable with I.T., and that in many schools the computer remains underused. There are a number of reasons why this may be so:

1. The teacher is not familiar with the equipment or the system.
2. The programs that go with the computer are dull and test low-level skills in a repetitive, uninteresting way.
3. Lack of supervision.
4. Lack of status given to technology in the school.
5. Lack of time.

We shall try to incorporate an awareness of these problems in the sections that follow. Number three is a classroom management and organisation problem, and would apply to any activity in which only two or three children could take part but having an interested parent in would be very helpful here. Number five is an indirect consequence of number

four: ultimately it is something that the I.T. co-ordinator would have
to draw to the attention of the senior management team. An alliance
of I.T. co-ordinator and language leader could make a very strong
representation.

Early decisions

As language leader, working with the Technology leader (if there is
one), you will have to remind new teachers in particular of the early
decisions that have to be made.

1. RESOURCES: PROGRAMS AND OTHER FACILITIES
It is beyond the scope of any book to give a really up-to-date 'Which'
guide to the best systems or the best programs. You really do need hands-
on experience of the kind that could come from a local authority I.T.
course, if there is one. There is no getting away from the fact that it
takes time to get to know a system, and that the rapid developments
in computer technology are daunting. Two of the more useful
introductions are *Children using Computers* (Straker, 1989) and *The
Integrated Classroom: Language, Learning and I.T.* (Moore and
Tweddle, 1992). From such books you can get a sense of how different
systems can be used – Anita Straker describes how the computer can
be used to control models made by the children (like a lighthouse, for
instance), while Phil Moore and Sally Tweddle include an account of
an electronic mail link between Year 7 children and student teachers
from a Birmingham college. The latter case describes how a whole day
was devoted to drama, maths and technology during which the children
imagined they had landed on a newly-discovered planet. The student
teachers played the role of the message-sending spacecraft, to which
the children replied at regular intervals throughout the day. E-Mail is
suddenly transformed from a buzz expression into a really useful
classroom resource. In both books, programs from Pen-down to Podd
are mentioned, and the next best thing to actual hands-on experience
is developing an eye for programs which keep receiving favourable
attention.

2. SHARED ACCESS OR IMMEDIATE ACCESSIBILITY?
Whether we keep several computers in the corridor for shared access,
or one in each classroom for immediate accessibility will depend on
the layout of the school, the extent to which teachers work in teams,
and perhaps other safety and security factors. It is something which
should be reviewed especially if teachers feel unable to use their

computers properly. There is little point in it gathering dust in the corner — and providing a neat little cloth to cover it is not the solution!

3. INTEGRATING I.T. INTO THE TEACHING PROGRAMME

You have one or, at the very best, two computers in your classroom, and three is usually the maximum number that can work on the computer at one time, if everyone is to get a look at the screen and have a go on the keyboard.

How long a task will take depends very much on what the task is. Tasks which require sessions of re-drafting and editing need to be spread over at least half a term in order to give the whole class an opportunity to work on the computer. This assumes three or four half-hour sessions per day, depending on how you organise your curriculum time.

This is not so much of a disadvantage as it seems when it comes to using the computer as a word processor because children can work on the printout (a printer is a must). With simulations children need to be working on the computer for longer periods — anything up to an hour.

I.T. as a word processor

As language leader you probably have your own computer system at home to practise on (if not beg, borrow or steal one). This is essential if you are to have a sense of what the computer can do as a word processor, even if the system you have at home is different from the ones you have in the classrooms. It will give you an understanding of the way a computer works, and the meaning of basic concepts like 'a file', 'pasting' and 'saving'. You will want to have a standard word processing program in all the computers in the school, as the word processor is a tremendous motivator for the production of language. Moore and Tweddle describe the enthusiasm and delight with which a group of Year 2 reluctant readers read out their own stories which they had previously dictated onto tape, and which had subsequently been printed out from the computer. It was not long before they were writing stories themselves straight onto the computer.

Practical Activity 2.3

Arguing the case for more word processors
If you need to argue the case for more computers in your school, in what will inevitably be the context of a tight budget, make sure you

include in your message to the Head/governors/parents the following advantages:
- The word processor gives children the confidence to know they can produce a piece of writing as smart as anyone else's.
- It removes the frustration which holds back many children when they realise that they have to rewrite their work — corrections are easy and quick on the screen and the print-out takes a matter of seconds.
- It encourages children to correct their own work, and have their work read and edited by others in a natural way.
- Parents are likely to be impressed by the quality of the book-making and display work which comes from the computer.
- This very process of production allows children to feel that they are professional writers.
- Perhaps the most persuasive point to stress is that it prepares children for a technological society.
Having argued your case, you now need to be ready for the inevitable queries:

ARGUMENT | COUNTER ARGUMENT

1. Wouldn't the money be better spent on books?
2. Technology is always changing: won't things be cheaper and/or better next year? (A difficult one — but see below*)
3. No one in the school is really knowledgeable enough to choose/mend the hardware, or select and classify the software.
Ask your colleagues to work in pairs and come up with a response to these questions.
Knowing your own school as you do, try to come up with other likely objections — and answers!
(*This is a difficult question, but not unanswerable. Try something along these lines: 'Yes, but if we wait too long children will be leaving this school who have had no computer experience at all!' Word will soon get around!)

Many primary schools have the Archimedes Acorn, and with it they use the word processing system known as Pendown. You may well know this click-on system, which allows children to write in a variety of colours, sizes and fonts. Not only can children write stories, poems and plays on it, but with the aid of additional programs on separate floppy disks they can make professional-looking posters and text book pages, with texts which include words and photographs.

Other systems in use include Edword, Wordwise, Quinley and Quad. Some systems are better than others, and for impartial advice write to E.T.C. (English Teaching with Computers: the association's address is at the back) or NCET, or NATE New Technologies Committee).

Some I.T. advisory teachers recommend the use of resource texts, which the teacher types in (or copies using a scanner), on which the children can work. Instead of starting from scratch, or being presented with inflexible texts in books, children are able to have something not only to which they can respond, but which they can modify and adapt. In other words it gives them power over the texts, which then become their own — whether it is a short story, poem, letter or piece of information writing.

I.T. as a language programme

There are good programs and there are bad ones. The best programs are interactive, provide a challenge and stimulate curiosity. These qualities are well recognised in the popularity of decision making adventure programs like 'Granny's Garden', in which the operator has to rescue some children from a wicked witch who has laid several traps for them. Working through the program children are involved in maths and language work, problem solving and decision making, the use of colour and graphics. In evaluating language programs — and there are those which improve spelling, encourage reading and writing, discussion and listening — good language leaders (Wilson, 1991) have suggested it is useful to ask the following questions:

What age range is the program intended for?
Can it be adapted to suit the future needs of children or children of different abilities?
Can it fit into other classwork?
What activities can it stimulate?
Is it necessary to do any preliminary exercises?
What do the children have to do during the activity?
Does any other equipment need to be provided to make the best use of the program (a tape recorder, for example)?
Would the program be better used with small groups of children, or on their own?
Is it necessary to discuss beforehand any points in the program?
How is a wrong answer dealt with?
Are the 'rewards' given sufficient to motivate children?
Are the child's responses recorded for the teacher to see at the end?
Is the reading age of the text below or above the expected reading age of the users?
Are colour and graphics used?
Once the program is underway, does the level adjust up or down according to the answer?
How is sound used?

If neither you nor the technology co-ordinator feel confident about which ones to use, it might be worth investing in a viewframe. This is a piece of equipment costing approximately £2,000 which allows text typed on a computer to appear on a screen big enough for the whole class to read. The verbatim text of an oral story told by a child is transformed into a 'written' text by a transcriber. In other words, the word for word version of the spoken story, as it was recorded on tape, has been written on the computer and it is the job of the transcriber to make it more easy to 'read'. The children watch the process of rewriting, and comment on what is being added, left out and changed, asking why and how it happened.

I.T. and simulations

A simulation program is based on a real set of circumstances, into which children can enter, making decisions and affecting outcomes without altering the original facts. These programs, which range from 'The Mary Rose' to 'Save the Osprey', are supported by worksheets and teachers' materials, and can be used as a focus for a programme of integrated work. Simon Lodge, a third year student teacher at Rolle Faculty of Education, carried out a survey of programs that were available for one commonly used micro-computer (The BBC Acorn) and selected one for particular praise:

Wagons West (Tressel)

This is an excellent program, as both children and teachers have testified. It simulates the experience of travelling West by Wagon Train as pioneer emigrants in mid-nineteenth century America. The package is generally suitable for pupils of ten years and over . . . and children take on the roles of men and women travelling to California in 1852.

On the way they will encounter real life hazards. Crises include dangerous river crossings, dealing with mountain men and coming face to face with Native Americans. Children's decisions must be discussed carefully as they will have a definite bearing on the outcome of the journey. Children are encouraged to co-operate and emphathise with the historical situation. The support material is excellent, with journey record sheets, group cards, 'fitting out' record sheets . . . and clear teacher's notes. The graphics are good and there is clear potential for a whole term's work. (Unpublished dissertation, p. 55)

For staff to get a feel of the way a simulation exercise can generate useful and productive classroom work the following staff development activity could be organised.

Practical Activity 2.4

This simulation requires access to a fax machine, and an arrangement whereby someone will fax through to the school two or three documents.

Colleagues are put into groups representing various pressure or working groups, such as The Linguistic Minorities Commission, editorial staff of The Sun newspaper, and The Society for the Preservation of Standard English. Each of these diverse groups is asked to respond to certain proposals about language use in trading communities, adjusting their replies as new faxed documents appear. Responses, which could be typed on lap-tops if these are available, or on desk-tops if they are not, should reflect the group's interest in content and style. Finish the exercise with discussion.

I.T. and newsdesk

This is a simulation exercise which contains some of the features of the staff development exercise described above. Groups of children act as editorial teams (editor, sub-editors, lead writer), and are given the basic details of a major news story to work on. At intervals a news update comes out of the printer, and the editorial team has to revise its stories in the light of recent developments. For example, a plane may have been hijacked, and at a later stage we learn that it has landed and fresh fuel taken on. Eventually the plane is stormed by an anti-terrorist squad.

I.T. and information collection and retrieval:
spreadsheets and databases

Information-handling software ranges from databases to spreadsheets, not forgetting that the word processor itself is an information-handling resource. Databases not only store information, but they allow that information to be presented in a whole variety of ways, from bar graphs to Venn diagrams.

A simple database can be constructed using questionnaire information, which might look like this:

Hannah

Gender: Female
Sister: Yes
Brother: No
Comic: No
Nintendo/Sonic: Yes
Own TV: Yes
Own computer: Yes
Reading: Yes

Bicycle: No
Sports club: No
Own radio: Yes

Once all the information for all the children has been logged, then questions like 'How many girls without brothers have their own computer?' (In this survey, at least one!) can be quickly answered by keying in the right instructions. Spreadsheets are particularly useful for work involving numbers, as a grid can be set up on the screen, with each box or cell adjusting to whatever has been typed in the first one. For example, if you started from the following headings:

Packets of crisps per day	Per week	Per year	Cost
X	$7 \times X$	$365 \times X$ ($=Y$)	$30p \times Y$

So that if a child types '2' under the first heading all the other numbers change automatically:

2	14	730	219.00

Promoting gender and bilingualism

The subject of girls and computers needs a special mention in this chapter. If, as is often the case, the boys in the school are inclined to dominate when it comes to interest in computer-aided activities, then there are certain things which the language leader could propose to advance the cause of equal opportunities in the computer-resourced classroom — that is, if no one else is recommending this already, because there is no special reason why it should come from the language leader. If we are committed to equal opportunities, however, we shall want to do things like making a girl the computer monitor, responsible for setting up the equipment at the beginning of the day, or asking girls to introduce an aspect of computer software to the class.

The gender issue may also crop up when it comes to the staff who are responsible for the computers in the school. If there is one person — a man — is there an argument for sharing the responsibility with a female member of staff so that girls can associate women with technology more readily? There may not be a problem of this kind in your school, and even if there is, and you are new to the school, you may not wish to become typecast by championing every curricular cause in your very first term!

There is one cause that the computer champions by its very existence, as long as the right programs are available. That is, encouraging children to write in their own first language, whether it is Hindi or Hebrew. There are opportunities to produce dual texts, and for children to learn from each other through the act of translating and creating in other languages.

If, in addition, Viewframe (described above) is available then work on standard and non-standard English can be done quite easily. For example, a nursery rhyme can be shown on screen in dialect and standard English, and using a list facility on Pendown, Standard English words can be listed, then patois words, frequency and word counts, with the two lists compared for similar meaning.

I.T. and special needs

There is considerable evidence that the computer assists the learning of children with special needs. In her article 'Learning Autonomy' Bridget Somekh (1991) describes how for one class of six- and seven-year-olds the computer was an important aid to reading. She notes that

> Perhaps the computer lessens the intensity of reading, because there are other things to do and notice; pressing the keyboard; making choices; playing the game, seeing bold and colourful graphics, some of them moving; hearing noises . . .

Another teacher mentioned by Somekh (as Wilson, 1991, observes) found that special needs children in his class related well to other group members, so much so that 'while operating the computer they did not seem to exhibit any special needs whatsoever' (Somekh, 1991).

Into the twenty-first century

We have considered the obstacles that hinder the development of I.T. in schools, namely that technology is advancing so rapidly that it is difficult to keep up. For the first time in our history the majority of children are likely to be more proficient in an area of skills than the majority of the adult population, which includes the majority of teachers. Yet the advantages that can acrue from using the computer as a tool — especially a language tool — are many and varied. Children collaborate and talk, they see how quickly a computer can respond, they begin to grasp the language of computers and see how they work. In the field of language it encourages children to read and write as they enjoy the satisfaction of having produced a printed, sometimes illustrated page. At all times the computer should be a piece of equipment that can be readily and easily visited and used, it should be seen as something that is interactive, and has the exciting potential of linking classroom with the outside world, so that when messages are sent and received there is a real sense of audience and purpose. Computers are not just a whim of fashion. They are not likely to go away, because their chief use is in the outside world, not the classroom: education has been a secondary consideration. Yet if children are not prepared for a world dominated by computers, they are at almost as great a disadvantage as the child who has never learned to read.

2.3 Cross-curricular language in practice: drama and role-play

Reflections and analysis

If there is one activity that brings together all the strands that we discuss separately in the next three chapters, and can be built around topics ranging from science to religious education, it is drama and role-play. We have deliberately positioned this section here. It comes as the conclusion to the part of the book which places particular emphasis on production, because role-play and drama represent most strikingly the active, dynamic element in learning. We have in mind the kind of role-play that emerges from the subject being explored in the classroom at the time, whether it is a history topic like evacuation in the second world war, or a science topic like light and colour. These are explored initially through talking and listening, reading and writing, and by building on this knowledge and language work the teacher can allow children to give expression to their knowledge through role-play. One obvious and simple example is the evacuation situation in which the children act out a scene at a station to which they have been evacuated, and are then selected (or passed over) by prospective host families.

Although occasionally we meet teachers who recall drama as one of the worst bits of their initial training course, students usually enjoy it because it is so cross-curricular, active, collaborative – and fun!

Drama appears in the Cox Report *English 5-16*, and although drama specialists were not very happy to see it subsumed within English, the original National Curriculum folder was stronger for the pervasive way that drama was meant to inform all language activities. In the section called 'Planning Schemes of Work for Speaking and Listening' the document says that 'teachers will need to provide opportunities for a range of drama activities' which might include:

- spontaneous play in a home-corner which reflects the theme of work being pursued.
- group improvisation of a story (heard or read).
- puppet play (where children can use the puppet as a means of communication).
- 'hot seating' in which either the teacher or a member of the group adopts a role and is questioned by the rest of the class. In exploring a fictitious 'future world' for example, a child or the teacher might agree to answer questions about decisions made by the astronauts.
- 'forum theatre' in which a small group improvise the next stage in the drama, in order that the class as a whole can explore and discuss how a dilemma might be solved, for example during work on 'the circus', two children might show what happens when the RSPCA inspector arrives to investigate a charge of cruelty to elephants.
- 'teacher in role' in which the teacher plays a key part in shaping the direction of the drama, in order to make learning more effective. The teacher might take the role of the circus manager, who discovered that the clown can no longer laugh, and ask for help and suggestions for resolving the problem.
- 'freeze frame' in which children in small groups devise a freeze frame which demonstrates what they want to say. The rest of the class is asked to interpret. The children might be asked to adopt positions that show the relationship between the various members of the crew on the voyage to the 'future world'.
- role-play and drama can be in two or more languages and can provide a very valuable way to enable children to use forms of language in English other than those already experienced. (DES, 1989)

All of this seems helpful and illustrates the cross-curricular nature of English. In the revised English Order this holistic approach appears to have been lost in a document which is very much informed by the notion of 'English' as a core subject made up of discrete parts.

Yet it is through drama activities such as role-play and problem-solving exercises that the Attainment Targets for speaking and listening are met, and from which reading and writing frequently develop. Other forms of drama may be informed by the language of gesture and movement as well as utterance, and although all of this comes well within the brief of the language leader, it may well be that there is another person in the school whose particular role is associated with putting on productions. Here it is useful to make a distinction between drama and theatre, the latter involving the idea of a performance to a public audience. Many teachers may think of drama in terms of performance, but most of the drama advisors we have spoken to prefer to emphasise the role of drama as a learning tool available to all children, not just the few gifted performers who shine in productions. This is the model of drama suggested by the activities listed above. Drama of this kind frequently involves the whole class, and often involves playing out narratives which emerge from other parts of the curriculum such as history, for instance. The teacher, too, plays a role — say the beadle in the workhouse, or the soothsayer in Ancient Egypt. Children not only enact roles in groups, but they are given opportunities to do other kinds of work in the role situation. So, for example, a child in the role of Victorian Headteacher may come to a point where he or she has to write a letter. Rather than mime it, the child can write the letter there on the spot, using pen and paper. When role-play needs to be suspended, the teacher comes out of role (one strike on the tambourine, for example, or standing up if it has been circle-time story-telling) and the children may move to a special corner of the hall for discussion or further directions. Of course, there are many ways of developing role-play work, such as 'freezing' a scene so that it can be taken apart, and perhaps acted out from the point of view of another character. Steve Cockett's suggestions built around Jan Needle's *The Rebels of Gas Street* explore a number of these techniques of miming and arresting action. More are suggested in the second half of this chapter. The point being made here is that primary-school drama is essentially for those inside it, not for those outside it, and, once again, the merit is in the process rather than the product. Such a distinction between the two aspects of drama could be the useful focus for a staff development session.

Practical Activity 2.5. A policy for drama

Beyond the School Production

General opening question: is it important to maintain a balance between drama as presentation and drama as experiential learning? What is the best way of ensuring this?

Specific questions:
1. Do we have a school production — too frequently
                                  — too rarely
                                  — at appropriate intervals?
If your school does not have a production which involves at least a year group, move on to number 3.

2. Why do we have a school production?

What are the advantages?
What are the disadvantages?
Are they inevitable?
Do they outweigh the advantages?

3. Why don't we have a school production? Should we arrange something?

4. Should the responsibility for the production:
   - stay with someone who is good at it?
   - rotate automatically?
   - involve the whole staff?

5. Do you use role-play as a learning aid in connection with any of the following areas of the curriculum:

i history?
ii music and dance?
iii poetry?
iv fiction?
v talking and listening?

6. Do you sometimes play in role?

7. How do you deal with the following problems:

| SPACE | INTERRUPTIONS | SHYNESS | CHILDREN NOT TAKING THE ACTIVITY |
| GROUPS OF THIRTY-FIVE | | | SERIOUSLY |

8. What was the best drama activity you did last year?

What is the value of drama

Following the discussion above you may be able to reflect on the value of drama, and agree some statements about its value. It seems particularly valuable when it:

successfully engages the whole class

allows children who are less successful at other forms of language work to show their ability

is exploratory

reaches a conclusion

is collaborative

You can probably think of many other points in its favour. Many teachers emphasise the possibilities it provides for improvisation, with children experimenting and developing roles in a free, collaborative way. Terry Furlong tells the now legendary story of the group of Wembley businesswomen and businessmen who were asked which subject they would put down first on a list of curriculum subjects, and much to his surprise after a brief conference they came up with the answer 'drama'.

Asked for their reason (and they clearly had in mind performance drama) they said that it required working in teams, it involved working to a deadline and it was assessed by a critical audience.

The school play and musical

Clearly there is a place for 'theatre' in school, for a whole variety of educational, social, developmental, community and public relation reasons. The big production can inspire a whole school, and everyone can be given some job or other, whether it's painting the scenery or being 'front of house'. Programmes are designed, the background researched, music practised. If the production can be seen to belong to the whole school, it serves a purpose well beyond that of language. And it is likely to be most successful in a school where drama activity in the classroom is encouraged from the very start.

Language and drama in the early years

Much early years work involves drama, although we may not always think of it as drama. Circle activities, in which children sitting in a circle hold a stone before they speak, or introduce a friend, or listen out for the name of an animal before they swap places with the other 'animal' of the same name, are frequently used as end of day activities, and involve a great deal of speaking and listening work. Here is a way of finding out more about circle activities:

Practical Activity 2.6

CIRCLE ACTIVITIES WITH EARLY YEARS CHILDREN

Ask two of your early years teachers to lead a session in which they introduce five circle activities to junior teachers (contact your feeder school if you are in middle school). Then discuss ways in which these activities can be adapted for older children.

One thought: the bigger the children, the more space you need!

Visual drama is an alternative to spoken drama, and works just as well with middle years children as it does with early years. Here are a few visual drama activities:

DUMBSHOW: This is the presentation of a scene without words, often using exaggerated gestures.

MIME: This is a form of dumbshow in which the audience is invited to imagine the missing object, whether it is a wall being painted or a meal being eaten.

DANCE DRAMA: Music can be used to encourage movement to illustrate a story or express particular feelings.

TABLEAUX OR FREEZE FRAME: This activity, which involves the use of a camera, can lead to writing and discussion work, but essentially it is a listening and movement session.

Take a topic which falls neatly into four sections — such as Time: The Day. Divide the class into four groups, one for each of the following: getting ready for school, at school, home again, time for sleep. In their groups children brainstorm the sounds and sights of their particular section:

Morning	School	Teatime	Bedtime
cleaning teeth	reading	watching TV	a star
milk-delivery	sandwiches	eating tea	sleeping
eating breakfast	skipping	cycling	book-time
dressing	answering a question	telephone rings	washing

We haven't listed the sounds because we wanted lists that would form the basis of a tableaux or photograph. So for 'bedtime' one child would assume a sleeping position, one child could be a star, one child washes her face, while another listens to a book which another appears to be reading to him — and so on. The teacher takes a flash photograph. After all the 'freeze frames' there is more talk about the pattern of the children's days, and then everyone waits for the photos to be developed. These are then mounted and displayed, and the children make labels, talk about the pictures and explain to the other groups what was happening. Children can then write about their days and the way they differ and resemble the daily routines of other children.

An extension of this involves more vigorous movement and choreography, where all the children actually act out their activity — so the washer washes and the television watcher reacts. With older children this can lead to more ambitious projects: I once saw a *commedia del arte* mime performer choreograph over fifty children on a stage: starting from scratch, and in front of the whole school, he created, in quick succession, two remarkable scenes: one was an orchestra in full flight, and the other was a frenzied scene of domestic activity, involving ironing, cooking, eating, painting, cleaning, and so on. It was unforgettable.

POEMS PERFORMED: Older primary and middle-school children are often given poems which they take away to the corridor or the reading corner to prepare group readings. Some preliminary whole-class work is necessary to illustrate what this means, for example one person reading the first line, two the second, three the third, four the fourth, five the fifth and then back to one for the sixth (or as appropriate). Children may wish to use props like chairs: somebody standing, somebody sitting with a group to one side. Children may wish to emphasise particular words with a single reader for most of the line, and then a group of six readers for one of the words in the line. Here is an example, showing in upper case the words read by all six. It can be very effective!

The Wind is LOUD
The Wind is BLOWING
The Waves are BIG
The Waves are GROWING
What's that? WHAT'S THAT? (from *The Rescue* by Ian Serraillier)

There are many more ideas in *Exploring Poetry 5-8* by Jan Balaam and Brian Merrick (1989).

Teacher in role

The teacher is surrounded by the children, sitting in a circle. Sitting down she is in role, standing up she comes out of role. She begins a story, and then gradually draws children into it, asking individuals questions, and they must reply in role.

Written drama forms: suggestions from New South Wales

The New South Wales Syllabus and Support Document *English K-6* (1992) lists a number of scripted forms of drama, many of which are already familiar in English classrooms. Docudrama involves presenting factual material in dramatic form, usually with a presenter or commentator linking the scenes. Anthology Drama involves the presentation of a linked sequence of scenes, drawn from stories or myths, but particularly from poetry. Collage Theatre is also a series of scenes, but this time the links are musical ones and the aim is to create an overall impression of an issue such as conservation. Readers' Theatre is given particular prominence in Australia, and simply involves groups of children giving prepared, scripted readings to the rest of the class, with accompanying gestures and movements. In Story Theatre a story is performed, and co-ordinated by a narrator, all from a rehearsal. No scripts are used.

Drama uses language in its widest sense, and draws together elements from the whole curriculum, particularly in the form we have called docudrama. Let us now consider the way that language itself reaches out beyond even the school, to the world beyond the school gates.

2.4 Beyond your school: wider liaison

Language across the phases — the early years

Many primary schools retain the traditional two-tier structure, which recognises two phases, infant and junior. Sometimes this is reflected in separate leadership, sometimes in separate buildings, sometimes even separate sites. If these phases are under separate management, or in separate buildings, it is important that the right hand knows what the left is doing — in other words that the language strategies being employed by early years teachers are being carried through to Years 4, 5, 6 and 7. This requires knowledge of the whole primary (or middle) school approach to talk, reading and writing, so that a developmental policy can be set in train. This, together with forming links with English Departments in secondary and upper schools, is a time-consuming business, involving regular contact with other teachers and classes in and out of school hours. It is time well spent, however, as the language leader will want to feel that there is continuity for children as they progress through the school, and move on to the later phases. It is sometimes useful, as well as comforting to have a huge roll of paper on which this evidence of progression is charted. Class teachers may be able to photocopy existing plans which can then be attached to the chart, rather than having to produce new summaries. The language leader can then see exactly how the language programme of the school develops.

Wider liaison

In the previous chapter we concentrated on establishing good relationships with colleagues within the school, of ways of working with them and ways of offering leadership. In this chapter we have addressed the question of why you are doing this, by considering what we mean by language across the curriculum and the school.

Yet as language leader your liaison role extends well beyond the school, and includes contact with parents, the local secondary schools, and advisors and inspectors. In each case the same general strategies that are appropriate within the school are likely to be successful outside of it. Drawing on your own practice you are able to talk about what you are actually doing in the classroom. If discussions with your colleagues have resulted in a whole-school approach, then discussions with parents and others start off on a firm footing, and can be followed by an invitation designed to draw them into a partnership.

Literacy out of school

Unlike some activities which are unique to school, language is not something that stops at the school gates. Children are generating and being exposed to language during all their waking moments, and it may be useful to include with your list of in-school activities a list of out-of-school language experiences, and circulate them both to your colleagues, again asking for additional ideas. Your list may look something like the following:

Reading with parents (all the way through the primary school: not just in the early years).

'Reading' and discussing television programmes.

Reading information at the post office etc.

Library and bookshop visits with the family.

Reading to younger brothers and sisters.

Making books for younger brothers and sisters at home.

Drawing attention to signs and notices in town etc.

The importance of parental and community involvement

Any discussion of literacy out of school immediately invites us to affirm the need for parental and community involvement. Contact with parents and the local community begins before a child is admitted to school. This occurs through home visits and liaison with a local playgroup or nursery, and continues through pre-admission sessions in school, and with parental involvement in the settling-in period.

Once a child is at school it is important to ensure that there is adequate information available to parents through letters, magazines, talks and open days, and that there are opportunities to meet staff, pupils and governors on both a formal and an informal basis. The language leader will be able to make a significant contribution to this process. Structured programmes such as home/school reading logs are valuable ways of encouraging parents to play an active part in the child's education.

There are many ways in which parents can help at school in specific subject areas – particularly in practical sessions and structured play situations. There are many parents who have specific skills which could be very valuable in school. For example, in the primary school where one of us teaches we have had invaluable help from parents qualified

56

as sports and swimming instructors.

For those parents who, for whatever reason, are unable to come into school to work with children on a regular basis, provision can be made for them to see 'the school at work' on an informal basis. This can be done by holding coffee mornings or open days. Of course, all parents must be made to feel that their attendance at PTFA or Home School Association meetings and events is valued by reminding them of the opportunities to help, or to observe how the school is run. By supporting such activities the language leader extends his or her knowledge of literacy out of school, and sets in train an important dialogue and communication process.

Let us now consider another way of developing the process of communication.

Parents and voluntary compacts

Parents are the top angle in the triangular partnership between children, teachers and parents, and many schools are seeking to involve parents more through the drawing up of compacts or contracts in which all three partners agree to provide and deliver certain things according to their responsibilities and role. The compact may state, for example, that the teacher agrees to keep a record of the child's reading progress, the child agrees to spend some time at home each week reading a book of his or her choice, and the parent agrees to provide an appropriately quiet space in which home reading can take place.

Practical Activity 2.7

Arrange an introductory meeting, with a view to drawing up a compact (with special reference to language skills). The aim is to produce a document, in partnership with parents who have consulted their children, setting out what responsibilities and rights each member of the compact − child, parent, teacher − has in the domain of developing literacy. In the initial meeting teachers will come together to draft a document, which will then be sent home to parents for consultation and revision. Such compacts have no legal status, but they help to remind all those involved in the partnership of their rights and responsibilities.

Divide the staff into three groups, preferably containing teachers of different ages. Starting with the early years, each group draws up headings to cover the appropriate range of language work, and the resources needed to enable children to develop as fluent talkers, readers and writers. Group one then lists the *parents* responsibilities under each of the three headings talking, reading and writing, group two, the *child's* responsibilities, group three the *teacher/school's* responsibilities. After ten minutes thought and discussion, groups should pass on the list, and add to or modify the one they receive.

There is obviously much more to parent liaison than drawing up and sending home documents. The importance of parental and community involvement was a subject we touched on in the previous chapter, and, as we all know, contact with parents is central when it comes to organising trips, explaining the school's reading and handwriting policy, having other adults in the classroom, organising performances and library days, appeal for 'historical' resources such as second-world-war gas masks, and meeting for informal chats before and after school.

Language across the phases

For many children the big jump from primary to secondary is made much easier if there is regular contact between local schools, involving preliminary visits from and to the secondary school. It is often the English/Language team that takes the initiative in establishing these links. Daniel Tabor, the continuity co-ordinator at Daventry William Parker School in Northamptonshire described one such initiative in his 1992 article. His main points were as follows:

1. The William Parker School English faculty has developed a partnership programme with all eight contributory primary schools.
2. Pairs of teachers work together: one English teacher from the secondary school will work with a partner from one of the primary schools.
3. Each pair plans a joint project involving children from Years 5/6 and secondary pupils from Years 7 to 9.
4. The projects run from one to three terms, with at least one of the joint sessions taking place in the primary school.
5. Topics include story writing, poetry anthologies, drama, media studies, Information Technology or environmental issues. Workshops with practising poets have featured successfully.
6. Teachers meet in the primary school at least once for a planning session.
7. Money is provided from a teachers' centre in-service fund.
8. Sessions take place within the structure of the secondary school timetable.
9. Buses and stationery are paid for by a special fund for continuity and liaison by the secondary school.
10. A co-ordinator who has an overview of all the projects is essential.

What are the benefits of such cross-phase liaison? Are there any disadvantages?

In his book *Curriculum Continuity in English and the National Curriculum* (1991) Daniel Tabor describes in more detail some of the joint projects which helped bridge the gap between the junior and the secondary school. Visiting secondary school children were paired off with top juniors, and, before beginning work on a joint project, children

58

filled in prepared questionnaires about each other — an activity which served as a successful ice breaker. Some of the joint activities focussed on poetry, with children picking poems and reading them to their partners when they came to visit. Then they were asked to write a poem to read to the partner, with discussion following. The centre of the poetry activity, however, was a joint workshop run by a practising poet.

Slightly less ambitious projects involved junior children writing stories for the older children, and vice versa. Again, this would happen only after the children had got to know each other, with similar ice-breaker activities to the one described above. The focus for the poetry or story-writing could be, for example, 'School'. The immediate advantage for the junior school children is that, as well as providing a real audience for the language work, it also allowed them to become used to the geography of the secondary school, something they recorded in their reflections and evaluations. One boy wrote proudly of how he was less nervous now that he knew where the toilets were, and how to negotiate his way around the school. Finally, joint junior/secondary activities could involve paired computer writing (see the I.T. sections) and drama work in which children write a script and then perform it together (for further examples see the drama and role-play sections).

Advisers, inspectors, and teacher education tutors and supervisors

Some primary schools are, or have been, used to regular visits from LEA advisers and University Faculty of Education tutors, while others, not necessarily the smaller or more remote schools, may feel neglected. Sometimes the school ethos plays a part in these perceptions: if the Head of the school, who will normally receive visitors, makes a point of calling in other members of staff for discussion and consultation, then you, as Language Leader, may find yourself involved in regular contact with a range of tutors. On the other hand, the visitors may be closeted in the Head's office, and you may remain unaware of the visit until a chance remark a week or so later.

If this is the case, or you find yourself in a school which is off the beaten track, then liaison will have to be preceded by initiative: attend courses, invite advisers in, ask the Head to enter in her or his diary the visits that have been arranged, so that you can have a quick word with the visitor before he or she leaves. Tact is the watchword, however!

2.5 The management of change: saving the baby

As a language leader you will sometimes hear yourself described as a curriculum manager. In the mid 1980s it became very fashionable to distinguish between proactive and reactive styles of management and leadership, the former being far more desirable than the latter. If we ignore the awfulness of the jargon, which probably makes you want to be known simply as a teacher, this is fine and good in principle, emphasising as it does the need for forward planning, vision, consultation and initiative. There are periods, however, when it is very difficult not to be reactive, and the present day seems to be one of those periods. With a complete revision of the English Order taking place, with forms of assessment that seem to change each year, with a shake-up of teacher education and a new emphasis on subject specialism in the upper years of the junior school, then it is no surprise that primary teachers will focus all their energies on coping with and reacting to the changes that all these developments involve. Yet there is a real danger that we lose sight of all that has been achieved in primary education in Britain over the last thirty years, developments that ironically, have made other countries envious of the best U.K. primary practice. As we do not want to lose sight of the expertise that comes from knowledge of good classroom practice, we shall look at the rich variety of approaches to classroom language in the primary school, which are sometimes neglected as discussion focusses on assessment and the content of the curriculum as determined by the Orders. To ensure that we do not throw the baby out with the bath water, in the next three chapters we shall look at the baby — or to be more precise, language and the child from birth to the age of twelve.

Summary

In this chapter we have considered the following:
- Planning language across the curriculum
- Language across the phases: theories that underpin whole school language policy
- The meaning of language across the curriculum
- Information Technology as a cross-curricular language resource
- Drama, role play and cross-curricular language
- Language across the phases: practical implications

PART TWO: LEADERSHIP AND EXPERTISE

In the three chapters in Part Two we concentrate on the aspect of leadership that springs from expertise − in other words the knowledge that the language leader will have about the role of language in education, the varied approaches to language acquisition and the significance this has for classroom practice. The possession of this knowledge is an important aspect of leadership and one which can all too easily be taken for granted. For many teachers these chapters will represent a summary of what they know and do already, but the validity of which they may have started to question in the current confusion of claims and counter claims about the teaching of language. Questioning established practice is a good thing, as long as the suggestions for change are the product of experience, research and public discussion. The chapters that follow build on these three processes, and are influenced by the three elements of the model which we offered in the introduction: production, scaffolding and reflective analysis. The language leader is likely to support an approach in which all the elements are in play, just as she or he will always insist on the unity of language, even when for discussion (and National Curriculum) purposes we separate the strands, in line with the Attainment Targets.

CHAPTER THREE

Producing Talk Together

Talking about talk

We start then with talk. In this chapter we begin by discussing the status of talk, and then go on to consider the development of talk from the pre-school years to the age of twelve. We consider the place of language games and storytelling in the talk repertoire, and the integrated activity of talking about books. We then discuss the subject of Standard English, move on to consider the nature of collaborative talk, and finish by referring to the more formalised talk activities the junior- and middle-school teacher will want to arrange. The assessment of talk is left until a later chapter.

3.1 Towards talking and conferencing policies: reflection and analysis

Most children arrive at school being able to talk. They have not been taught how to do this, although they may have been encouraged by parents or other adults to speak and say words in a particular way. The lips, the tongue, the teeth, the voice box and the nose undertake the most sophisticated operations which often requires the most technical descriptions in books on language. Yet this all comes naturally to most children who grow up in a social environment. They have no formal lessons. Quite often they do not seem to be making any progress at all, and then out will come a stream of language showing that things have been happening inside their minds all the time. In a case reported recently, an exceptionally precocious child appeared to be able to read at once, before he could talk. But who is to say that he was not mentally registering all the language he was hearing?

Through learning to talk, children simultaneously use talking to learn. In saying that talking is a fundamental activity on which most learning depends, we are taking the LINC defition of 'talking' as the integrated process of speaking and listening. It is indicative of the former status of talk that, as Anthony Burgess points out (1992), in many languages the word 'tongue' is a synonym for 'language'. The painful process of recovering this status is suggested by the need for terms like 'conferencing' and 'oracy'.

Yet the National Oracy Project, the National Curriculum and the LINC project acknowledge that talk is central to our use of language — in fact it is the very foundation. In the LINC materials (unpublished), the section called 'The Process of Talk' begins with this question from *English 5 – 16* (1989):

> In addition to its function as a crucial teaching and learning method, talk is also now widely recognised as promoting and embodying a range of skills and competence — both transactional and social — that are central to children's overall language development. (15.4)

Earlier — it forms the very first page of the Cox Report, despite being headed '15' — *English 5 – 16* had this to say:

> Our inclusion of speaking and listening as separate profile component in our recommendations is a reflection of our conviction that they are of central importance to children's development. The value of talk in all subjects as a means of promoting pupils' understanding, and of evaluating their progress, is now widely accepted. For instance the Cockroft Report (1982) on the teaching of mathematics drew attention to the importance of learning through talk. (15.1 and 15.2)

It is the National Oracy Project which has done more than anything to give talk the recognition it deserves. Established in 1987 by the School Curriculum Development Committee it completed its own development phase in 1991. Between 1991 and 1993 it passed through the dissemination phase, spreading the findings of the project by means of videos, books and files for classroom use. As Gordon Wells says in the concluding essay of *Thinking Voices:*

> The centrality of talk is finally being recognised. Not simply in theory — in the exhortations of progressive minded academics — but mandated at all levels and across all subjects in a national curriculum (In Norman (ed.), 1992)

Although reading and writing are not necessarily adjuncts of speech (a fluent speaker may not be a fluent writer) it is inconceivable that they would not have been preceded by it. Leaving aside the science fiction fantasies of a writer like Kurt Vonnegut, can we imagine a human society that has books but no conversation? Such a society has never existed. The private acts of reading and writing must follow the social act of talking and conferring. At the end of this chapter there is an opportunity to consider constructing a policy for talk and, as an introduction to the activity, it could be useful to explore the status of talk with your colleagues. Most of us consider it very important, but how much status do we actually give it in our classrooms?

3.2 The stages of talk

Pre-school talk

The social nature of spoken language — as adults we don't talk unless someone is listening — is well understood. In *Thought and Language* (1962) Vygotsky articulated what now seems a commonplace — learning takes place in a social context. In very young children, however, language, and the sheer delight of being able to make and shape language, becomes an extension of play and enjoyed for its own sake. There are young children all around, even as this is being written, and some of the children are just howling and shouting for the sheer pleasure of it as they enjoy their play under the trees. The play is social, but language is being used as a sound system to express mood rather than as a semantic system to express meaning. None of them are saying things which they want the others to listen to — and the others aren't listening anyway! Another group of children, led by an adult, has just passed chanting a marching song as the group makes its way to the swimming pool, happily enjoying the song-like rhythm as the teacher calls the refrain:

Adult: Everywhere we go-oh
Children: Everywhere we go-oh
Adult: People want to know-oh
Children: People want to know-oh
Adult: Where we all come from
Children: Where we all come from
Adult: This is what we tell them
Children: This is what we tell them
Adult: Mind your own business!
Children: Mind your own business!

Although the majority of these were school-age children, this incident draws attention to another characteristic of early language experience — its interactive nature. The parent will respond to the young baby's noises and facial expressions with words — it will conduct a 'conversation' with the baby. The pleasure of sound, the enjoyment of talking or singing for its own sake, which is first manifested as baby's babble or language play, is a stage in the developmental process (a stage which we as adults return to when we sing in the bath or talk to ourselves). Young children initiate talk — they do not wait until others speak, unless the context is one in which they do not feel confident. Context is all important — the child who chatters in play or in the bath may be shy with strangers. But no child is silent all of the time: such a silence would suggest some unusual cause.

Early years children

The following inventory has been drawn up by Maggie Maclure (1992) to show what many children will be able to do at the age of five:

- draw on a vocabulary of several thousand words
- control many of the major grammatical constructions of their language
- speak with adult-like pronunciation
- talk for a range of purposes
- use talk to further their own learning
- express feelings through talk, and understand the feelings of others
- know many of the cultural and procedural rules for talking with different kinds of people
- engage in role-play
- deploy a range of rhetorical strategies to persuade others
- have some metalinguistic knowledge
- get pleasure out of playing with and through language
- have a developing sense of genres of talk, for example jokes, stories, 'news', etc

Although there is a debate as to the extent to which language play can be classified as evidence of metalanguage awareness, Juliet Partridge of the University of Tasmania has described how texts used by early readers which utilise aspects of language play such as rhyme, riddles, puns and alliteration may facilitate language development (1992, UKRA presentation). Most would accept that children, through language play, become familiar with the linguistic structures which they will reflect upon later.

Practical Activity 3.1

The following suggestions come from Alison Nealy, a Year 1 teacher. If you are a Year 1 teacher, you could add to this list and talk to the teachers from Years 4 upwards about the kinds of things you encourage children to do. If you are a teacher of children aged seven and above, then you could arrange to take a Year 1 class to try some of these out:

a) IN PLAY ACTIVITIES:
Lots of role-play — house, shops and so on. (Other fruitful scenarios are a bus/train using rows of chairs in the hall or playing schools — it is amazing what you learn about your own habits and sayings!)

— playing/co-operating with toys. Construction toys are particularly useful where methods of building/design/function of each part of the 'model' can be discussed/argued about/dictated by the bossy one! It's important to limit the number of children allowed to play with some toys otherwise fragmentations of the group can occur, following dissent over the common aim. Dividing the materials between the factions never works because no one gets enough to do anything properly.

— free play with classroom displays and equipment. Often children can choose to 'play' with an experiment or apparatus they have been 'working' with earlier. I have found that children doing this with friends verbalise their thoughts about the results as they go. If playing by themselves they will quite often want to report to the teacher at the end of the activity.

b) IN GROUP SITUATIONS:
— circle-time ice-breakers such as — introducing yourself (Clap! Clap! Li-sa!), then saying one true and one made-up thing about yourself.
  — telling news.
  — telling stories: group contributions to a common story, either a well-known one such as *The Three Bears* or a story made up by a group leader (for example, the teacher) and adapted to include children's suggestions as the story unfolds.
  — rhyming words, examples, suggestions from children.
  — towards the end of the Year 1, I've had some success with rhyming couplets. I supply the first line, the children help out with the second.
  — description games: one person describes something or someone, others guess.

c) IN 'STRUCTURED' SMALL GROUP SITUATIONS:
  — recording conversations, finding out about people (asking questions). Expect a lot of giggling to start with. Familiarise with tape recorder if necessary.
  — taped poetry/stories for quiet listening
  — taped news/stories by children
  — board games/card games

d) CHILDREN WITH SPECIFIC LANGUAGE DIFFICULTIES:
Once specific language difficulties have been noticed — and there are striking differences in children's achievements, even as early as Year 1 — then it is important to find out if the cause is physical, neurological or social. In an ideal world, the best strategy for dealing with these problems is a daily, one to one, five minutes uninterrupted chat about anything at all. Practically this is less easy than it sounds, for having an *uninterrupted* five minutes in an infant classroom is very difficult. This is where a good classroom assistant or parent helper is invaluable, either to have the chat or to field the rest of the class

while teacher and child are incommunicado.

Playground duty can afford good opportunities for talking informally with individuals. In the classroom context, any activity which involves working with or helping an adult, who can talk with children as they do the job e.g. washing paint pots, sorting out mixed up pieces of jigsaw, tidying a cupboard. Finally, small groups can use board games alongside a parent helper.

'Oracy and Play' is not something that should be restricted to the early years. Here are some ways of working with older children.

Practical Activity 3.2: Working with Years 3 to 8

Invite children to try one of the following, collaboratively, in groups. The emphasis is on talking rather than writing, though someone can volunteer to do the writing down.

1. Backwards rhyme: start with a list of eight rhyming words (for example, crown, town, frown, brown, gown, drown, down). Now produce a very short poem:

A smile then a frown
As she thought he could drown
Weighed down by his crown
And heavy brown gown
Far, far from the town.

2. Always alliterate: use the initial letters of your name for some alliterative nonsense:

Madeline makes merry
Ann actively aids archers
Rebecca returns rooks relentlessly
Yasmine yodelled yesterday.

Richard relishes raspberries
Oswald outshines Oscar
Benjamin betrays bitterness
Ian is ill
Nigel never neglects newts.

Not all acrostics (as these are called) need to be nonsensical:

Helen likes clothes
Especially bows
Last Saturday it rained
Easy she thought
Nice day for dressing up.

Language play itself is accompanied by several years experience of an environment in which the children hears adults addressing or talking to each other. As Garton and Pratt have demonstrated (1989) pre-school children of two, three and four years of age have often picked up a great deal of knowledge about the differences between sounds (say between a 'k' sound and a 'd' sound) even though they cannot reproduce that sound, as the following extract shows:

A four-year-old is talking about what he wants to be when he grows up.
Adult: What do you want to be when you grow up?
Child: A dowboy.
Adult: So you want to be a dowboy, eh?
Child (irritated): No! Not a dowboy, a dowboy!
(Garton and Pratt, 1989. Also quoted in LINC, unpublished, p.12)

The stages in the development of language were described by Gordon Wells in *The Meaning Makers* (Wells 1986) and adapting the diagrammatic form in which they appeared in the LINC materials they can be summarised as shown overleaf.

Ages five to eleven: foregrounding talk in the primary classroom

How easy is it to measure and describe the changes that take place in children's speech between the ages of five and eleven? For a number of reasons, it is not very easy at all, even though we could easily tell by listening to a tape whether the speaker was five or eleven. Brooks (1992) concludes that despite the thorough language development research of the Bristol Study of Language Development (Wells 1985a 1985b, 1986) and the empirical findings of Durkin (1986) and Neville (1988) we know remarkably little about the development of children's speech through the primary and middle school. This may be a legacy of the 1960s belief, following Chomsky (1959), that language development was largely complete by the age of five, and that what followed was largely an unfolding or revelation of patterns already in place. Yet common sense tells us that most eleven-year-olds are more sophisticated speakers than most five-year-olds, and that there are some things that eleven-year-olds are still not at home with, whereas at fifteen they will be. Assessment and Performance Unit surveys (Gorman *et al.* 1988) have shown that eleven-year-olds are more proficient at narrating a personal anecdote, telling a story or describing a picture than they are at presenting a point of view based on written notes or discussing a technological problem. From Neville we learn that a child's vocabulary at least doubles between early primary and mid secondary. But as yet we have no model or oral development other than the implied one in the National Curriculum Order for English.

STAGES OF EARLY LANGUAGE ACQUISITION

FUNCTION	MEANING*	STRUCTURE
What the children are trying to do with their language (e.g. make requests, ask questions, make statements.)	The states, events and relationships the children talk about	The way in which the language is put together – its grammar
Stage I Children's first utterances usually serve three purposes: – to get someone's attention – to direct attention to an object or event – to get something they want – a thing, or a service done for them. Next, they begin to: – make rudimentary statements ("Bird's gone") – make requests.	Children begin by naming the thing referred to. Soon they move beyond this to relating the object to other objects, places and people, e.g. "Daddy car", "There Mummy", as well as to events, e.g. "Bird's gone". They are concerned with articulating the present state of things. Because of the very limited structures children can control at this stage, much meaning is conveyed by intonation.	Many of the remarks of this stage are single words, either the names of things or words like "there", "look", "want", "more", "all gone". (These are often referred to as "operators" because (whatever their grammatical function in adult speech) they serve here to convey the whole of the child's meaning apart from the name of the object.) Other remarks consist of objects name and operator in combination: "Look Mummy", "Daddy gone", "There Mark".
Stage II At this stage children begin to ask questions; usually only "Where?" questions.	Children are very concerned at this stage with naming and classifying things (and drive parents made asking "Wassat?"). They also begin to talk about locations changing (e.g. people "coming" or "going" or getting "down" or "up"). They begin to talk in simple terms about the attributes of things (e.g. things being "hot", "cold", "big", "small", "nice", "Naughty doggy", "It cold Mummy").	Children's questions at this stage tend to consist of "What?" or "Where?" (the interrogative pronoun) and the object begin asked about (e.g. "Where ball?") "A" or "The" starts appearing in front of nouns. Basic sentence structure begins to be used: subject – verb e.g. "It gone", "Man run", or subject + verb + object e.g. "Teddy sweeties". (Teddy wants some sweeties). The apostrophes of possession begin to be used: "Sarah's doggy", "Man's bag".
Stage III By now, children are asking lots of different kinds of questions, but often signalling that they are questions by intonation alone (e.g. "Sally play, Mummy?"). They are also able to express more complex wants: "I want Daddy take it to work" as they begin to use more grammatically complex sentences.	Children now begin to talk about actions which change the object acted upon (e.g. "You dry hands"). Verbs like "listen" and "know" begin to appear as children start to refer to people's mental states. Children, by now, refer regularly to events in the past and, less frequently, in the future. They can talk about actions being on-going ("Mark doing it", "Shish still in bed") and enquire into the stage of actions (e.g. as to whether something is finished). They are beginning to articulate clearly the changing state of things.	The basic sentence structure has expanded: Subject + verb + object + addition is regularly seen: "You dry hands", "A man dig down there". Children at this stage are beginning to use auxiliary verbs: "I am going" and phrases like "In the basket" (i.e. using preposition + article + noun).

Stage IV As children begin to use increasingly complex sentence structures (see "Structure" column) they begin to: – make a wide range of requests (e.g. "Shall I cut it?" "Can I do it?") – explain – ask for explanations – the dreaded "Why?" question makes its appearance!	Because children are now able to use complex sentence structures, they have flexible tools for conveying a wide range of complex meanings. Perhaps the most striking development is their grasp and use of abstract psychological verbs like "know" to express the intangible operations of their mind. Children also, by this stage, begin to express meaning indirectly – e.g. replacing the direct imperative request "Give me..." with the more indirect "Can I have..." when it serves their purpose or the situation better. As well as saying what they mean, they are now saying it appropriately for the context.	Children by this stage are handling questions – "Can I have one?" – and negatives – "He doesn't want one" – with ease, and are no longer reliant on intonation for these. This is because they are now fully able to handle auxiliary verbs: 'do' is the first to appear in children's talk, followed by "can" and "will". By now too, children are using one part of their sentence to refer to other parts e.g. "I know you're there" or "I want the pen Grandpa gave me". Now that they can do this, the sentence has become a very flexible tool for them.
Stage V By now, children are frequently using language to do all the things they need: – giving information – asking and answering questions of various kinds – requesting directly and indirectly) – suggesting – offering – stating intentions and asking about those of others – expressing feelings and attitudes and asking about those of others.	Children are now able to talk about things hypothetically or conditionally: "If you do that, it will ...". They are also able to formulate the conditions required for something to happen: "You've got to switch that on first". Often they are talking about things which are always so – i.e. they are able to talk about generally applicable states of affairs. As well as general references to past and future, children now begin to talk about particular times; "after tea", "before bedtime", "when Daddy comes home". They are able to make estimations about the nature of actions and events, e.g. that things are habitual, repetitive or just beginning, for example. *NB "Meaning" here refers to meanings which children *express*. They may *understand* more.	By this stage, children are quite at home with all question structures including those beginning with words like "What?" and "When?"; "What does it mean?", "When is she coming?", where the subject and verb have to be inverted. They are also fluently using sentences made up of several clauses; consequently, the flexibility and variety of their sentence structure has increased considerably. Up to now, grammatical developments have added to the length of the sentence. Now, children begin to use processes which make for great economy of expression (these are collectively referred to as a *cohesion*).

By the end of stage V, a child's language is in place and s/he has a basic vocabulary of several thousand words. From now on, what is learned increasingly depends on experience – on opportunities to use the language and to hear it used, for a wide range of purposes to a wide range of audiences in a wide range of contexts.

(LINC, unpublished, pp. 14–45)

We have already drawn attention to the key place given to speaking and listening in *English 5-16*, and it is interesting to see that the authors of the report, having established that talk is central to the learning process, then go on to consider the way that communication is a keystone of the community, whether we are defining the community in terms of the social group in which we live, the economic environment of industry, commerce, business and the professions in which many go on to work, or the immediate community of school. Let us consider two of these communities, the two which featured in the LINC television programmes — school and a hospital.

Practical Activity 3.3: A day in the language life of the school

This is an activity for older children. An activity for early years children, one which also involves older children, follows.

A group of five/six children, together with an adult and a camcorder, are commissioned to make a short video of the daily language life of the school, concentrating on a variety of Year groups. The preliminary meeting of the commissioning agency agreed that the following locations/scenes should be included:
1. Starting the day 2. Registration 3. Assembly 4. Waterplay
5. Making a circuit 6. Playground Talk 7. Shared Reading 8. Lunch
9. Pastoral Talk 10. Learning a game 11. Talking about some aspect of geography or history 12. Describing movement 13. Staffroom 14. End of day (caretaker) 15. Playground/parents

Children then show the film, stopping it after each scene to comment on the importance and purpose of the spoken language at each stage.

Practical Activity 3.4

Two Year 5 or Year 6 children go into the home corner in the Year 1 class and act as participating observers as the children there act out a day in the language life of a hospital.
The home corner should thus have a bed, medicine cabinet, charts, kitchen area, and so on. Provide paper for notes, charts and notices, etc. The older children then meet back in their classroom to discuss and record what they have observed about the way young children use language.

Role-play and public speaking

For children in Years 5, 6, 7 and 8 a more formal kind of speaking will be included in the talk repertoire. Discussions will become debates, there will be oral presentations to small groups if not the whole class, and role-playing situations in which adult situations such as a public enquiry into the routing of a motorway will be enacted. Some of this work will come under the umbrella of drama, some under the heading of language or English work.

3.3 Story-telling in the classroom

Arguably story-telling is the most natural and universal reason for speaking with an awareness of audience. Narrative is not only a 'primary act of mind' to use Barbara Hardy's phrase, it is a fundamental way of structuring experience and something encountered and practised by children from the earliest age. The ability to retrieve the past and talk about it is a significant stage in children's language development, as they discover that they are able to break out of the present. At home children will hear stories, they will recount to their parents stories of what has happened to them while they were playing, they will tell each other about their experiences. When it occurs naturally in conversation story-telling requires children and adults to possess considerable social skills, because it breaks the normal rules of turn taking. As Harold Rosen has pointed out, when someone says 'Did I ever tell you about the time I . . .' they are signalling that they would like you to listen more than the usual amount of time. Children telling stories onto a tape recorder, writing them, and examining the difference, can unearth a tremendous wealth of knowledge about the way language works and can be used, and is a rich resource for the teacher to draw on in the classroom.

Practical Activity 3.5: Oral story-telling in the classroom

Most of the following activities involve retelling stories that children have previously heard.

i) CIRCLE ACTIVITIES: Chain Stories: sitting in a circle, children retell bits of a story, passing on a story stone or shell when the next person takes up the narrative.

Fortunately/Unfortunately: The teacher starts by saying something like 'When I woke up this morning my car would not start. Fortunately I have a bicycle and live near the school.' The first child continues with a statement beginning with 'unfortunately', and so on.

ii) PAIR STORY-TELLING: Sitting opposite each other, pairs of children tell each other a story they have heard or read. They then move on to make another pair. Do this three times.

Mixed age children tell each other stories, or children are paired with adults.

iii) GROUPS: The teacher tells a small group of children a story, and they go and tell it to their own small groups.

iv) AUDIENCES: Children prepare a story-telling session to be presented to parents. Parents in turn tell their own favourite stories.

v) TEACHERS: tell stories to their own class, or to someone else's class.

vi) VISITING STORYTELLERS: invite a professional story-teller into the school.

vii) DRAFTING STORIES: Using a tape recorder, children tell stories and then listen to them. They then improve the story in some way.

viii) NON-FICTION STORIES: Children are asked to record onto a tape recorder a report of a project or experiment they have carried out. With younger children, a recorded report is likely to be a fuller, more structured and carefully thought out report than a live one.

What are the educational reasons for story-telling in the classroom?

Apart from the obvious fact that story-telling provides opportunities to carry out many of the speaking and listening Attainment Target activities in the National Curriculum, it also provides an opportunity to develop work in art, drama, music and writing. Children can present stories against a painted background, or write versions of the stories they have heard. It extends their knowledge of stories which come from a wide range of cultures, and offers them a chance to hear traditional tales from many parts of the world. It allows discussion of the way stories end or develop, and the issues of power or gender that characterise many stories. It allows children to use their own language, and speak in their own voices, rather than one imposed on them. In so doing it plays an important role in the provision of equal opportunities in the school.

3.4 Talking about books

Although talk may precede reading, pre-school and early years children, as well as proficient readers from junior and middle schools, will enjoy talking about books. The language leader is often in a position to recommend books which will stimulate children, and lead to lively, enthusiastic discussion. For younger children there are interactive books like Janet and Allan Ahlberg's *The Jolly Postman* and *The Jolly Christmas Postman* and picture books like Sarah Garland's *Doing the Washing* and *Polly's Parrot*. Older children can talk in groups with or without the teacher, having collectively read Robert Westall's *The Scarecrows* or *Fathom Five*, the sequel to *The Machine Gunners*. Preparation will ensure that the talk has some structure (What does Polly see in this scene?) without being constricting.

3.5 Codes and registers

Much is made in the National Curriculum of children being able to speak and write in appropriate circumstances in Standard English. In other words, children should be made aware of the conventions of Standard English, and in certain contexts asked to stick to them.

Standard English is a dialect, but a dialect which is privileged above all others. It is a matter of power, beautifully illustrated by an old black and white film called 'The Franchise Affair' in which a witness is told by the Judge, who leans over the bench in disapproving way, to stick to 'Standard English, or at least basic English'. The witness, who has been using what the Judge regards as slang expressions, wilts and conforms. Even today it is unlikely that a witness would say 'No your honour, I wish to stick to my pattern of speech: I would like you to adjust yours' because of the unequal position of the powerful judge and the nervous witness. So that in saying that Standard English is simply a dialect that cannot be said to be better or worse than Geordie, West Country or Norfolk dialects (not to be confused with accents − a child can speak Standard English with any accent under the sun) we are not saying that it doesn't matter how you speak. Everyone accepts the need for the appropriate register − that is the appropriate pattern of speech for the appropriate context. Formal contexts, such as interviews, and many careers, require the speaking of Standard English. Once familiar with this children are able to move from one register to another with great ease. After all, they already possess not one but a number of languages, in that they move naturally from the register they use with their friends, to that which they use with their parents, and to that which they use with adult strangers.

At the same time it is important to recognise the rich variety of non-standard dialects, and the way that each regional dialect has a fully worked-out system. One consequence of Bernstein's notion of elaborated and restricted codes (Bernstein, 1964) was that some teachers took this to mean that some children didn't have a developed language system at all, and this became associated with the idea of class. This was fatally patronising, but in validating and valuing all the language children bring to the classroom in a constructive way, the teacher cannot ignore the realities of the world. Ownership of Standard English is like owning a car − you can survive without one, but getting everywhere on public transport can sometimes be extremely difficult, even though trains and buses are better for the environment than cars.

Some children in the class may be bilingual, and for these children school may be the only place where they use their English. There are tremendous opportunities for comparisons of languages in exercises such as the 'language play' one above, and we have more to say about bilingualism in chapter 6.

3.6 Group discussion: collaborative talk

Research (see, for example, Nicholls J. and Wells G. (eds.) 1985, *Language and Learning*; and Maclure, M., Phillips, T. and Wilkinson, A. (eds.), 1988, *Oracy Matters*) has shown that children are often rather good at collaborative talk, even though transcripts of the conversation can make the talk look extremely undeveloped, unfinished and muddled. It is only when hearing (and sometimes seeing) the talk that it is possible to appreciate the strenuous working towards clarification of meaning that is taking place, using a whole series of linguistic and non-linguistic cues.

The structured alternative to collaborative talk is teacher directed talk, which consist of the teacher asking the whole class questions (Initiation), getting a response (Response) and providing a comment (Feedback). Hence the initials I.R.F. to describe the process. With a lively, sensitive teacher it can work well, but it's amazingly easy to fall into the trap of 'guess what the teacher has in her mind'. Language specialists can easily fall prey to suggesting things like 'There's a word for being frightened of being shut in − does any one know what it is?' The problem with closed questions is that the questioner has only one answer in mind, and so quite enterprising suggestions have to be turned down, leading to deflation. This is not to suggest that teachers should never ask specific questions, merely to point out the dangers of this technique if handled badly.

Finally, on this point, if there are colleagues who are suspicious of group talk on the grounds that children can waste a lot of time by not concentrating on the point, and I.R.F. on the grounds that if the teacher had told the children the answer straight away it would have saved a lot of time, don't talk merely about the value of process. Instead, quote the CBI which has endorsed a problem-solving approach (on the grounds that problem-solvers rather than academics with memories full of information are what industry needs) and two teachers, one of whom said that collaborative talk shows what children have learnt rather than what they have been taught, while the other commented that children sometimes don't concentrate when they are writing: it's just not so noticeable. Yet we must be careful. In *Thinking Voices* (Norman, 1992) there is a salutory chapter by Terry Phillips with the title 'Why? The Neglected Question in Planning for Small Group Discussion'. Terry Phillips describes how one group of children, asked to reach agreement on the objects they would put in a time capsule, simply traded off suggestions quickly and drew up a rushed list. Why not? They were simply doing what they had been asked. The lesson for the teacher providing the scaffolding is clear: make quite explicit what the purpose of the activity is. Let children ask 'Why are we doing this?' so that there is a shared understanding of the purpose of the group discussion. If the intention is for children to reflect on their decisions, to evaluate their choices, and to consider the choices of others in a thoughtful and negotiated way, then say so! Otherwise we end up with hastily drawn up lists!

Here is an activity which moves us in that direction.

Practical Activity 3.6

REFLECTIONS: CHILDREN REFLECTING ON THEIR OWN TALK

Children work in pairs recording on tape a rehearsed but unscripted advertisement for one of the following:

a) Bottled mineral water   b) sun glasses   c) latest film

MARKET RESEARCH: Test on a group of other children. Listen to their comments.

Children then revise their advertisement, discussing ways in which they could improve it.

Most teachers find it pays dividends to manage and arrange their groups carefully, ensuring that there is a gender mix and a mixture of personalities and abilities in each group. Friendship groups are not always the best groups for challenging and productive oral discussion.

3.7 'Improving the Quality of Argument'

Improving the Quality of Argument (Andrews *et al.*, 1993) is the title of the final report of a project which sought to explore ways in which the learning and teaching of argument in schools can be improved. It is generally agreed that this is a neglected area in the primary school curriculum, and in 1988 an Assessment and Performance Unit report noted that only 8 per cent of a substantial sample of eleven-year-olds regularly engaged in this kind of work (Gorman *et al.*, 1988). There is clearly a problem about finding space in an already overcrowded timetable, but the evidence of the Andrews report is that primary age children are capable, in Stephen Clarke's words, of 'far greater powers of argument than may often have been assumed' (Andrews, 1993, p. 233). Projects in primary schools ranged from Year 5 and Year 6 work on topics such as bullying and school rules, to projects with Years 1 and 2 on the moral issues in *Burglar Bill*, and *Jack and the Beanstalk*. With younger children discussion of whether it was right for Burglar Bill to do certain things and whether it was right for Jack to take the Giant's gold had to be backed up by *reasons*. With the older children it was possible to look in a more systematic way at the nature of argument, at both adversarial and collaborative approaches, and in one school a Friday Club was formed to focus on issues for debate. Children not only produced writing, but reflected on ways in which the foregrounding of argument had influenced them. All seemed to enjoy it, and one of the most interesting findings was the way that poor readers were sometimes very skilful when it came to oral argument.

3.8 Speaking and writing

It is usual to point out that there are several important differences between speaking and writing. Speaking is unrehearsed, unedited, unrevised. It is also ephemeral: writing is a permanent record. The differences are best illustrated by comparing the transcript of an actual conversation around a meal table with an equivalent scene from a novel or play.

It is hardly surprising, however, that in very young children the differences are not so marked. There are clear connections between speaking and the early patterns of writing. Halliday (1989) discusses some of the similarities and differences in his *Spoken and Written Language*. On the other hand, as Katharine Perera (1990, in Carter (ed.), 1990) has argued we may not be fully aware of how often children are omitting oral constructions from their writing, simply because that which has been mentally discarded in the writing process never gets to be seen.

3.9 Strategies for talking and listening from New South Wales

We shall end each of the three chapters in this section of the book with some practical suggestions from the Support Document for English: *Kindergarten to Year 6* in New South Wales. Here are some for talking and listening: many of them will be familiar to you already.

BARRIER GAMES: a physical barrier is placed between pairs of children, who then have to describe a picture, ask questions about an object or tell their partner how to arrange objects.

PROBLEM-SOLVING ACTIVITIES: in groups children are given a problem to solve, in the context of information which they are given. In *The Desert Island Game* they are given a list of objects, songs, videos, books or food, and they must then agree on six or ten which they would have with them. In *The Gift Game* children are given a list of people and a catalogue, list of gifts or collection of 'junk' mail from which they must choose an appropriate gift for each person. In *Twenty Questions* a child takes on a role (For example, a lawyer, a bricklayer, a fire-fighter) and then the other children have to ask up to twenty questions, for which the answer can only be 'yes' or 'no', to discover their identity. An actual person such as Ned Kelly or Cleopatra may be preferred. *Hot Seating* is a stage on from this, involving detailed interviewing, with teacher acting as intermediary.

LISTENING GAMES: these are often best organised as circle activities. In *Memory Games* one person starts by saying 'I went to the zoo and saw . . .' or 'I went on a picnic and ate . . .' or 'I went to the shop and bought' and then the next person repeats the statement and adds an item. When it breaks down the game starts again. In *Dictagloss* the teacher reads a passage or poem at normal pace, and the children write down key words or phrases. The teacher rereads, again at normal pace, and in groups children try to reconstruct the passage as they heard it. They then compare it with the original.

3.10 Summary

Before we turn to reading and writing let us summarise what we have discussed so far. We shall do this through a practical activity.

Practical Activity 3.7 Writing a School Policy on Talking and Conferencing

Introduce this brainstorming activity to your colleagues by summarising some of the points about the status of talk made in the first section of this chapter. If there is general agreement on the importance of talk in the context of both learning and the National Curriculum, then hand out and consider the appropriateness of the following questions when planning talk activities:

Making Space for talk: Purpose and place

What is the point of the activity?
Will the fruits of the discussion be passed on to others?
What materials and activities will have been used to introduce the activity?
How will the furniture be organised?

Talking within a framework

What kind of ground rules?
How should groups be selected?
How long should be allowed?
Will there be opportunities to reflect on their ideas?
Will they want to record their conversation, on either a computer, paper, or a tape recorder?

Practical considerations

What will the role of the teacher be? Will the teacher be available as a consultant?
Will children have different roles? Are any of them 'experts'?
What about the reluctant speakers: how can they be encouraged?

Outcomes

The children will consider the activity to have been worthwhile if . . . what?
I shall consider the activity to have been worthwhile if . . . what?

Finally, proceed to small group discussion of the following:
What should the school policy be on:
1. The status of talk within the classroom and school.
2. Knowledge of pre-school talk.
3. Talking about books.
4. Standard English, register, accent and dialect.
5. Collaborative talk and I.R.F.
6. Role-play and public speaking.
7. Story-telling in the classroom.
8. Speaking and writing.
9. The assessment of talk (see chapter 9).

Ask each pair or group to report its findings, and then take these ideas further, issuing a consultative reading policy which staff are asked to comment on and modify prior to a follow-up meeting. You will probably want to adapt the eight sections proposed above, adding or subtracting as your school thinks appropriate.

CHAPTER FOUR

Producing Readings Together

Reflection and analysis

> People say that life is the thing but I prefer reading (Logan Pearsall Smith
> *Afterthoughts**)

In this chapter we continue our survey of the subject of language in the primary school by focussing on reading, one of the key areas on which the language leader will be assumed to have some expertise. We begin by reminding ourselves of the holistic approach to language, and then address the key question of why we want children to read. We briefly consider the impact of television, before going on to stress the importance of literacy. Next we consider ways in which the development of children's reading can be supported, and reflect on whether reading schemes and the concept of emergent literacy enhance this development. We briefly consider the role of group readings, reading recovery and reading information books, before concluding with a brief reference to advanced reading skills and the assessment of reading. Once again our survey is influenced by our model, which sees reading as an interactive process, in which a text (scaffolding) leads to reading (production) which is then enhanced by discussion (reflection and analysis). First, however, a reminder, if any were needed, of the dangers in separating reading from talking, listening and writing.

4.1 Questions about reading

Whole language and USSR

There is something terribly misleading about the signal a new chapter sends in a book about language in education. We have separated talking

---

*Our thanks to Sally-Anne Mitchell for drawing our attention to this quotation.

and listening from reading, as if they were discrete entities. We package language for discussion purposes, and for assessment purposes, which is why the Order for English has separate strands and attainment targets. In his original report, however, Professor Cox and his committee stressed the interrelatedness of reading and writing, speaking and listening. From their classroom experience most teachers would confirm that Kenneth Goodman (1986) was right to argue that language emerges in different but interconnected forms often in a single situation. The extension of this belief in whole language is that children do not learn by being taught a discrete hierarchy of language skills, so that we should resist, or realise the limitations of, the images of three ladders, speaking, reading and writing, which children have to climb separately until they reach the top. We can see this tendency to move from part to whole by looking at the historical development of the teaching of reading from the end of the nineteenth to the end of the twentieth century which would look something like this: alphabetic, syllabic, phonetic, look and say, and 'real books'. Although it is generally accepted we experience language as we experience things we see − recognising that a shoe is a shoe from its appearance, rather than mentally assembling the heel, sole, toe and laces, until we have constructed a complete shoe − we obviously have to make sure our plans cover the National Curriculum with its separate Attainment targets. And for classroom management reasons there will be sessions in which writing is given prominence, and sessions which focus on reading. Obvious examples of this are DEAR − Drop Everything And Read, ERIC − Everyone reading in class, USSR − uninterrupted, sustained silent reading, and SQUIRT − sustained quiet reading time − in which during a timetabled period lasting up to half an hour (depending on the age of the children) both teacher and class read silently together, and then talk about what they have been reading. The practice, popular in many schools, gives status to reading and allows the teacher to convey her own enthusiasm for books.

The School Council Project *Extending Beginning Reading* (Southgate *et al.*, 1981) recommended that all seven- to nine-year-olds should be given a period of sustained silent reading each day, and there is a considerable debate at the moment about whether teachers' concentration on core activities such as this has been at the inevitable expense of the rest of the National Curriculum, or whether the rest of the National Curriculum has eaten into the time formerly devoted to reading. In many junior schools silent reading continues to provide many children with a very pleasurable part of the day. The follow-up talk and discussion supports a social, interactive model of reading, in which children and books are seen as shared producers of meaning. As well as dialogue with the teacher follow-up activities in which children articulate their responses can include group reports, reading logs, or charts and diagrams. Such activities may help some children more than others make progress in their reading, and should be used sparingly – not all reading has to lead to writing! The point is that children learn in a whole variety of different ways, and draw on a whole variety of skills and knowledge. To separate reading from the other aspects of language may be useful from the point of discussion and planning, but for children and adults alike these separations are not reflected in the way we produce, reflect on and use language. No one model will serve the diverse needs of a whole class, let alone a whole school.

Why do we want children to read?

From our own research (Peel, 1992) it is clear that for many children the utilitarian aspect of reading is the one that has impressed them. A selection of Year 2 children from Plymouth and South Devon Schools said that, among other things, they needed to read wiring instructions to avoid electrocution, to help a blind mother, and to help them get a job. Pleasure did not enter the equation very much. Yet most teachers, even those enfolded in critical theory, would put pleasure quite high on the list of the benefits to be gained from reading. It is quite likely that the one thing that has made us want to take on the role of language leader is the enjoyment we derive from reading fiction, magazines and newspapers. In drawing up a reading policy, we need to address the question of the kind of readers we want children to become, and why we want them to read.

It may be that we want to give children access to alternative, imagined worlds.

> The reader absorbs and makes pictures from the writer's words; it is therefore a superb aid to intellectual development. Reading fosters mental alertness because it is active; watching (television) is essentially passive. (Elkin, 1992)

The teacher who wrote this is expressing a widely shared view. Would we want to challenge any of the assumptions expressed here? Is gender an issue we would want to consider? How would we respond to the view that the problems is not that boys read too little, but that girls read too much? And what about the disparaging remarks that are often made about the influence of television: is there a shared view in your school?

Has television supplanted Reading?

Television needs to be mentioned quite early on, because it usually enters discussion about the supposed problem of reading standards. In the 1990s, television, and its library of videos, is the source of narrative pleasure for many children. Susan Elkin mentioned above, was expressing misgivings about a recent serialised version of Mary Norton's *The Borrowers*, which she saw as a second-rate experience for children, compared to reading the book. People are usually divided in their response to the influence of television. Parents who regret the fact that their children do not read more usually lament the quantity of television that they consume. On the other hand, for understandable reasons, television features in most homes, and in many children's bedrooms. Critics, too, are divided over the significance of this. A survey carried by N.F.E.R. (Cato *et al.*, 1992) found that one in five seven-year-olds had a television set in the bedroom, and that these children were less likely to be good readers. But as we reported previously (Peel, 1992) children do not necessarily value the pleasure they get from television above the pleasure they get from books, and there are those such as Margaret Meek (1991) who suggests that some children may learn to read from television. They do this by seeing words in advertisements, and titles announcing programmes. And we should not assume that frequent television watching turns children into listless addicts. In the Leeds Education 2000 project many children, especially from disadvantaged neighbourhoods, were so keen to learn to read that they were willing to come into school during the holidays (Strickland, 1992). When a school is a caring, reflective learning environment children value it, and school, like reading itself, can become a refuge from the more intimidating facets of growing up in the nineties. Television programmes, like books, can be channels for these disturbing facets, but again like books they can surprise, delight and inform. If we view the arrival of the television as we view the arrival of the printing press in the fifteenth century, we put it in its proper perspective. It is a technological tool that can be used for a whole variety of purposes − most schools use television programmes as part of their teaching repertoire − and a recognition of this fact must surely make us as language leaders want to bring the language of television into the educational frame. That is why we have a separate chapter on Media Education in the section called 'Scaffolding', in which we argue that children should be taught to 'read' television actively.

The importance of literacy

We all know that a literate child is not necessarily a happy or successful child, any more than a child who has problems with reading and writing is necessarily unhappy and unsuccessful in the broader sense. Yet it is the exceptional child who has the reserves of character and imagination to overcome serious literacy difficulties. In taking on the responsibility for co-ordinating the literacy policies in the school the language leader's heart is likely to miss a beat from time to time as she or he reflects on the awesomeness of the responsibility. The supervision of a literacy policy is indeed a role central to the importance of learning, but it would be quite wrong to think that literacy begins at five, or even four. Children arrive at school already having been made aware of the processes of reading and writing, and already able to talk and express themselves in speech and gesture. In some cases children arrive at school already able to read.

How do children learn to read?

This is the question we have heard on the lips of a student teacher hunting for an answer on the shelves of the library, and from the lips of a wise experienced teacher who had concluded that there was no universal answer that applied to all children. Cliff Moon (1988) relates the story of how a puppy was taught to overcome his fear of descending the stairs. A boy who had been left to look after the puppy for an evening solved the problem by putting the puppy on the first step and encouraging him to step down to the second step, and so on. The problem with this as a model for reading development (it works as a model for certain learning activities) is that it doesn't describe how children learn to read by doing the whole thing first, and then coping with the individual steps. For the story to work as a parable of reading the puppy would have to be encouraged in a supportive way to tumble down the stairs to get to his bowl, and having done that a couple of times he would then be invited to improve his technique of descent to make the experience even more enjoyable.

There are those who would argue that the step-by-step approach is the right model. It is what is often called the bottom-up model (the puppy story in reverse), with children being taught sounds, then words, then sentences, and so on. It may be that some children do learn to read that way: just as the puppy dog became increasingly adventurous with each step he took, so some children are able to progress as readers if this approach is used. As Ian Michael explains in *The Teaching of English from the Sixteenth Century to 1870* (1987), this was the approach adopted in the seventeenth century, with reading being taught through concentration on the letters, dividing a word into its component syllables, and stressing their obedience to a number of rules. The practice was very popular around 1675, but then fell into decline, and had been abandoned by 1820. Nevertheless, the link between spelling and reading never really died because it was based on the assumption that short things were easier to learn than long ones – hence the move from letter to syllable, and syllable to word. In the middle of the nineteenth century, Comenius's idea that we perceive objects and words in their wholeness belatedly took root (Comenius's *Orbis Sensualium Pictus* dates from 1659), and in the twentieth century the move in the direction of wholeness has continued. The analogy of how we learn to swim or ride a bicycle may be a useful one to explain how most children learn to read. We learn not by practising swimming strokes on a chair, or by riding a tricycle but by taking the plunge, and actually riding a bike. Similarly, a couple of years ago we saw learner hang-gliders taking off with an experienced hang-glider sharing the controls. So that is how you launch yourself off a mountain for the very first time! This seems to be the way we learn to read – by experiencing early on the thrill and joy that the whole experience can supply, but in the company of others who are more expert than us. The step-by-step approach, which as a twentieth-century model of learning has its roots in Piaget, Behaviourism and the work of Chomsky, has to be reconsidered in the light of the research of Bruner, Goodman and Donaldson, who emphasised the social, interactive and holistic nature of language learning, a point re-emphasised recently in *Learning to be Literate* (Garton and Pratt, 1989). As we saw in the last chapter, Gordon Wells in the Bristol Language Development Project found that children learned to talk not by being instructed and corrected by their parents but by being immersed in talk. In other words they learned to communicate by communicating. This principle has clear echoes in Frank Smith and Margaret Meek's suggestion that we learn to read by reading. In other words we move from whole to part and not from part to whole. This is the top-down model.

Most teachers take a pragmatic view and incorporate both approaches in their curriculum planning. The role of the language leader is to encourage colleagues to discuss the approach they favour, and where there is evidence that one approach is being favoured to the exclusion of others, to encourage reflection and dialogue. This can be done by having meetings in each other's classroom, or by asking someone to visit from another school. If evidence were needed that we use a variety of strategies when we read, a letter written by Peter Donnelly and published in the T.E.S. (29 March 1991) perhaps made the point. It started like this:

RXXL BXXKS DXBXTX XS PXXNTLXXS
Whxn wxll thx rxxl bxxks xrgxmxnt xnd?

and so it continued, demonstrating the wide variety of cues that we use when making sense of words.

The only problem with this is that adult readers have already developed these strategies: beginner readers would have difficulties with 'rxxl bxxks' because they have not had enough encounters with the expression 'real books'. So it is safe to conclude that children build on what they have seen, so that the more words they have seen and registered as meaningful, the greater is the chance that in fresh encounters with print, these words will be recognised and 'read'.

4.2 Towards production

First readings: emergent literacy

As we know, young children do not wait to be taught in the helpless way that fledgelings in the nest wait to be fed. They forage for themselves, and take what they want from the world as the fancy moves them. On shopping journeys in the push chair they will notice words, will see adults reading shopping lists and signing credit card slips. In play and interaction with their parents they will pretend to read books, and produce real or imaginary pieces of paper that constitute important 'letters' they have written. They will see words on television, and though they cannot read them they know that others can. They will be able to pick up the right sweet packet because they can 'read' the shapes and colours sufficiently well to know that it is sweets and not toothpaste! Anne Washtell, in a talk called 'Reading in the Early Years' (1991) argued that children should be encouraged to develop this awareness

88

of print from the very earliest age. In Shirley Payton's *Developing Awareness of Print* (1984) the child in the case study was spotting that the letter C in her name Catherine was also in the shopping logo 'Co-op' at the supermarket. Once in the nursery and reception class names and the names that form the register become invaluable aids to phonic and letter awareness. Rhymes and scrabble games serve a similar function. The teacher can build up confidence by encouraging children to suggest words for her to write on the board, words which they have seen in visits to the shop and the café, and so on. At the same time very young children's awareness of book's conventions should be recognised. Carol Fox (1983, 1984 and 1988) has shown how children 'talk like books' in the way that they tell and rehearse long, often quite complex narratives. At this stage they probably think that reading and writing are quite easy, just as older children often assume that driving a car must be easy. The language leader will want to encourage the parents of pre-school children to maintain that enthusiasm and natural willingness to experiment. In some cases this will mean reassuring parents that what they are doing already is exactly right, in some it will mean encouraging parents to give reading a higher profile in the home, and for a few it will mean tactfully suggesting that the parents curb their own enthusiasm if it is resulting in too stiff a regime. It may be that the early years teachers in your school organise home visits to prospective parents, and carry out baseline assessments. There will almost certainly be a meeting for such parents. Below is an activity which could produce a page of advice for parents of pre-school and early year children at either kind of meeting.

Practical Activity 4.1 So you want to help your children to read?

As a staff development exercise, consider ways in which the advice you send out to parents of pre-school children provides answers to the following questions. If it has not been the practice to send out advice, discuss the advisability of doing so, and use this activity to draft a document.

At what age should I introduce my child to books?
How should I introduce them?
How can I best choose appropriate books?
Should I buy these books, or can I get them from the library?
Should I try to teach my child to read, or can that be left to the school?
When is a child ready to start reading?
Should we read together at particular times of the day, and for how long?
What if my child wants to go back to the same book again and again?

Producing readings together: active emergent reading and writing

Reading and writing are not only inter-related, they are both active processes — hence the idea that children and adults together *produce* readings. To say that stories stimulate the imagination is to tell only half the story, for it makes the child's mind sound like a bell that is waiting to be rung. As Shirley Brice Heath says in 'Separating "Things of the Imagination" from Life: Learning to Read and Write' (1986):

> In the western tradition, debates over the role and power of imagination have continued since the earliest Greek writings. Samuel Coleridge's treatment of imagination in *Biographia Literaria* (1817) stimulated European and American writers of the past century to question whether imagination is a synthesiser or a multiplier of images. The image-making power of language has in recent decades been as debated for the reader as for the writer. Both use imagination to separate themselves from the natural world; every work of imagination is an analogue made up of only the fragments of life available to the imagination of the cocreators of text-reader and writer. (p. 156)

Reading is the making of meaning, the miraculous process whereby apparently arbitrary and meaningless symbols are taken in combinations from the page to the mind and there translated into pictures, ideas, stories and imagined worlds. As we have seen, oral language does this too in an equally wonderful and miraculous way. And the cycle is completed when the child reverses the process, and takes the pictures and thought from the mind and converts them into words, just as is happening now as we write this sentence. It is the mind of the learner that is at the centre, or rather the mind of the learner interacting with the text. This interaction is what characterises all language work, and underpins our model of learning. The unity of this process, which sees talking and listening, reading and writing as a continuum, is, as we have seen, known as whole language, or a holistic approach to literacy. It is important to stress this again, before we move in to the detail of how teachers and parents can induct children into reading, so that we do not lose sight of the wood as we examine the trees.

4.3 Scaffolding: help for beginner readers

Although children may come to school with a considerable understanding of how texts work — knowing about beginnings and endings of books, left to right directionality, front and back, even the difference between letter and word, we do not assume that things will take care of themselves and that the process of learning which seemed to occur automatically at home will continue without the continuing provision of an appropriate environment. For between the age of five and seven many children will make the most enormous progress in reading and writing — more than they ever make in their whole lives. For some children, and in certain schools this may be the majority, the school may be the first place that provides the kind of environment in which print awareness is encouraged, and so the rituals of the literacy club will have to be introduced from scratch. This is why the scaffolding produced by the class teacher is crucial for the language development of so many children. As Garton and Pratt (1989) conclude:

> A supportive person, prepared to talk to the child, to read to the child, to encourage attempts at literacy activities, is a prime ingredient in the development of spoken and written language. Such interaction need not always be one-to-one, but sensitivity to the child's needs, sensitivity to the child's accomplishments, and a readiness to assist the child's efforts when talking, writing or reading are essential. (p. 220)

What else needs to be considered during these early years?

Establishing the home corner and the book corner

A clear signal to nursery and reception class children that reading matters is the presence of an attractive reading area, well stocked with colourful picture books, some with and some without print. The book corner needs to be freely available and accessible — and children should be encouraged to take books home (and told that the books should live in their special plastic bags). Although it takes some setting up, a ticket scheme is advisable, and children should not feel that there is pressure from the teacher to take books or limit choice. Equally, the home corner, the area in which children will do much role-playing, can be supplied with writing materials, books and magazines, telephone directory and posters which children feel they can make free use of.

Print awareness in the classroom

Even though many children will not be able to read their names, it is worth combining their name with a picture above their peg, or on displays of their work throughout the room. There will be name labels on drawers or boxes, and words on the colourful displays throughout the room, especially on a wall display of a scene involving characters from a shared book. Children are curious about the world of print, and this curiosity is a natural step along the road to emergent reading.

Producing readings together

For the very young child reading is a shared activity with an adult. At the very beginning the child will probably want to tell the story from the pictures, ignoring the print, and predicting from the illustrations what is going to happen next. At the next stage the teacher will read all or part of the printed words, pointing to them as she does so. Gradually the child will take over, getting the sense of a line even if not getting every word right. In shared readings the adult and child take it in turns to read pages or lines. We all love stories, and this is what makes children persist with a reading, that and the sense that adults they care about value this activity and derive pleasure from it themselves. It requires effort — as adults we know how hard it is to make sense of a notice in a foreign language we are not familiar with. It is even more difficult if the letter forms themselves are unfamiliar to us. We can cope with 'Verboten' because it is like 'forbidden', but unless we are familiar with the Russian alphabet, this expression will baffle us:

Автомобили, для управления которыми выдано настоящее разрешение

So familiar letter shapes are important.

Textual cues

As readers we use the following cues:

pictures;
our own previous sight and knowledge of words;
knowledge of narrative structure: predictable story shape.

Beginner readers use the same strategies and so it is very important that they have had plenty of pre-reading experiences of this kind.

Reading methods: varieties of scaffolding

As language leader you will probably want to organise a staff development session in which the various 'methods' of teaching reading are discussed, even though some of them are not really 'methods' at all — they have simply been identified as such by some critics. Some of the following have been in use for nearly twenty years now, some have been superseded, some only recently introduced. Some involve strategies that are discernible in approaches to literacy adopted over one hundred years ago.

USING 'BIG BOOKS', 'SENTENCE MAKERS', 'LETTER TRAYS': 'LANGUAGE EXPERIENCE'

The 'language experience' approach emphasises the active nature of learning to read and produce readings, and the social nature of language. In reading from an enormous book, with very large print, the children can share in the experience of seeing and hearing a story unfold, and the teacher can point to different features of the words as she reads. The book is held open on an easel, facing the children who sit on the mat, and the children see the teacher behaving as a reader. Alternatively children can follow in their smaller versions of the book. The trouble with Big Books is that they soon lose their newness unless they are kept in a large plastic wallet which some suppliers sell. And then there is the problem of finding somewhere to store them.

The Sentence Maker is a way of integrating reading and writing. In method it goes beyond the practice by which the teacher intially writes down the child's dictated story, for it allows the active involvement of the child. Supported by an adult, early years children select words or letters from a tray or folder and place them on a display stand to make up sentences and narratives. Children are thus being readers and producers of new texts at the same time, and this activity became extremely popular through the 'Breakthrough to Literacy' materials of the 1970s. Having produced their sentences they then copy them down. If they want a word that is not already printed on the card the teacher simply makes a card with it on, so that there are no limits to the vocabulary being used. These words can be kept on the wall in pockets, and children can check that they have the right word by running it through the language master — as long as it is a word in common usage. The language master system is not so flexible when different words are required. However, at the same time as doing this kind of story and sentence making, children would be encountering a wide variety of printed stories, information and picture books, thus addressing any concern there may have been about children not breaking through to discover the richness of language. Teachers who still use this method frequently sound a note of caution about organisation. The sentence maker needs to be kept tidy or the whole things becomes a farce. Even then some children find it irksome to copy down a story they have already composed on the stand, while others find the little cards too small to handle easily.

RECOGNISING WORDS WITH FLASH CARDS

In the late nineteenth century there was a switch from learning to read through spelling and syllables to whole word recognition. In the twentieth century this led to the widespread use of the flashcard, which has a whole word on it and is flashed before the children who are then asked to say the word together. Words that can be accompanied by pictures are not so much of a problem as 'it' and 'go' which have no object with which they can be associated. So although some 25 per cent of our vocabulary is made up of a relatively short list of between ten and thirty words, a lot of these words (like 'the') do not have useful meaning when they are decontextualised. Another problem is that this method does not help children when they encounter a new word, and books with a limited number of words can become very dull and repetitive. The 'look and say' method remains popular in some schools, however, particularly those in which great stress is laid on phonic awareness, and can prove successful with children who have a strong visual memory.

WHAT ABOUT PHONICS?

Although a knowledge of phonics does not help us when we learn to talk, it is useful to know that the English language is broken up into sounds, represented by the sounds of the twenty-six letters of the alphabet and various combinations of these letter sounds. The National Curriculum Council argued that the revised Order for English should place more emphasis on the role of phonics in the teaching of reading, and this can be traced to the influence of Martin Turner's *Sponsored Reading Failure* (1990) which argued that evidence is available to suggest that reading development can be encouraged by phonics teaching. Although this evidence is not conclusive − in the seventeenth and eighteenth centuries there was a great vogue for phonic-based reading books, but when they proved ineffective they were replaced − most teachers will include some phonics work in their teaching repertoire. This may include 'I Spy' games, card games, board games, letter-writing practice as a formal class lesson, wall displays, pictures, colouring sheets and television programmes such as 'Words and Pictures' on the BBC. For certain words − is Reading a town or an activity? – we need the context, and so need to go beyond phonics.

UNNECESSARY SCAFFOLDING? READING SCHEMES

This is one issue which tends to divide teachers, and like many other things in education it has its ups and downs. Reading schemes are sets of books whose language and subject matter has been staged and structured in such a way that they provide a programme of reading which the teacher is able to monitor easily. The early criticism of such schemes was that the books were ridiculously artificial – hence the term 'real books' which is applied to stories written as stories rather than to conform to a level of language. Publishers have tried to answer this by commissioning 'real writers' to produce books for the schemes, which are now livelier and more colourful than their prodecessors. Few people are wedded to schemes in an evangelical kind of way: teachers use them because there is a continuing tradition in their school for using them, and they appear to offer something measurable in an uncertain world. Many schools use schemes such as Story Chest, Oxford Reading Tree, Ginn 300, and Fuzz Buzz, and in 1993 publishers reported a sudden demand for phonics-based reading schemes, no doubt in response to the proposed revision of the Order.

Critics of reading schemes would argue that they are totally unnecessary because they do not reflect the omnivorous way in which we read: plodding through a series of prescribed books kills the joy of reading, and turns texts into leaf fodder for caterpillars. Better to make available to children a John Burningham, a Jill Murphy or a Babette Cole. Those committed to this approach will take the bold step of throwing out all the schemes, allowing children free choice. In reply, those in favour of schemes argue that sometimes children choose inappropriately hard or easy books, and waste a lot of precious reading time either staring at meaningless pages or skipping through pictures. Colour coding of books is a kind of compromise, which allows children a choice, but allows the teachers to have some sense of the reading progress the child is making. The 'real books' approach can be made to work, and when it does it can generate an excitement for books that is infectious. There has to be whole school agreement if such an approach is to be adopted, and a complete enthusiasm for it. The language leader could test the waters by arranging a staff development session in which the matter is debated, using a discussion document which looks something like this.

> **Practical Activity 4.2 The Pros and Cons of Reading Schemes**
>
> | Pros | Cons |
> | --- | --- |
> | Allows teacher to monitor progress more easily. | Sometimes they are not 'real stories'. |
> | Some schemes are lively and colourful. | Children may find them too narrow and restrictive. |
> | Children experience a sense of achievement as they progress. | Differences between children are highlighted with a damaging effect on the children who are making slower progress. |
> | Something to build on: permits transference of vocabulary, phonic progression. | Gender stereotyping in Ginn 360 and 'One, Two, Three and Away'. |
> | Gives sense of 'comfortable familiarity'. | Focuses on one aspect of language, when we actually read by taking diverse elements from the whole book. |
>
> In pairs, add to, or challenge items from this list, to discover whether there are more pros than cons, or vice versa.
> As language leader you will need to gauge the position of your colleagues, so as to develop a whole-school approach and policy. It may be that the school has abandoned schemes, and relies on the teacher's ability to choose 'real' books. In that case discussion will focus on ways in which the real book approach can be improved so as to win the support from teachers that it demands.

Although most schools will favour a variety of methods, if they accept a model of learning which, like the one we offered at the beginning of this book, starts with the notion of production, but recognises that learning takes place where production intersects with supportive scaffolding and reflection, then the emphasis is likely to be on lively book discussion, creating a stimulating environment in which children's work features, and only using scaffolding where reflection considers it supportive and ennabling. Some teachers view reading schemes in this light: others teach successfully by doing away with schemes and colour coding altogether. If this is the case, it will need to be a whole-school approach, and the scaffolding will appear in the form of a sustained programme of literacy awareness and events rather than book resources alone.

Listening to children read

For years the practice of listening to children read has been favoured in the primary school as a way of ensuring one-to-one contact. Research has shown that in many classes during the two minutes attention that each child is likely to get, no more than thirty seconds passes before an interruption of some kind. This is of limited benefit to a child, and so teachers have decided either to encourage parents to come in and take part in shared readings, or they have so managed the class that there is an understanding that when the teacher is reading with a child no interruption is permitted. Children soon adapt and recognise the reason for this. The trouble with 'listening' is that there is no way of understanding if the child understands what is being read. Children may read out loud quite skilfully, without having a clue what they have read — but this can be true of adults as well! The teacher will normally find out whether this is the case by asking the child questions about what has been read.

Some teachers hae introduced the system of partner reading, where children read to each other, or paired reading where children share a text and come along to read to the teacher having prepared a reading. It is also possible to make use of any visitors who come to the class — student teachers, students on work experience, children from higher up the school, or the middle or secondary school — who in most cases will be happy to hear children read, or to read to them.

Reading support (1): reading recovery

It may be that your school has introduced a Reading Recovery Programme, the aim of which is to help those who are experiencing reading difficulties. It involves shared work — one-to-one tutoring — with adult and child producing readings together according to a set programme such as the following, as outlined by Howard Crossland:

A TYPICAL TUTORING SESSION (30 MINUTES)
1. Rereading two or more familiar books
Aims: boosting confidence, orchestrating skills.
2. Rereading the previous day's new book
Aims: check developing skills using a running rercord (see 'miscue analysis' below).
3. Letter identification using plastic letters and magnet board.
Aims: relate problems to context; build comparative strategies.
4. Writing a story using ideas from familiar books. As much as possible to be written without the teacher's help.
Aims: establish connections between reading and writing; expand the number of letters and words the child can write independently.
5. Hearing sounds in words
Aims: to help the child think about the order of sounds in spoken words;

help the child to analyse a new word into its sound sequences. (This may use material from child's writing, sometimes not.)

6. Cut-up stories – dictated by the child to the teacher, or copied by the teacher onto card from the child's (corrected) written story.

Aims: practise assembling sentences; one-to-one correspondence of sounds spoken and words written; directionality; checking behaviours; segmenting oral language; word study.

7. New reading book introduced (chosen by the teacher). Aspects of plot, pictures, words, letters, sentences, writing style are pointed out.

Aims: assist the child to orchestrate complex reading behaviours; apply strategies to new texts, with support.

8. New reading books attempted

Aims: practise the complex range of reading behaviours; continuity with the following day's lesson (recheck for accuracy).

The system was devised by Marie Clay, and the evidence from New Zealand is that it works well, not least, perhaps, because of the one-to-one support and attention the child is getting! But it is more than that: it provides a highly structured example of 'scaffolding' being used to help children with their own language buildings, and is an example of the partnership or apprenticeship to the production of readings. In New Zealand teachers praise the method for the way it improves children's self-esteem. On the other hand, in Britain critics object to the fact that it can mean removal of the child from the classroom, and that those using the system have to conform to the methodology prescribed by Marie Clay. Parents are given no significant role, despite all the evidence to suggest that parental involvement is crucial in early reading. Finally, critics point out that it does not take acount of social or cultural conditions, nor acknowledge the linguistic experience of non-English speaking children. Basically the criticism is that it offers a very narrow view of reading, and one that we should not endorse unreservedly.

Reading support (2): specific learning difficulties

Parents are sometimes told that children who confuse one word or figure with another, make careless reading mistakes between the age of eight and twelve, or are confused between left and right, may be suffering from a specific learning difficulty called dyslexia. In many cases there are other explanations for these difficulties, and teachers have been reluctant to 'classify' children in this way. Early research was inconclusive, but the latest evidence is more convincing. It is now clear that a malfunction of the brain can cause left/right confusion over which

98

the child has little control. Expert diagnosis is necessary, and this may be possible through your LEA, which should have a policy on dyslexia. Parents may wish to know of the address of the British Dyslexia Association at 98 London Road, Reading, Berkshire RG1 5AU, or The Dyslexia Institute at 133 Gresham Road, Staines, TW18 2AJ.

Producing group readings together

In the field of education reader response theory owes much to the work of Louise Rosenblatt. In *The Reader, the Text, the Poem* (1978), drawing on the shift in emphasis in critical theory from author to text to reader, she argues that the text only comes alive, and thus becomes complete, when the reader carries out a reading. This emphasis on the active role of the reader has clearly changed the way we perceive reading, and in the classroom has led to the practice of small group reading sessions in which a common text is read (in a variety of ways) and then talked about. The advent of the Big Book means that group readings can begin as early as the reception class to Year 2, with predictions as to what the book is to be about followed by readings from volunteers (rather than in a set order which can have the effect of children concentrating solely on 'their bit'). Regarding Years 3 to 6, the class can be divided into groups of between three and five, usually friendship groups, facing each other and possibly supplied with a tape recorder. Each child takes a turn at reading, and the stories should be ones which can be completed in five to ten minutes. Give the children a specific task to complete once they have finished the reading. For narratives this could be a story map, a time chart, or a list of opposites. Children could discuss openings, endings, points of view, and the relationship between picture and text. These ideas and others are explored in *Group Reading in the Primary Classroom* (Bentley and Rowe, 1991).

Other group readings can take place on a smaller scale. These can involve prepared readings, shared readings and paired readings, with children reading together at times, or alternately, or both.

Types of reading and response: Key Stage 1 to Key Stage 3

Slightly different end-of-reading tasks of the DARTS kind could be appropriate, particularly for older primary children. DARTS are directed activities relating to texts, and include cloze exercises (deciding which word would best fit a gap in the text — children are given several choices), prediction exercises (what will happen next?), sequencing exercises (jumbled paragraphs which have to be rearranged), and underlining and labelling various sections of texts (facts or opinion, for example). Response activities can range from paintings to maps, from Wanted Posters for characters in books, to drawing up indexes for information books.

With information books children should be encouraged to use research skills by completing graphs and charts produced by the teacher. Many of the books which the children will be encountering in your classroom, both information books and popular children's fiction such as Dick King-Smith's *Hodgeheg*, Gene Kemp's *The Turbulent Term of Tyke Tyler*, Susan Cooper's *The Dark is Rising*, Janet and Allan Ahlberg's *The Jolly Postman*, or Robert Westall's *Blitz Cat* can be applied to the following activities suggested by Hilary Mason and Stephanie Mudd (1992).

ANTHOLOGY-CARTOON-CONTENTS-CREATIVE WRITING-DIARY ENTRY-EPITAPH-FACTION-INVITATION-JOKES-LYRICS-MAPS-PEN PORTRAIT-PERSONAL WRITING-PERSUASIVE LETTER-PICTURE BOOK-POSTER-PROCLAMATION-PROGRAMME OF EVENTS-PROMOTIONAL WRITING-RECIPES-RIDDLES-SIGNS-STORY-TELLING-TALK/PRESENTATION-TITLES.

For a fuller explanation you will need to consult the article itself but with a little bit of ingenuity you will be able to work out the kind of activities that each of these involves. A recipe for the 'boys' in *Piggybook* for example?

Reading information books

We have mentioned information books several times, and the language leader will need to stress the importance of developing children's skills as readers of what are sometimes called 'non-fiction' books. In *Making Facts Matter* (1992) Margaret Mallet offers a valuable account of the need for the careful selection of information books, for an awareness of the density of some information books, and the difficulties posed by some indexes. Familiarity with the organisation and structure of information books can be the subject of pre-reading activities. To assist and focus the reading itself a number of activities are useful. The group reading activity described above can be used in a slightly modified way, for example. With information books children should be encouraged to use research skills by completing graphs and charts produced by the teacher. Using a book such as *No More Butts: Tobacco and Smoking*

(Collins, 1988) children can be asked to complete summaries with the aid of the following table:

Place	Time	Event
North and South America	Earliest	Native Americans use leaves for smoking
Mexico	1578	Spaniards see Native Americans smoking
England	1584	Two of Raleigh's men bring tobacco to England

As Margaret Mallett observes, 'the more subject-centred approach of the National Curriculum makes information books a key genre in the primary years' (p. 38).

Advanced reading skills

In *The Teaching and Learning of Reading in Primary Schools* (HMI, 1991) a number of points were made about the need to extend children's reading, particularly at Key Stage 2 where bright children are often capable of much more sophisticated scanning and skimming techniques than they are either given credit for, or opportunities for. The same point was made in the revised document *English 5 – 16* (1993) where the introduction to Attainment Target 2 (reading including literature) says:

> More advanced reading skills enable pupils to recognise key points and issues in texts and to select and organise information efficiently. They comprise:
> – identifying key points and ideas
> – seeking information
> – skimming (for an overall impression of a page)
> – scanning (looking for specific items)
> – summarising
> – putting together material from different sources
> – cross referencing (including the use of an index)
> – distinguishing fact from opinion
> – reading literature with increasing insight
> – using library skills

Although it might be thought that children should only progress to this more advanced work having become 'free readers' after the successful completion of an initial reading programme, this assumes a linear model of reading development, whereas there is evidence to suggest that progress is cyclical. Some so-called advanced reading skills, such as reading between the lines, reading for information, distinguishing between important and less important elements in a text and discussing the structures of literary texts, can be introduced at the earlier stage.

Monitoring and intervening

Teachers can monitor children's development in reading (and writing) by:

Listening to children read aloud (sometimes useful).
Talking to children individually.
Looking at children's reading logs and reading journals.
Listening to children as they talk in small groups.
Noting voice and finger pointing (indicates a reliance on directional and visual attributes of text, as opposed to whole meaning).
Noting pauses and hesitations (as children search for a strategy and cue).
If possible, resisting intervention.
Noting repetitions: children may find this useful to recover a sense of the text they are reading.
Noting – and encouraging – self-correction.

It is also useful to keep a running record. This, a variation on miscue analysis, is described in chapter 9, and is a form of monitoring employed in the pilots for both the Key Stage 1 and the Key Stage 2 SATS in England.

Strategies from New South Wales to support reading

The following list was drawn up for teacher librarians in New South Wales. Although it is assumed that such people will be based in the library and not have a class to teach, there may be some ideas here which an enthusiastic school will want to take on and modify. On the other hand, it may be that there is something here on which you as language leader feel you can take an initiative.

TEACHING STUDENTS TO SELECT AND USE LITERARY, FACTUAL AND MEDIA TEXTS.
Activities to stimulate children's interest in, and enjoyment of, reading include the following:

author of the week corner	book character 'This is Your Life'
displays	author 'This is Your Life'

author visits

fancy dress

story-telling

reading stories

puppets

publication of children's own writing

readers' clubs

poem of the week display

book review mobiles

library 'graffiti' noticeboard (in which children write lines from favourite poems, comments on books, etc)

auctioning favourite, popular books

quiz shows

book talks

library magazine

book fairs

children's book review files

panel discussions

character guessing games

twenty questions

Summary of Topics

All of the following have been discussed, and knowledge and experience of each contributes to the expertise which we have identified as one key aspect of leadership:

- The concept of whole language
- The importance of literacy: why do we want children to read?
- Television and reading
- Reading development
- Supporting reading − reading schemes and emergent literacy
- Group reading
- Reading recovery
- Reading information books
- Advanced reading skills
- The assessment of reading (more in chapter 9)

CHAPTER FIVE

Producing Writing Together

Knowledge about writing is an essential part of the language leader's repertoire, and although it can be convincingly argued that every teacher should or does have this expertise in the context of their own classroom, it is the language leader who will have the global, cross-phase view that is essential for curriculum development. We begin the chapter by considering why we want children to write and then go on to consider the stages of writing – both in terms of the developmental stages, if such there are, and the stages in the process itself, from draft to finished product. We consider the issue of emergent writing, and the debate about whether process or product is more important, and the issues surrounding genre theory. We consider audience, purpose and context. This is followed by sections on the reluctant writer, spelling, information writing and other genres in the junior and middle schools, and we conclude with a brief look at poetry and advanced reading and writing skills, leaving the assessment of writing to a separate chapter once again.

Reflection and analysis

The length of this chapter is partly a reflection of the central role writing has in the process of learning. It also reflects a reality, namely the dominant role writing has always assumed when it comes to assessment, even though in many lives fluency in speech and reading are more immediately empowering. As teachers we have to balance these conflicting demands. Let us begin by deciding why it is we want to develop our own writing abilities and encourage them in children.

104

Preliminary Activity 5.1

Research in the early 1980s (Southgate *et al.*, 1981) suggested that writing is an activity which occupied primary school children for about 20 per cent of their curriculum time. But whereas upper juniors spent the majority of this time on writing related to topic work, the opposite was true for lower juniors who spent the majority of their writing time on free writing. Has the position changed in the 1990s? And are there significant differences in the answers to the following questions depending on the age of the children involved? In the following activity, keep these questions in mind, and see if you can draw some conclusions about the current status of writing in your school.

A question for teachers: why do we ask children to write?
A question for children: what do children think about writing?

1. Staff development session
Ask staff to write down three reasons why we ask children to write, or to learn how to write. Put these in order of importance. In groups of three compare findings, and negotiate. As a team draw up a statement on the purpose of writing in your school.
2. Classroom activity
Ask children in your class why they think they should learn to write.
Ask them what they think is happening while they are writing: ask them to write and reflect at the same time, talking to a response partner.
Ask them if they can say what each of the following is: a letter, a word, a sentence, a paragraph, a story, a form of writing that is not a story.
Ask them what they enjoy about writing.
Ask them what they find most difficult.
Finally, ask them how they think they could become better writers.

This could be done as a questionnaire, either written or oral. It could lead to group discussion, followed by whole class discussion leading to an agreed series of statements about what writing is for. Display this on the wall, to remind you, the children and visitors to your classroom about what you agreed, and the need for shared understanding.

5.1 Why bother to write: why not learn to type? Or why bother to do either?

Computers are still struggling to make their presence felt in schools in the way they are felt in the office: they are not yet cheap enough or handy enough for every child to keep a lap-top in his or her locker. It could happen soon, but it is not happening now. So we have reserved a special section for a discussion of writing and I.T., and here we shall address the issue of writing with the non-computerised primary and middle school in mind. In other words, we shall be acknowledging the fact that most children are still introduced to writing through paper and pencils, progressing on to pens and folders with the occasional access to the computer.

Will the first two stages soon become obsolete? It is not inconceivable, but it is extremely difficult to imagine that the art of handwriting will ever be lost, however pocket-sized computers become. The microprocessor may become the equivalent of the pocket calculator in dimensions and cheapness, but whereas a calculator's work often yields a single number which is either spoken or recorded on a small piece of paper, the equivalent work done by a computer requires several sheets of paper if the product is to be passed on to someone else. There is electronic mail, of course, which sends texts through the telecommunication systems to receptive terminals and screens, but if that becomes the sole means of written communication then we are at the mercy of technology, and we have lost as much as we have gained. Put simply, if the act of written communication is to remain as popular and universal as it is, it *requires* the survival of the familiar form of handwritten marks on paper. The analogy of the car is slightly helpful here. Driving makes life easier and more manageable for many people, but if the price we paid for having cars was the gradual loss of the use of our legs then the trade off would not be worth it. Walking is something you need to do in a place like a café where you cannot take a car. The same is true of writing, for it would be cumbersome to take a printer or satellite dish into a café. Writing produces a product, and you may need a hard copy instantly. Lap-tops may become as small as biros, but it is hard to imagine printers as thin as paper.

But why do it?

So far we have talked about the physical and utilitarian aspects of writing, which are undoubtedly important. But writing is also a psychologically controlled process that allows us to use our imaginations and cognitive abilities, to give expression to the affective part of life, expressing delight, wonder or sorrow. Being able to write gives children the optioin of a second voice that in terms of empowerment may be at least as important as their spoken voice, either now or later in life. Teachers in primary or middle schools may wish to give emphasis to person-centred writing – privileging what Cox characterises as the 'personal growth' model of English. They may want to give greater emphasis to the social function of writing, claiming for the primary and middle school what Cox, with the reference to 'adult needs' model, sought to provide time and space for a combination of the two, seeing writing as a crucial enabler, not only for the future lives of children, but for the here and now of childhood. Writing – and by writing we clearly do not just mean the accurate copying of text − is not only the means through which most learning is expressed, but as with reading it is the medium through which learning actually takes place. As readers we become better writers, and as writers we become better readers. This is the case argued by Frank Smith (1982) who maintains that not only will writing survive the rivalry of television and cinema, but that for many of us it is through writing that we come to know what we know. Put another way, by writing about experience we come to know that experience. Although most would accept this, following the pioneering work of Britton *et al.* (1975a), Barnes (1976) and Martin *et al.* (1987) there are now fierce arguments (surprise, surprise!) about the approach to writing that is most likely to empower children, and whether functional or purpose driven categories such as transactional, expressive and poetic (Britton, 1975b) or narrative, description, explanation and argument (Wilkinson, 1986) are really helpful or distinguishable concepts for the language leader.

How and what then?

These arguments have led to a debate about the kind of writing that older primary and all secondary children should be encouraged to attempt, and in many ways this debate parallels the one about how − or whether − early years children should be *taught* to write. Both debates − one about the acquisition of the physical, scripting skills, the other about the form and content of the writing process − are similar in some ways, and are more complex than the reading debate which has been easy to represent as new versus old, or as progressive versus revisionist. The writing debate sees the *process writing* model that teachers have adopted following the work of Barnes, Britton, Harold Rosen, Donald Graves and James Moffett, challenged internationally by two opponents − the Key Stage tests and Australian genre theory. John Dixon, who reported the findings of the influential Dartford Seminar in his *Growth Through English* (1967), and is associated with the personal growth model mentioned in the 1989 Cox report, said at the time that a new model would eventually be needed 'to transend its descriptive power'. He has opposed Australian genre theory, which argues that children ought to be taught to imitate specific genres such as science writing in order to learn the language of form on the grounds that it sets up an authority of fixed textual form that is not only rigid but inaccurate. We shall develop this point later. None the less, in Britain at least, the large majority of research findings and commentaries on English over the past twenty years have supported a child-centred model of education which presupposes that children need to find their own voice and language through expression of their own experience. In the early years this means the encouragement of emergent writing, that is the very young child's first attempts to make marks on the page, whether these are lines, squiggles or recognisable words. Gradually the child is drawn into the writing culture, because complementing the notion of child centredness is the recognition, deriving partly from the works of J. S. Bruner (1986), Frank Smith (1982), Margaret Spencer (1986), and Barbara Tizard and Martin Hughes (1984), that literacy is socially constructed and involves interaction with others. It is a developmental model of language acquisition, and has involved a shift in emphasis from product to process (see Wray (ed.), 1988). So the National Writing Project (1985-89) attached great importance to issues such as the following:

- a target curriculum which provides children with purposeful writing activities for specific audiences
- a child-centred view of learning which sees children learning through experiment, building on past experiences
- activities which reflect the rich experiences of writing available in the home and the community
- tasks which recognise the complexity of the writer's behaviour from initial jottings, through many revisions, to a final outcome
- the collaborative nature of writing activities in which thoughts are written down after much discussion and texts take shape through others reading and reacting to them
- a social view of writing where practices are linked to cultural norms and expectations
(From National Writing Project, *Ways of Looking*, 1990)

In passing these extremely influential points on to the English working group (the Cox Committee), the National Writing Project reported that they represented the views of thousands of teachers around the country. As we shall see below these views have created a model of the teacher of writing as one whose role involves, among other things, modelling writing for children and facilitating writing activities. Because the 'other things' are sometimes not spelt out, it is a model which critics such as Margaret Donaldson have characterised as the product of 'the minimal teaching movement' (1989). There are indeed those who argue very strongly that writing is 'caught' rather than taught. Here is a paragraph from Frank Smith's *Writing and the Writer* (1982), a quotation which is cited in the equally influential *The Primary Language Book* (Dougill and Knott, 1988):

> My own recommendations for how writing and reading should be taught is perhaps radical; they should not be taught at all. Not in any formal sense, as subjects. All the busy work, the meaningless drills and exercises, the rote memorization, the irrelevant tests, and the distracting grades should go . . . in their place teachers and children together should use writing (and reading, spoken language, art and drama) to learn other things . . .
>
> Children should learn to write in the same manner that they learn to talk, without being aware that they are doing so, in the course of doing other things. (p. 211)

In 1988 Dougill and Knott were able to quote this without comment, but in 1993 it is hard to consider an ideological position more at odds with the system of assessment procedure that primary and middle school teachers are required to implement, nor the model of the role of the teacher that these assessments seem to assume. This is a tremendous source of conflict for many teachers, especially language leaders.

How and why has the position changed so quickly? How has one prevailing ideology come to be overtaken by another? There are many possible answers — the inevitable nature of reaction, cultural nostalgia, anxieties about economic failure, the hijacking of the curriculum by a small group driven by dogma, literacy 'standards' as scapegoat or diversion, the failure of progressivism to respond to cultural change, the abuses of an ideology being used to discredit that ideology, the unworldliness of that ideology and so on. You will choose your explanation according to your beliefs. Instead of trying to provide simplistic, polarised answers, let us try and trace a change in attitudes to writing caused by educational rather than political forces.

Although the National Writing Project pointed towards the need for a variety of types of writing, in the past the emphasis on child centredness has encouraged teachers to give children in the junior, middle school and secondary school years opportunities to produce personal chronological writing in particular. In the 1960s and 1970s this kind of writing was invariably called creative writing, and in the preface to *Creative Writing in the Primary School* (Lane and Kemp, 1967) we can glimpse the assumption that underpinned this emphasis on personal writing. The preface begins by quoting from the evidence the National Association for the Teaching of English presented to the Plowden Committee:

The first concern of the English teacher should be to allow children's own private experience to stimulate them to write (and talk) out of their own interests, so that they themselves, and other people . . . may enjoy the result. Thus children will use the material of their personal relationships with family and animals; their experience of home, play, school, shopping and incidents which have made a strong impression on them . . .

It is a point developed by Stratta, Dixon and Wilkinson (1974) in *Patterns of Language*, which has section entitled 'The Uniqueness of the Self'. Fifteen years later and the privileging of the terms 'creative writing' and 'personal response' was challenged by those, Australian genre theorists among them, who argued that all writing involved an element of creativity. The genre theorists, who argued that children could only be empowered as writers if they were introduced at an early age to a range of genres, argue in favour of a system of scaffolding to support the production of children's writing, transcribed or not as the case may be. Inspired by the linguistic theory of M. A. K. Halliday (1975) which emphasised the social context in which meaning is made through language, genre theorists have proposed that at an appropriate stage in their development children are explicitly taught the conventions of genre, which in terms of language can be anything from label, observation, comment and recount, to narrative. A recount, for example, is a narrative which lacks a complication and a resolution. Other neglected genres are instructional, argument and reports. Dissatisfied with the categories of writing identified by Britton and Wilkinson, genre theorists such as Martin, Christie and Rothery (in Reid (ed.), 1987) have argued that genres can be identified by their characteristic use of language. They further insist that a familiarity with structure precedes creativity — and reject the claims of their opponents such as Dixon (in Reid (ed.) 1987) and Britton (1978) who have argued that this is a narrowing, restrictive and counter-productive approach. Genre theorists such as Martin *et al.* (1987) have countered with the claim that children are not in a position to choose until they are aware of the conventions that determine the forms from which their choice is going to be made. It is not a case of privileging product over process, it is more a case of not being able to engage meaningfully in process until you have been made aware of product. Our model of learning, which applies to writing, tries to reconcile these two positions.

Audience and purpose

As with the reading debate, for most practising teachers this will be a false polarity. Most teachers use a mixture of methods, and as we have seen the National Writing Project, in advocating variety, explicitly endorses a social rather than a private model of writing. Emergent writing will be encouraged, but there will also be times when word making practice is appropriate. Some children will seem to develop writing skills intuitively, while others will need coaching. Attainment Target 3 of the National Curriculum Order for English, announces in bold letters at the head of the page that its aim is to foster: 'A growing ability to construct and convey meaning in written language matching to audience and purpose.' Further up the primary school the same principles apply. Although the United States and Canada may appear to be more influenced by a linguistic model which situates them closer to the Australian model than the writing Attainment Target of the Order for English in England, all four countries share a number of pedagogical assumptions in their approach to writing, differences being those largely of emphasis. Older children will be encouraged to write poems, to make their own illustrated story-books and to write about their own experience but they will also be writing in a variety of other forms with particular audiences in mind. In a recent project on homes and housing a Year 6 class examined house descriptions from estate agents, and then wrote similar descriptions of their own houses. This kind of non-narrative work calls for a different order of skills, and its place in the primary curriculum has been increasingly stressed in government reports over the last twenty years. The National Primary Survey conducted between 1975 and 1978 (DES, 1978) concluded, in the words of a recent HMI survey, that although 'the older, abler children were capable of using writing to argue a case, to express opinions, or to draw conclusions, most of them had little experience of this kind of writing' (DES, 1990). By the end of the eighties the position had shifted, but not dramatically. This is what the DES Survey of 'The Teaching and Learning of Language and Literacy', following the usual HMI visits and inspections, has to say about writing in primary schools in the 1980s:

> Throughout the primary age range the majority of children write about personal experiences confidently and competently, especially when their ability to narrate or to describe is called into play. By the age of 11 about half are reasonably proficient in adopting style and form for particular purposes and readers. It has become evident in schools participating in or influenced by the National Writing Project that considerable improvement in the range and quality of children's writing is possible. (DES, 1990, p. 10)

Setting the parameters

Research and common sense tells us that children need to know the kind of writing that is expected of them before they write. Sometimes this will involve storying, involving a person or people, a temporal sequence and narrative in form — what Katherine Perera (1984) describes as chronological writing. Very often it will involve what Perera calls non-chronological writing, such as notes, labels, notices and descriptions, and characterised by a factual content, a logical sequence and impersonal tone. Both the National Curriculum and the National Writing Project are informed by this kind of distinction in which audience and purpose dictate the kind of linguistic discourse: in other words different situations require different forms of language.

The National Writing Project was set up in England and Wales by the School Curriculum Development Committee and ran from 1985 to 1988. Its findings were published in a series of theme packs and in-service materials, which identified a range of strategies to encourage writing for different purposes and audiences across the school. Before we go on to consider some of these, let us consider a model of the teacher of writing, through a practical staff development activity taken from one of of the in-service booklets. We need to be quite clear about the underlying assumptions that inform the approach that is currently regarded as 'good practice'.

Practical Activity 5.2

The following model of the teacher of writing was produced by the Manchester Writing Project, which was part of the National Writing Project. In groups consider ways in which you would adapt or modify the model to match the approach you would endorse:

observer
|
facilitator ———————— TEACHER ———————— adviser
|
model

The teacher of writing will at various times assume the following roles:

– observing children, noting the experiments they are making with writing and the hypothesis they seem to be drawing about its structure and uses.
– observing how children respond to the various classroom writing tasks.

- observing the classroom itself and the messages it is transmitting.
- facilitating the child's exploration by creating a literate environment which draws on the child's own cultural and linguistic resources.
- facilitating the child's experiences by providing relevant purposes and audiences for writing and ensuring that children experience a full range of literacy activities.
- advising the writer by providing a reader-response, giving editorial support when it is asked for and providing an experienced writer's viewpoint.
- modelling the writing process by writing for and alongside the children.
- modelling by inviting writers into the classroom: parents, older children, published authors.
- modelling by giving access to different forms of writing in all subject areas.
- supporting the writer through the provision of as many resources as possible: pens, felt-tip pens, note pads, class books, zig-zag books, magnetic letters, word processors, typewriters . . . and more.

(From National Writing Project, 1989, *Becoming a Writer*)

The majority of teachers are likely to endorse these aims, but the increasingly prescriptive assessment arrangements for English at Key Stages 1, 2 and 3 are inspired by a pedagogical model that seems to assume far more intervention, and is perhaps influenced by memories of the formal methods of instruction that characterised teaching in the past. Now there are different kinds of intervention. Modelling, as described above, is one kind. The provision of writing tables and writing corners, fully equipped places set aside for writing to be used whenever the child feels she or he wants to write is another. The teacher is intervening by creating an appropriate environment, what the National Writing Project calls 'the careful structuring of context'. But we should not be so intimidated by threatening phrases such as 'transmission model of teaching' that we become too timid to admit that the careful structuring of instruction is also occasionally important. The National Writing Project accepts this, but even in the excellent *Becoming a Writer* this is not met head on. We do not know if writing is better 'caught' or 'taught', but we do know that an ever emphasis on the teaching of a reading skill such as phonic cues or a writing skill such as the 'correct orthographic reproduction of conventional written language forms' (Fisher, 1992) gives children a limiting view of language (Clay, 1979). Naturally enough this has led to a 'whole view' of language, and in taking a whole view the taught skills element has usually been taken for granted. Assuming that they do not accept Frank Smith's non-interventionist strategy, new teachers will need to make up their minds whether they want to intervene on a one-to-one basis according to children's separate needs, or whether there is a case for whole-class teaching at certain fixed times. What needs to be kept in mind is that a series of initiatives from the 1970s onwards — those famous red folders issued by the Schools Council Project (Doughty, 1971), the Bullock Report (1975), Kingman, Cox and the National Curriculum Order for English — assume that the social nature of language is recognised through a rejection of set, corrective exercises in isolation from normal language work. Children should learn about how language works through tasks and activities organised by the teacher, but not through separate drills. Projects like *Language in Use* (1971) and *Language in the National Curriculum* (unpublished) have encouraged a pedagogy which involves what has been called a 'fieldwork approach'. This approach to knowledge about language, the belief that children can evolve naturally as writers and readers if they experience an environment rich in literacy, and the emphasis on discovery methods has created a theoretical model of education which is more honoured in the breach than in the observance. This can be disorientating for student teachers, particularly those teachers of early years children. They will be unsure about what interventionist strategies, if any, they should employ. So let us address this subject now, and begin by making a distinction between the various stages of writing, for intervention and direct class teaching may be more productive at some stages of development than at others.

5.2 Towards production

The stages of writing

The expression 'the stages of writing' can be understood in two senses. In this section we shall be concentrating on the way children have been observed to pass through a number of recognisable stages in their development as writers. But for children themselves the discovery that even for published authors writing itself is a process which evolves through several stages can be something of a surprise.

DRAFTING

Show children copies of Roald Dahl or Anthony Browne's initial drafts, with alterations and deletions in pen, and they will often be surprised. Here, for example, is a draft version of a page from Anthony Browne's *Gorilla:*

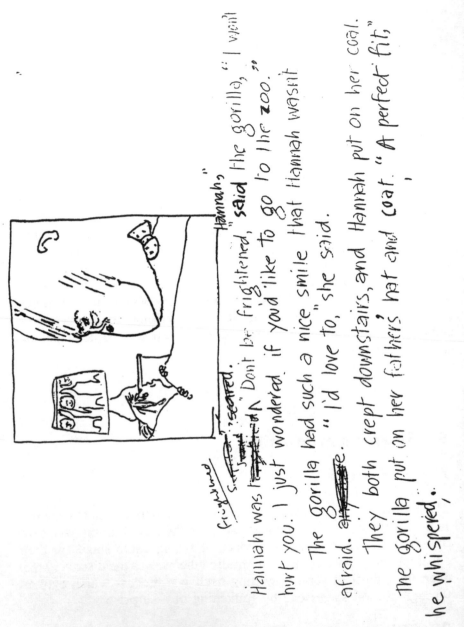

Children often express surprise that writers like Anthony Browne do not just write their books and have them printed. So it is useful to show them the drafting process, to encourage children to see writing in the same way that a potter sees clay — something that can be worked on and shaped, before finally being fired in the oven. Donald Graves has encouraged the practice of conferencing, whereby a reader of the child's text indicates how it might be developed, in conference with the child. The reader, usually the teacher, is recommended to approach the conference with specific goals and questions in mind. Laverty (1986) suggests that the child should underline parts which he or she is pleased with, thus giving the teacher the cue to stress what is good. Wray and Gallimore (1986) lay stress on the need to start the conference by getting the child to articulate the purpose of the writing, and then to move on to revision, which should involve crossing out, arrows, circling and underlining, rather than rubbing out. Another procedure is for children to organise response partners, sometimes called critical friends: having read the writing produced the children then discuss what was good about it and where it could be improved. Through these strategies the interactive, social and public nature of writing is acknowledged, and children begin to accept the idea of redrafting. A note of caution has to be introduced at this point because reasearch such as that by Bereiter and Scardamalia (1987) has suggested that children are reluctant to rethink the content and structure of their work, preferring instead to provide additions or alter the surface features. It is a good idea to give children some guidance on what can be expected of a good response partner. For example:

START BY READING THROUGH THE PIECE OF WRITING
FIND TWO 'GOLDEN' LINES
WRITE DOWN TWO GOOD THINGS ABOUT THE PIECE OF WRITING
WRITE DOWN ONE WAY IN WHICH IT COULD BE IMPROVED
HERE ARE SOME OF THE THINGS YOU COULD SAY ABOUT SOMEONE ELSE'S WRITING:

This is a good beginning. I like these words. You need a stronger beginning. I liked this character. Why did you write this bit like that? I liked the ending. You need to say more about this character. There's a jump here – you need a connection. The golden lines are . . .

The great advantages of these partnerships, apart from encouraging children to evaluate writing and encouraging them to write about writing, is it enables them to see writing as a 'collaborative activity' in a 'community of writers', to draw on expressions sugested by Morag Styles (1989) and John Richmond (1990).

DEVELOPMENTAL STAGES
In Eric Carlin's 'Writing Development – Theory and Practice' (1986) there is a useful summary of theories of writing development, from

Moffett (1968; 1981), through Britton (1975), to Bereiter (1980). These
do not so much identify the stages of development, as the parts, which
when integrated, constitute this development — drawing, handwriting,
transcribing, and revision of our 'inner speech'. More recent
descriptions have led to an emphasis on the difference between the
development of speech and writing, differences which can be
summarised as follows:

SPEECH	WRITING
ephemeral	fixed
immediate	delayed
unrevised	can be edited and revised
fast	slow
gesture, vocal emphasis	punctuation fulfils this function
and pauses indicate structure	

Some of these differences are distinguishable whatever the stage of
development, others more marked in younger children who may find
writing exceptionally tiresome, slow and frustrating — an obvious case
for allowing them to tell stories on to tape. But as Wells and Chang
argued in 1986, there is a strong case for encouraging children of all
ages to have task-focussed oral activities, as there is evidence to suggest
that this gives them confidence and opportunities to develop the skills
of composing — which they list as pooling, selecting, marshalling and
organising ideas — that are employed in writing.

At the end of his article Carlin concludes that of the two models he
used in his study to assess the language development of primary school
children, an abbreviated version of the Wilkinson (1980) model for
the analysis of writing is more useful than language count that features
in the Australian Language Ability Test (Wilson, 1980). Although recent
pedagogical developments over the past ten years have favoured
Wilkinson's holistic approach to language — his developmental criteria
includes such concepts as the thinking and feeling involved in writing,
recent linguistic based research has found these broad descriptive models
imprecise and unquantifiable. There is a detailed description of the
linguistic features of children's writing in both Perera (1984) and Tann
(1991), and both descriptions assume a staged development which is
quite different from, and possibly more demanding than, speech. An
understanding of the stages of children's writing does not necessarily
require a knowledge of linguistics, however. The stages of writing
identified by Kroll and Wells (1983) are relatively clear, and have been
summarised by Sarah Tann as follows (we paraphrase):

i Preparatory stage: During this stage children are acquiring the ability to produce handwriting and to spell.

ii Consolidation: this stage is normally reached at about the age of seven, by which time handwriting and spelling usually becomes less of a chore, and easier to produce. 'Writing (at this point) is still personal, colloquial, situational and context bound. Children are willing to rub out and alter letter shapes or spellings, but are rarely willing to revise or edit.' Between the ages of seven and nine children become productive and prolific writers of stories.

iii At about the age of nine children become aware of the idea of having an audience. In other words they begin to develop the ability to distance themselves from their writing, and are willing to draft and edit their work. They achieve what Donald Graves (1983) calls 'decentring', and are able to pay more attention to the structure. Children will continue to produce stories, but the satisfaction of the self is not the only aim — there is a genuine attempt to communicate through the writing. This stage is what Kroll and Wells have called 'differentiation'.

iv By the end of the middle school, in Year 8 or 9, children then achieve the final stage, called 'integration'. The child is able to produce a range of styles for different purposes and audiences. Some children may well achieve this stage before the age of twelve or thirteen, so opportunities for a range of writing should be provided throughout the primary school.

The danger with any model of development is that it can easily become too stratified and hierarchical, while our experience as teachers tells us that children do not progress in this neat, systematic way. This is a point made by Roslyn Arnold (1991) who offers us the visual metaphor of the spiral of writing development, starting from the 'core self', and constantly encircling this centre with increasingly sophisticated language forms. This raises separate questions about the authenticity of the 'core self' from which this personal voice comes, but this is not the right place to introduce the whole issue of deconstruction!

Starting to write

Children bring to school a considerable knowledge about writing. In many cases they will have seen their parents writing, they will have encountered books which show characters writing, and in their play they will have pretended to write or deliver letters. They will almost certainly have seen characters on television engaged in writing, and they have gone further. In drawing, painting and colouring they may have included marks to indicate words, they may have produced pages of scribble writing, and by the time they start school at the age of five many will be able to write their names. Making recognisable letters is hard, exhausting work and it is generally accepted that their difficulties should not be increased by making them write on lined paper or discouraging them from behaving as writers in their emergent writing.

To encourage children to develop their own emergent versions of writing and evolve into successful communicators the teachers can take a number of initiatives. As the first picture in *Becoming a Writer* shows, the teacher can write on giant sheets of paper, perhaps folded to represent the pages of a book, to show children how words are made, how sentences are written, how stories unfold. This is a more public version of the labelling process that teachers will do on individual pieces of work. But what about other practices that you may remember from your own childhood − copying from the board, tracing over letters and words − or copying under letters and words − in special books, attempting joined up or cursive writing, using a pen rather than a pencil − is there a place for any of these? And what do early years teachers mean by dialogue journals, pencil play and pattern making?

If you are an early years teacher, the following account from a teacher of Reception/Year 1 will sound very familiar. To a non-early years specialist this may not be the case − and sometimes most of the staff in a primary school, including the language leader, will not be early years teachers.

In her classroom and school Jan had successfully created an environment which announces the importance attached to reading and writing. In her role as Reception/Year 1 teacher and Language Leader she fulfills all of the roles identified by the Manchester Working Group. Below, however, she was asked to say what interventionist strategies she adopts to help children become more proficient writers:

> Children start school with a wide range of abilities. The first thing is to encourage them to feel comfortable with a pencil, so we have pencil play activities. Children want to make marks on paper. They like the feeling of being able to make symbols, and that is the beginning of writing. They love making pretend letters which they put in envelopes. I'll talk about a topic like the tadpoles in our school pond, or the leaves falling outside, and the children will draw and write around the drawing. But they also want to make the word shapes they see in books and so we practice letter forming not by copying from the board because the distance makes this very difficult, but first by patterning and tracing, and then by modelling sentences that the children have dictated to me or one of the classroom assistants. The children have special dialogue books for this, and they can contain little stories, or something the Assistant has said followed by

something the child said. We'll talk about matters like reversed letters, capital letters in the wrong place, missed letters and full stops when it is appropriate, when we know the child has the confidence in herself as a writer. A few of the children are even ready to try joined up writing. You would be astonished by the differences in ability by the time they are six.

In her study of emergent writing Kathryn Falkner (1991) reports the following comment made by a nursery teacher in response to the question 'What assumptions and beliefs underpin "emergent writing"?':

'That writing should be allowed to emerge and develop in the same way as any other skill that the child might have, like learning to walk, learning to talk, and so it is actually dependant on you giving the child the right environment and the right input at the right time — it is very much to do with attitudes really.'

Over lunch she reflected on what she had said, and was concerned that it sounded too simplistic, and neglected the role of the teacher. She explained:

'If you are trying to get the children to use the skills that they have got, then you've got to encourage them to take risks and that the teacher doesn't always know best, so you'd have to operate a curriculum that would encourage them to take risks for themselves in all areas, writing included.'

She was then asked how this was demonstrated in the planning and practice of the nursery curriculum:

'I suppose this gets back to knowing how to develop potential. We've already talked about children needing to have access to books, and people being around to read with the children, and discussion with the children when you're looking at books. We often actually talk about who has written the book . . . so that they get an idea that "it is words" as well as pictures that convey meaning. We will quite often, when reading with a child, run our fingers along the print, and we sometimes even talk about the fact that the words are helping us to know what to say, but the pictures also tell us the story. So it's through our attitudes to books and allowing the children to use the books, but also that we are prepared to spend time looking at books with the children and it is not just the children looking at the books on their own. When they've drawn or painted something, we will often write the story that goes with the picture which the child tells us. Quite often when I'm doing this writing, I'll say the words as I'm writing them. When we're giving out pictures at group time, we'll quite often get them

120

to 'read' the stories back to see if they can remember any of them. Lots of things in the nursery are labelled both with pictures and writing so that they're getting the message that labels convey meaning as well, and there are notices about in the nursery which we talk about, there are notices for their parents . . . So it is these two things really – firstly the books and second the drawing plus writing. And that they see us doing writing – I think that's very important. We've also provided different shapes of paper, for example, long paper to encourage list making. We've given them blank forms which have already got some writing on and they do squiggles in the boxes that are inviting them to write there. I haven't ever provided envelopes becuase they are too expensive, but we do make them up sometimes, and books too . . . And they do letters and stamps.' (Falkner, 1991, p. 61).

Falkner then conducted her own case study of a group of nursery children, using the Ahlberg's *The Jolly Postman* as the stimulus for letters from Goldilocks to The Three Bears. Below is an example of a letter and envelope produced by Samantha, who changed from the slow production of individual letters (see line 1) to the production of a whole letter when she discovered that what she called 'pretend writing' was acceptable. She signed off with a squiggle (see line 10) and positioned the words on the envelope (which she read as 'To the Three Bears', so showing an understanding that a letter needs to be to someone, from someone, and to have a message:

line 1

line 10

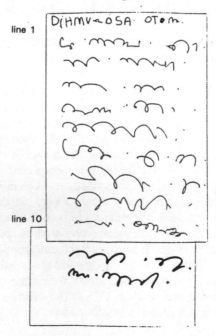

What is the rationale behind emergent writing?

Advocates of emergent writing emphasise the way that it encourages children to take risks, and develop confidence in their ability as writers. The emphasis on production of the whole rather than correctness of every part means that for children like Samantha it can have an unexpected effect, but Falkner was able to conclude from her case study that the majority of children she worked with showed awareness of function (for example, what the letter is for), form (for example, how the letter is laid out) and social action (for example, who the information in the letter is for and why). In this respect it had acheived the value effect of *decentring*, that is shifting children's perception of the world to beyond a merely *egocentric* one.

In her case study Kathryn Falkner cites Hall (1987) who recommends the use of the term 'emergent writing' as it implies that:

- development takes place within the child . . . and therefore instruction is not the only means of encouraging the emergency of literacy.
- 'emergence' is a gradual process: it takes place over time.
- for something to emerge there has to be something there in the first place.
- things usually only emerge if the conditions are right. (Hall, 1987, pp. 9–10)

The reluctant writer

Some children may be reluctant to write. To give them confidence to move beyond emergent writing, teachers encourage reluctant writers to draw a line every time there is a word they find difficult. They may begin by drawing more word-space lines than actually writing, but it is a step in the right direction. Another strategy is to get reluctant writers to write the initial letter of words that they find difficult.

Patterning: starting to form letters and words

Children make patterns such as OOOOOOOOOO in the sand, with forefingers or with paint. Fingers can be used to trace round letters, or to make the shape in the air.

Writing messages

Young children are taught lower rather than upper case (capital) letters because they are more distinguishable from one anther. Joining letters in a cursive script can help spelling, but some teachers prefer to let children develop at their own pace. When children are having difficulties with writing early years teachers always look to see if this is caused by:

a) posture — which may involve holding the pencil too tightly, or too near the tip, or sitting in their own light, or using too much pressure, or not sitting with the arms on the desk, and so on.

b) materials — writing materials need to be varied (crayon, pencil, felt tips, pens) and of the right size. The debate about lined paper for young children remains unresolved: many teachers consider lines inhibiting: some young children will develop more self confidence if they have the support of lines.

c) being left-handed, loss of shape due to speed, absence of spaces between words.

Stages in development

The problem with handwriting development, as with speaking and reading, is that it is not linear, and therefore it is dangerous to present rigid models of what should be achieved at certain ages. Children learn in spurts, and not all aspects of learning take place at the same pace. For detailed examples of the kind of handwriting that can be achieved at various stages see *The Development of Handwriting Skills* (Jarman, 1979), which gives examples of children's writing at various ages. Most teachers would be happy with the following broad descriptions of four phases in writing development:

EARLY PHASE: students engaged in personal, drawing, scribbles and letters.
TRANSITIONAL PHASE: students move from scribbles and invented letters as they learn to form individual letters and numbers.
DEVELOPING PHASE: students learn to link letters to form words, and begin to develop a rhythm and flow to their writing.
PROFICIENT PHASE: students move towards developing a personal handwriting style that is fluent and legible and shows the individuality of the writer.

The fact that this comes from a document called *English K-6* (1992), which in National Curriculum terms means Reception to Year 6, suggests where the early phase should appear and where the proficient phase is normally achieved.

Teaching handwriting: context and audience

There is a strong case for teaching handwriting, but doing so in a context which means that there is a real audience and purpose. This means writing with the intention that the work will be 'published' either as a display or a finished book. One very positive effect of the National Curriculum document for English is that teachers now think very much more about making explicit to children the context in which their writing is taking place — either real or imagined — and the audience for whom it is intended — again either real or imagined. An imagined audience and context is provided by the newsroom situation described in *Becoming a Writer*. A real context and audience was provided by the Newcastle reception class which baked cakes for the nursery, and received a thank you letter, asking for the recipe so that they could make the cakes! They then had to consider how to reply to an audience who could not read! Another real audience was established by a teacher in Somerset who set up a postbox in the classroom and encouraged the children to write to each other. Another situation arose from classroom observations of the differences between real caterpillars and the caterpillar in *The Very Hungry Caterpillar* by Eric Carle. Having noted the differences, the children then wrote to Eric Carle, asking him if he had ever observed the differences. In each case handwriting practice is taking place, but towards a particular end: this is preferable to copying exercises done simply to practice style.

Other real contexts and audiences involve writing notices, books, signs and letters for other chlidren or adults to read. Book-making, especially with the aid of the computer, has become a particularly popular and successful activity over the past few years. Newsroom was the name given to a classroom activity in which the whole of the classroom was turned over for use as a newsroom, with children at different tables with different functions. A whole wall was taken up with a giant front page that the children put together. This can work with beginner writers just as much as it can with children who have more advanced writing skills. The role-playing elements remains the same, although with Year 5, 6, 7 and 8 children it is possible to use more advanced computer simulations which print out news stories: contact your local language and I.T. adviser, or the New Technologies Committee Chair at NATE, for more details.

Towards a handwriting policy

It is important for a school to have a handwriting policy so that there is a basic style throughout the school, for it is generally agreed that children should not be asked to change their style as they mature. The formulation of a handwriting policy is an appropriate activity for a staff development session, which we shall approach through a practical task.

Practical Activity 5.3

See if agreement can be reached on each of the following issues:
1. A style to be adopted throughout the school.
2. The extent to which teachers should intervene and teach handwriting.
3. A policy on writing implements.
4. The case for writing corners.
5. Lined paper − when, and with what space between the lines.
6. Writing skills that should have been acquired before the transfer at eleven or thirteen.
7. The demands of different subjects.

5.3 Ghoti and chips: does spelling matter?

In answering what may appear to some to be a facile question we cannot do better than quote Bill Mittins, a crusader for common sense on the subject of grammar and spelling for more years than he cares to remember. In response to the question 'Does Spelling Matter', he writes:

> It did *not* matter until (late 15th century) printing invented *mis*spelling. Today it *does* matter. Colin MacCabe, for instance, in 1984 delivered a lecture entitled 'Righting English or Does Spelling Matter?' His short answer was: 'Obviously immediately and emphatically, Yes'. However, he insisted on making that answer 'seem a little less self-sufficient' by shifting from the usual context of widespread current decline in 'standards' into 'a historical and linguistic context which makes it clear that although spelling matters, writing cannot be considered in isolation from other questions about language. (1991, p.5)

This reflects the thinking of recent research following the work of Donald Graves (1983) and the views of most teachers of language. But it is not the way that spelling is perceived by those who organised the Key Stage 1 tests for 1992: spelling, for all children of average ability and above, is to be assessed separately. Mindful of this, how should of a book. To improve spelling children can be encouraged to reveal how they read words — whole words, not looking at the parts?

Spelling strategies for children (2)

The New South Wales Board recommends the following strategies

experimenting and inventing   memorising visual patterns
listening to sounds and sound patterns in words (auditory memory)
pronouncing words with artificial correctness to reinforce memory of structure (articulatory memory)
use of syllabification
use of analogy
use of spelling rules   use of memory cues (mnemonics)
use of morphemic cues   exploring word origins (etymology)

Are some of these more helpful than others?
    Below is a technique widely used in schools:

SACAWAC: Spell and cover and write and check. Alternatively:
1. LOOK ((a)Teacher writes the word, (b)child looks and says it)
2. COVER (Child covers the word)
3. REMEMBER (Child remembers the word)
4. WRITE (Child writes it)
5. CHECK (If wrong, go back to 1(b))

This technique helps to develop the kinaesthetic memory, which allows children to recognise and recall the feel of words. Other activities which aid this process include:

— using handwriting to reinforce spelling patterns.
— writing words in sand or paint.
— using the whole body to make letter and word shapes.
— writing letters and words in the air with fingers, hands or feet.
— tracing over letters.
— tracing over templates of words.

Mnemonics may be of limited use, but children sometimes find it useful to know that 'There is A RAT in sepARATe.' You can encourage children to make up their own: 'There's GUM in ArGUMent.' Other examples are 'A pIEce of pIE' and 'hEAR with your EAR'. Give Year 4 children ten commonly misspelt words and ask them to make up the early years teacher approach spelling? Firstly, through an awareness that diagnosis is important: different children will have differing reasons for misspelling words. Gentry (1987) identified a series of stages through which children pass in their spelling development, from an early reliance on phonetics and aural memory, through visual memory to a mature stage in which a range of strategies are employed. Sarah Tann has some excellent advice encouraging teachers to identify exactly who is finding a child's misspellings problematic. Is it a problem for the child, in that it discourages story-writing because it undermines confidence; is it a problem for the reader, because it is difficult to understand the meaning; or is it a classroom management problem for the teacher because children are queueing? Each of these situations requires a different strategy. Rather than the 'ten words a week' spelling test alone, spelling can be encouraged through games such as letter, pattern, or word lotto, 'I Spy' 'phonic' games, alphabet books, word-within-word spotting (for example, h-eat, sep-a-rat-e) and handwriting (there is some evidence that cursive handwriting improves spelling).

'Ghoti', by the way, was offered by George Bernard Shaw as a spelling of fish. 'Gh' as in rough, 'o' as in women, and 'ti' as in nation.

Spelling aids and strategies (1)

As Angela Redfern (1992) says, research has shown that:

- spelling is active not passive.
- spelling is a developmental process, like talking, and accuracy will increase as children mature.
- spelling is a visual skill.
- the visual memory can be trained.
- motor skills can also support spelling.
- writing for a purpose is a crucial factor.

Redfern suggests a number of strategies which teachers can offer children. She recommends plenty of work with rhythm and rhyme, including clapping rhythms, skipping rhymes, reciting nursery rhymes, alphabet songs, and alliterative poems. Another strategy involves focussing on letter strings, words within words and rules about double consonants. The overall plan is to use a variety of methods, some exercising the audio memory, some the visual memory, some the audio-visual memory. Words can be given to children in advance, written on pieces of card which are kept in an envelope, or written in the back memory aids like the above for these words.

It is important to note that different children have different needs. Because there are different ways of looking, some children will need whole words, while others will want bits of words. Some children will benefit from being given the syllables which make up words, particularly if this is done through prefixes and suffixes (syllables aren't useful for words like usually, whose syllables are U-SU-LY):

PREFIX	ROOT	SUFFIX
mis	tak	ing

Do children need to know spelling rules, such as the one illustrated above, whereby the 'e' is dropped in front of the suffix, 'ing', or are there too many exceptions? We debated providing a list of twenty-three rules in an appendix to show just how many exceptions there are, but decided against it. Individual children who have particular problems may benefit from knowing such rules, however (for example, 'i before e except after c').

Spelling tests or spelling games?

Both are frequently used by teachers in the belief that practise should improve spelling. Evidence that it actually works like this is hard to come by, but as long as it does not become a fetish or dreary and dreaded start or finish to the day, spelling activities can enliven the week and foreground the importance we attach to spelling. Rather than decontextualised spelling tests, which rely on short-term memorising, spelling can be taught through an explanation of some of the rules, which children then put in sentences that make a crossword puzzle. Some children may improve their spelling by being encouraged to imagine the sound of the word − in others words, its phonic make-up. If words like 'apple' are muddled in the visualisation in the head − and come out as 'alppe' then sound it out. For words like 'Wednesday' the best strategy is to sound it out as it is pronounced: Wed-nes-day. This can be done rhythmically, using a rap style, if the teacher feels up to it! By the way: it is unlikely that children will start to pronounce the word this way in ordinary conversation.

Some of the above would count as 'spelling games'. Books of such games are published regularly, *The Puffin Book of Spelling Puzzles* being a lively recent example (Edmonds, 1992). Until we have discovered a strategy that solves the problem of spelling for the many children who have difficulties of this kind, there will be a place for language games.

Spelling and the very young

Most teachers of the very young would confirm the findings of research that shows that children learn to spell by writing, inventing spellings, and refining and understanding their print. Early years teachers provide a variety of writing experiences and support the writing of individuals through a variety of techniques ranging from word banks, through tracing and drafting techniques to mini lessons on children's common errors.

A cautionary reminder: two timely quotations

> Although there is a need to focus upon . . . technical accomplishments of the writer, we must not forget that the child's purpose in writing (and any pleasure . . . derived from it) sprang from the need to give shape to powerful feelings on the page, rather than the demonstration of practical writing skills. (LINC p. 36)

> Teachers provide the greatest encouragement for children to communicate in writing when they respond more to the content of what is written than to . . . errors, and when they share a child's writing with other children. (Ibid.)

5.4 Writing in the junior and middle school

Genres and contexts   Outside audence

Although writing in certain genres (such as autobiography and biography) is perhaps more appropriate for older children it would be wrong to think that young children should always be expected to write stories. One Year 1 class described by a member of the National Writing Project team (1990) tackled a non-chronological writing activity by putting together a booklet for newcomers to the school. Ideas were brainstormed as the children thought about the problems they faced when they started school, and the children then wrote down a sentence and a picture to illustrate such difficulties as the size of the lavatories, the need to remember where you had put your coat or lunch box, and the difficulty of writing! The teacher used the children's language, and the ideas for the pictures, to put together a book which was actually sent out to newcomers.

Writing for an audience outside the school is becoming increasingly popular. For older children the material for a genre such as 'biography' is very likely to come from outside the school. Children can be encouraged to interview older relatives or friends of the family, and use the information they gather from the interview and related research to construct an account of a life which also gives insights into the community.

Another form of writing that can lead to the production of a book is autobiography. Here is an example, described by a Year 6 teacher:

> The purpose of the autobiography was to provide their mentors at secondary school with some information about themselves. The children were asked to collect some materials first: photographs, old clothes and toys, and in one case even the wrist band the child wore when she was a baby! They interviewed their mothers and other relatives or carers about their childhoods, and then brainstormed the incidents they most remembered, using the materials as a stimulus. They then chose an incident with which to begin their autobiography, flashing back to the details of place and date of birth at a later stage. This enabled us to talk about structure and chronology. The autiobiographies were then enclosed in card covers designed by the children, and spiral bound by the classroom assistant. Several of the children used their autobiographies with Year 1 children, concentrating on those bits which talked about their experiences as infants.
>
> If children were reluctant to write about their lives because they had traumatic experiences, then I asked them to write the biography of a relative instead — a cousin, for example.

Much of the writing from Year 3 to Year 8 or 9, in the junior and middle school that is, will emerge naturally from cross curricular topics such as 'The Victorians', 'Structures and Forces', 'The Second World War', and so on. In covering these topics older primary children and middle school children who have more of a subject-based curriculum will provide scientific writing, empathy writing in history, imaginative diary writing in response to 'The Way We Used to Live', and report and evaluation writing for technology. Writing in response to music will have been given new emphasis by the demands of the music syllabus in the National Curriculum: one enterprising school approaches this through Disney's *Fantasia*, thus incorporating art, media, music, language history and technology work. But we shall end this section on writing with a brief list of suggestions for writing for a real audience.

Practical Activity 5.4 Writing for real situations

Non-chronological

Safety regulations; recipes; classroom inventory; description of bedroom; description of favourite toy; school prospectus (for parents); school report (for governors); letters to radio presenters, M.P.s, Road Safety Officers, authors and poets, other children in another school and/or country; shopping lists (children are sent on a shopping expedition to the local newsagent for a number of items ordered by the teacher — children keep receipts, and on return discuss items and experience. They also take a photograph of the shop and the shopkeeper. If old enough, they write up an account of their visit — but we have moved onto our next heading.

Chronological

Instructions: how to work the computer, camcorder, video recorder (test these instructions on a reader); picture stories for younger chlidren — with a) three words per picture b) a longer sentence per picture c) a paragraph per picture; fifty-word stories for a competition; report of a scientific experiment; autobiography and biography.

5.5 Poetry

In his *Defense of Poetry* (1579/80) Sir Philip Sidney argued that poetry could never be accused of telling lies because it never pretended to tell the truth. The liberating thing about poetry is that it is not obliged to imitate the 'real world' in the way that stories or information writing are. A poem can be about anything, including itself, but it does not have to represent that something. It can have form (poets like Patricia Beer insist that it must operate within some known genre, whether that be syllabics, sonnet or haiku), but is not obliged to. One starting point for poetry is word games, acrostics, jingles, and shared readings and performance — language games and language listening. One language co-ordinator at a North London School (LINC, 1992) produced some remarkable work with her Year 1 class. The children produced shared colour poems based on science work involving refraction and colour tables. Here is one of them:

Indigo Poem

Indigo sky in the middle of the night
Space is indigo
Indigo sea, far away
Indigo dolphin, splashing through the waves, where an
Indigo mermaid flaps her indigo tail.
Indigo slates on a roof
Indigo bruise on my knee
Indigo blood to my heart
Indigo bluebottle flying to the meat
And putting germs on it

No less remarkable is a poem produced by a six-year-old after the same teacher had read the class a twelve-year-old's poem called 'The Magic Box'. Children were then asked to close their eyes and imagine the most amazing box in the world, in which magic could be stored. The poem had to begin 'I will put in my box' and then this had to be followed by three things that could not be held in the hand, the whole process done three times and then rounded off with a statement about the box itself. This is one of the poems:

Alice's Magic Box

I will put in my box
a bubble of a fish
the beam of the sun
the smell of a flower.

I will put in my box
the dust of a butterfly's wing
the puff of a web
the darkness of a hole.

I will put in my box
the purr of a cat
the blueness of the sky
the sneeze of a human.

I will put in my box
the look of a horse
the colours of the rainbow
the sadness of a boy.

My box is a treasure chest
To hold these treasures.
(Alice, aged 6)

There are a number of starting points for poetry writing, ranging from class poems built up by the whole class about a rainy or a windy day, for example, or picture poems which repeat a shape and repeat a phrase around that shape, with something stated in between. Children enjoy working with partners and producing poems like the following:

Active ants
Boring bees
Clever cats

Dangerous dogs
Enquiring elephants
Furious foxes   and so on   or Autumn fruits
                                                     Plumper than grapes
                                                     Poison for Snow White
                                                     Lesson for Newton
                                                     Eaten by teachers

There are several ways of working with very young children, and poems can emerge quite naturally from drawings and follow-up discussion. Here are two from children attending Birley Nursery School:

Two Robins

There once was two robins
That lived on a tree
They had two babies
And lived quite happily
(Julian aged 4 years 7 months)

Crocodile

Crocodile will bite you
Be careful
You will fall in
You'll get wet
Snap snap snap snap
(Sarah aged 4 years 6 months)

These two poems are among several that feature in a poetry supplement in NATE News, Autumn 1991. There are many other useful starting points. Geoff Fox and Brian Merrick's *Thirty-Six Things to do With a Poem* (1981), starting from the premise that poetry is something to be experienced before it is analysed, contains a variety of useful suggestions ranging from group presentations, to visual representations in the form of frieze or art, personal anthologies and desert island poems activities (children choose their eight favourite poems, which are read and recorded). Brian Merrick's two books, *Exploring Poetry 5-8* (Balaam and Merrick, 1987) and *Exploring Poetry 8-13* (1991) both contain a range of exciting and novel ways of encouraging children to respond to poems. Other ideas include pairs of animal silhouettes (framing animal poems in the outline of the animal, the first poem being a published poem, the second one by the child); footprints (children select a poem from an anthology, and write it on a cut-out footprint, which is then placed on the floor. Children then walk along the footprints, stopping to read the poem they are standing on when the music stops.) Both Michael Rosen (1989) and Sandy Brownjohn (1980, 1982 and 1989) have written books with plenty of practical suggestions, and accounts by Calthrop and Ede (1984) and Benton (1988) focus on teaching and young children's responses respectively. Finally, *Poetry 0-16* (Styles and Triggs, 1988) is a useful guide to poetry which has proved popular and successful in the classroom. Many of the ideas for poetry suggested by these writers are reflected in the list of suggestions from New South Wales, which include the following:

> Creating poems determined by a) shape (as in concrete and Dada poems, for example, a poem about fish in the shape of a fish); b) the number of words in a line, or number of lines, for example, couplet, quatrain, haiku, cinquain, Dylan Thomas portrait, limerick, sonnet; c) specified line beginnings, for example, acrostics and list poems.
> Performing poems, both in the form of multivoice recitation and choral dramatization, where movement is added to the multivoice reading.
> Responding to poems through a) response logs; b) jigsaw-cloze where lines are cut up and jumbled up like the pieces of a jigsaw; groups reassemble them; c) setting poems to music; d) making anthologies; e) adding favourite lines to graffiti walls; f) collage presentations of the kind described earlier in the drama section in chapter 2.

Finally, there is a great deal to be said for getting a live poet into the classroom, although writers like Roger McGough, John Hegley, Michael Rosen and Wendy Cope (who may be persuaded to do her finger rhymes) have to be booked well in advance, and are best made use of when groups of schools work together on a Book Week.

5.6 Advanced reading and writing skills

It would be a mistake to assume that the word 'advanced' used in this context means skills that will be more appropriately learned by older children or young adults. The reading skills of scanning and skimming, or reading for a particular purpose can be introduced to upper juniors and practised by them. Equally some nine-, ten-, eleven- or twelve-year-olds will show a real ability to write in the style of someone else, or in the detached style of non-chronological forms such as description

134

and advertisement. Examples and opportunities to produce their own should therefore be given. Some children – often children you would think least likely to – are capable of producing the most amazing advanced work if it is a subject and form that they suddenly find themselves at home with.

5.7 Writing activities from New South Wales

To support *non-narrative* writing, modelling, followed by writing conferences is recommended. In other words children are presented with texts produced by the teacher – a piece of report writing for example – and then asked in either group conferences, peer conferences, or whole-class conferences to talk about the piece of writing, clarify and rework it. The children then do the same to their own texts.

To support *narrative writing* the following suggestions are made:

Story maps – individuals or groups make a visual representation of the main features of a story.
Storyboard – the narrative is told in frames which act as a shooting script for video or film.
Retelling – the most significant feature of their own story, in speech or writing.
Reading logs and journals – logs are records which the teacher can use to gain an insight into reading. Journals are opportunities to give a more personal, private response.
Detective activities – children are given an ending, and then asked to construct a series of events which lead to this ending.
Prologue and epilogue – incidents which happened before or after the events in a book which has been read.
Letters to characters, biographies of characters, interior monologues. These are all ways of developing the relationship between reading and writing.

Too much writing?

It is arguable that we ask children to do too much writing in school. We need to make sure that we know why we are asking children to write, that they know what they are meant to be doing, and that there are opportunities during the term for writing in a whole variety of forms.

Conclusion?

The issue of assessment is dealt with in a separate chapter, but there are valuable sections in both Fisher (1992) and Graves (1983) on the assessment of younger and older children's writing respectively.

Some children find writing frustrating, difficult and confidence-sapping. Others find it liberating, comforting and enjoyable. We want all children to be competent writers, and to discover the pleasure of writing. As long as we keep the above points about form, purpose and audience in mind, and the points made earlier about revision and editing on the word processor, we will ensure that we avoid the danger of overloading children with unhelpful writing for its own sake.

Summary

In this chapter we have considered the following:

- Reasons for writing.
- Emergent writing.
- The genre debate.
- Audience and purpose.
- Chronological and non-chronological writing.
- Stages of writing and stages in writing.
- Context and audience.
- The reluctant writer.
- Spelling.
- Information writing and other genres.
- Poetry.
- Advanced reading and writing skills.

PART THREE: REFLECTING ON LANGUAGE AND EQUALITY

CHAPTER SIX

Flagging Issues

The title given to this chapter is deliberately ambiguous. The subject of language and equality, which forms the core of this single chapter, is such an important one that it needs to be flagged by the language leader at all stages of her or his work.

Using the other sense of the word 'flagging', in England the issue of equality is one that has perhaps flagged in the public consciousness over the past few years, as the local management of schools, and Standard Assessment Tests have perhaps unwittingly emphasised the differences between schools and between children, rather than the things they have in common. This is something that the language leader should be wary of, because, as Michael Newby (unpublished) wrote in *Rachel Writing:*

> Making language is part of being human, a biological given, and so its growth will conform in some measure to some pre-ordinated set of procedures as it buds, unfurls and blossoms into maturity . . . It is only by making this assumption (that children, though each with a unique set of experiences, and so with a unique set of things to express, are as much similar as they are different) that any kind of research into the development of behaviour can occur. (p. 3)

This sense of a common bond which transcends differences in culture, social class, gender and age has implications for children's entitlement. The National Curriculum acknowledges this:

> In order to make access to the whole curriculum a reality for all pupils, schools need to foster a climate in which equality of opportunity is supported by a policy to which the whole school subscribes and in which positive attitudes to gender equality, cultural diversity and special needs of all kinds are actively promoted. (*Curriculum Guidance 3 − The Whole Curriculum*, NCC, p. 3)

138

Although the issue of equality operates across the curriculum — and has implications for management and organisation, the governing body and staffing, as well as curricular areas such as art, geography, history, mathematics, modern foreign languages, music, P.E. and dance, R.E., science and technology, it is within the area defined as English that we are primarily concerned.

Practical Activity 6.1

Below is a summary of seven draft criteria suggested by the Runnymede Trust for Equality Assurance in English. Staff could work in pairs and consider their response to each and then in plenary see if there is any collective agreement on all or some of the statements:

1. 'Literature is drawn from a wide range of times and places, and refers to a wide range of human conditions experiences and achievements.'
2. 'Pupils (should) have opportunities to use language, drama and literature to explore aspects of personal and cultural identity.'
3. 'Poets, story-tellers and other writers who visit the school are from a diverse range of cultural and ethnic backgrounds.'
4. 'Pupils see that languages, oral traditions and literary heritages significant to themselves and others are valued.'
5. 'Staff have clear criteria for the choice of texts, and have agreed on how they will deal with racist language and assumptions which may occur in texts.'
6. 'Pupils develop . . . skills in challenging stereotypical images, languages and concepts.'
7. 'There is appropriate and accurate use of a variety of accents, dialects and languages in books, including displays, and in written and oral work.'

Some, or perhaps all of these issues may have been addressed already. It is after all some years since the Swann report *Education for All* (HMSO, 1985) appeared with its recommendations, summarised in the D.C.C. paper *Education for a Multicultural Society*, that we should:

– ensure an education for all our pupils and students which prepares them for the challenges of life in a multicultural society;
– provide education specifically matched to the needs of minority group pupils;
– equip young people, and schools and colleges as institutions, to counter racial prejudice and ignorance in whatever form it appears.

Many schools and colleges already have an Equal Opportunities Policy statement, and such a policy statement addresses whole-school issues, and is not specific to language. But language underpins whole-school issues, and this particular issue merits a section in a language leader's book just as it merited a chapter in *English 5-16* (1989).

6.1 Language and variety

It is a rare (and in some senses impoverished) school which has pupils all of whom have the same background in terms of ethnic origins, regional upbringing and family lifestyles. Apart from some rural primary schools, and independent preparatory schools, most schools have an enormous diversity of children in each class. It is worth quoting from the opening of a paper by Mark Halstead (1991), written for a Moscow audience, but a salutary reminder for those of us who teach in Britain:

LINGUISTIC DIVERSITY IN THE UK

Great Britain has a population of about 55 million people and is made up of three constituent countries: England, Wales and Scotland. The United Kingdom consists of Great Britain and Northern Ireland. England is by far the biggest country, with over 47 million, while Scotland has over five million, Wales nearly three and Northern Ireland one-and-a-half. All citizens of the United Kingdom have British nationality. Of the total population of the UK, rather more than three million were born overseas, and many of these fall into the category of 'ethnic minority'.

Use of the English language is undoubtedly one of the most important factors in being British. It is widely claimed that English is the key to participation on equal terms as a full member of British society. On the other hand, the more the importance of English is emphasised, the more the other languages of the United Kingdom are likely to be undervalued. Indeed, to describe them as 'other' implies that they are a deviation, and that monolingualism is the 'norm'.

The minority languages of the United Kingdom fall into three categories: indigenous languages, languages of the new ethnic minorities, and dialects. First, there are the indigenous British languages. Although there is only a tiny number of monoglot speakers of these languages, bilingual speakers of Welsh and Gaelic form a significant minority, and may even be increasing in number. Estimates suggest that there may be 80,000 speakers of Gaelic, and over half a million Welsh speakers.

The second category comprises the minority languages whose presence in the UK results mainly from the influx of ethnic minority groups from many parts of the world (especially the Indian sub-continent) since the second World War. When questions about linguistic diversity are raised in the UK, it is usually these languages on which the discussion is focused. No precise statistics are available for the population as a whole, but a number of surveys of bilingualism have been carried out in schools. A language census carried out in 1984 for the Inner London Education Authority, for example, showed that 16% of schoolchildren in that district spoke a language other than English at home, and altogether 147 different languages were recorded. The 12 most commonly spoken languages (in descending order) were Bengali, Turkish, Gujerati, Spanish, Punjabi (Panjabi), Chinese, Italian, Arabic, French and Portuguese. In Bradford, . . . 69 languages were recorded in 1987, and nearly 25% of the city's schoolchildren spoke a language other than English at home. Four-fifths of these spoke Punjabi/Urdu or Punjabi/Gurmukhi, and the other main languages were Gujerati, Bengali, Pushtu, Italian, Polish, Hindi, Cantonese, Ukranian and Creole. Some children, particularly those of Asian origin, may indeed be multi-lingual; in one piece of research, a ten-year-old girl is reported as saying:

I speak English at school, Gujerati on my way home with my friends, I learn Urdu at mosque, I read the Quran in Arabic, and my mother speaks Marathi.

Speakers of minority languages are distributed unevenly through the UK, however, and there are very many places, particularly the villages and the countryside, where English is the only language spoken or understood.

The third category consists not so much of other languages as of dialects other than standard English . . . In addition to the regional dialects within the United Kingdom, this category also includes the language form used by many British citizens and children of West Indian origin.

The children we teach live and will work in a society that is multiethnic and multicultural. On a recent visit to Australia we were told that up to 40 per cent of the population had a language other than English as their first language. In the U.K. as a whole ethnic minorities comprise some 6 per cent of the population. The language variety in many British schools is immense: children whose mother tongue is not English, children whose first language is a regional variation of Standard English, children like the one growing up in Devon whose mother is Italian and whose father comes from the Channel Islands. In many of our cities the language variety is even greater, and a rich resource on which schools can draw. It is important that we are educated so that we do not lump languages together as 'Chinese' or 'Indian', ignoring the complex, but important, distinctions between identification with the language of religion rather than the language of speech, the fact that the version of the language spoken in Britain may be very different from the version spoken in the mother country, and the fact that Panjabi speakers from East Africa may speak yet another variation of that language.

All of us — teachers and children — can benefit from the fact that we have experience of multilingualism. We live in a multilingual society, and variety of language links us to other parts of the world. It prepares us for the fact that we live in a mobile, culturally diverse society. Because of under-resourcing, there are undoubtedly times when the problems faced by schools, children and parents seem more apparent than the rewards. There needs to be proper classroom support for all of us — children and teachers alike — to benefit fully from the richness of each other's culture.

6.2 Bilingualism and multilingualism

Like Equal Opportunities, this topic was the subject of a special chapter in *English 5-16*. The chapter makes many of the points that have been made already — namely that bilingual children should be seen as an advantage in the classroom rather than a problem, that stimulating materials for those who are just beginning their acquaintance with English are essential, and that integrated support rather than withdrawal is the recommended method for help with their English. Finally, the report calls on the school community to have respect for the languages of others, and to recognise that all languages have a fully worked out system, and a literary tradition, whether oral or written, which is itself a rich resource to be tapped. A sizeable proportion of schools — about 5 per cent will have a significant population of children for whom English is not the mother tongue, while in Inner London, for example, 23 per cent of children came from homes in which a language in addition to, or other than English was spoken. Some children of mixed parentage will be used to speaking in three languages, and the multilingual nature of our society is at last recognised in official publications. The government's booklet on the Council Tax, for example, was available in the following languages: English, Urdu, Bengali, Punjabi, Gujerati, Hindi, Chinese, Vietnamese, Turkish, Somali, Greek, Arabic. One of the first things a teacher should do is to find out just how many languages are spoken by the children in the class, and how many their relatives speak.

Practical Activity 6.2

Show the children a diagram showing the many languages spoken in Britain, and ask them to write down a) the language(s) they speak at school, (b) the languages they speak at home (c) the language(s) spoken by their relatives. There may be some surprises. A Haringey survey showed that the most popular language other than English spoken at home was Greek (34.1 per cent).

In readiness for a follow-up session, ask the children to bring in an example of the languages they have mentioned. If necessary, allocate a language to individual or groups of children. It may be helpful to focus the activity asking the children to bring in a written version of 'The moon' (or anything else being covered in a topic) in a language other than English and to display this in the room.

The Swann Report

The Swann Report (1985) suggested that children will learn more English through socialization in the playground than in the classroom, and that children for whom English is not the first language should share in all the activities of their contemporaries as soon as possible. If there are several non-English speaking children in the class it is easier for the new arrival to settle in, and as soon as the child seems settled the use of English in the classroom can be encouraged. A special language teacher can provide invaluable support, working in the classroom alongside the teacher. In planning work on a whole-school basis the following suggestions, taken from an article called 'Strategies for supporting Bilingual Learning' (Hackman, *et al.*, 1993) may be helpful:

Ensuring integration into the oral life of the class
- plan to greet and address all pupils in each lesson.
- learn and use names, even those which are unusual to you.
- make use of visual cues, gestures, and props and anything which gives cues to meaning.
- create opportunities for speaking and listening in secure contexts, for example pairwork.
- pay particular attention to eye contact and sight lines but be prepared for different social responses, for example, formal silence, dropped eyes and gestures which may have a different meaning in different cultures.
- seize opportunities to verbalise tacit language, for example, distributing books 'Here is your book, Ahmed.'

Support for the bilingual (child) when reading a text with the whole class
- taped versions, for example, listening corner for reinforcement or catching up what has been missed.
- paired and grouped readings.

The Reading Culture
- different cultures read in different ways, for example, they may read for ritualistic purposes rather than personal empathetic involvement.
- use picture books.

– we need to allow rereadings: bilingual children have special needs to familiarise and consolidate literacy experiences in another culture.

Units of Work
– some titles offer richer and more equal opportunities for the multilingual classroom:
  Ourselves (as opposed to Myself);
  Autobiographies including language autobiographies;
  Travel/journey/quests;
  Growing up.
– avoid spurious themes (dogs, castles).

Playing a duet with the support teacher
– use support for teaching sequences which are rich in opportunities for intervention and development work, for example, individual projects or exploratory group tasks.

Logs and Journals
– guarantee all pupils access to the teacher's attention.
– yield both learning and teaching insights.

There are many more suggestions in the original article, but it could be a useful staff development exercise to use these headings and draw up your own lists.

Multilingualism

For a large number of children in our schools the term bilingualism is inaccurate. Many children whose parents or grandparents have their roots in the Indian sub-continent are multilingual, being fluent in Urdu, English and a form of street language which is a combination of the two.

Marilyn, an advisory teacher from Bradford, argues strongly that schools need to build bridges with the Asian-British community by having parents rooms, shared outings, and community schools ideally housed in the same buildings as health centres. For a long time Bradford had special language centres for children who could not speak English, but not only was this found to interrupt their education and integration, but as the schools themselves were often far from where the children actually lived it actually prevented home-school contact. She believes that such contact is crucial, even in cases where the teacher speaks no Punjabi and the Punjabi speaking parents speak no English. Communication between interested human beings is always possible.

What else can be done, particularly in the classroom? The language leader will want to explore the advantages of conducting certain curriculum sessions in a language other than English, not only as a way of drawing this language into the classroom but using it as a means of learning more about English. In Scotland, France, Lithuania and Belgium children of primary school age are taught a second language, while in Canada they are immersed in French — and this does not affect the English they speak in the playground at all, despite what some parents may fear. All the evidence available suggest that children, whatever their first language, *benefit* from experiencing a diversity of languages. The price of monolingualism was painfully revealed on a television programme recently, with the story of the British company that had gone bankrupt and called in the receivers. The receivers went through the company's papers, and discovered an order from a German company, the biggest order that the company had ever received. The order had been in German, and since no one at the company could speak German it had been filed away and forgotten.

Revised Orders

Recently there has been an attempt to give greater emphasis to Standard English. *English 5-16* always argued that English would be the medium of education in England, and children's entitlement to Standard English is emphasised both in the report and in the original form of the National Curriculum Document for English. As we saw in the Introduction, English is an emotive subject, and the danger of defining Standard English as 'correct' English is that it has the effect of devaluing other forms of expression which in the appropriate context are perfectly valid and successful forms of communication. It imposes a hierarchy that is not intrinsic to language itself, and this runs counter to the Cox Committee's earnest wish that other languages are given the respect they deserve. This is one of the greatest challenges for language leaders at the moment.

This is such an important issue that it will almost certainly come up at a non-teaching day session. All we would say here is that it is culturally revealing that if their languages are, say, English, French and German then the children are invariably seen as very clever, whereas if their languages are English, Urdu and Bengali this is not necessarily the case. Children have sometimes felt it necessary to conceal the language they speak at home because the school (and consequently the other children) does not accord it any status. Children then become wary, suspicions arise, children who do not have this second language seem to think that they are being discussed by the other children and what the school should be developing as an asset becomes a source of friction. In the past the situation was made worse by teachers who told parents to use only English in their homes, because they believed that it could be blamed for slowing a child's progress in reading. No research has supported such a belief. As this section is being written a mother is telling off her child on the other side of a canvas screen. They are talking in Dutch and they are concealed so I cannot tell what he was doing wrong. The mother is very angry indeed. The child is now talking to himself, consoling himself with language. I can guess what is happening because the situation is familiar: a child being told off, the tears which subside into sobs and quiet mutterings, and eventually, the reconciliation. I have spoken to the parents who are fluent in English, and their bilingualism makes me envious. I don't think they are talking about me when they talk to each other (although they may be!) because we have sat and chatted together. That is all it needs, that and the mutual respect for each other's culture.

Increasing knowledge about language and increasing respect

In October 1992 the Association of Headteachers renewed their call for the teaching of modern languages in primary schools – meaning languages like French and German. The Kingman Report argued that children should be given opportunities to increase their knowledge about language – meaning English. Neither had in mind the languages already spoken by bilingual and multilingual children from ethnic minorities, and yet an increase in the knowledge of these languages is surely appropriate in a multicultural society such as ours, as a means of broadening cultural awareness and increasing respect for the richness of cultures.

How can this be done? In primary schools which contain Hindi or Punjabi speakers, for example, group discussion led by these speakers can explore the way that the language is spoken and written, thus contributing to a demystification process for non-speakers in the group. If there is no ethnic mix then the kind of pairing of schools described by Bob May, a primary school teacher from Hampshire, can be set up. In a section from *A Rich Resource: Writing and Language Diversity* (National Writing Project, 1990) he describes the many advantages and occasional pitfalls of such a pairing, with a visit arranged on a day which focusses on some kind of festival or celebration. He emphasises that the children should be paired one to one, that there must be much pre-visit correspondence involving the exchange of pictures, letters, invitations, cassettes, videotapes, dual language books, photographs, and so on, in order to avoid the visit with its focus on a ceremony having the effect of re-inforcing stereotypes. Clearly this is an activity which has to be handled with skill and sensitivity: but the dividends can be enormous.

We shall end this section on Bilingualism with a practical staff development activity.

Practical Activity 6.3

The following extract from Redbridge's policy on bilingualism was written with secondary schools in mind. To what extent do you think that the points raised apply equally to a) primary schools in general b) your school

> The term 'bilingual' refers to any use of more than one language. Users can vary from those who understand several languages but prefer to speak one of them, to those who are fully fluent and literate in more than one language and move naturally and unconsciously from one language to another (code-switching). The majority of people in the world are bilingual, and one in three Redbridge High School Students is bilingual.
>
> Bilingual learners already have competence in one language and are adding to the repertoire. They already have a full range of cognitive abilities.
>
> Children in the early stages of learning English need the opportunity to talk and read and write in their home language to maintain their conceptual development and to help their understanding and acquisition of English. Research has shown that maintaining and developing the first language, far from interfering with the acquisition of English, helps students to become more competent and confident in its use.
>
> Bilingual students have the same rights as monolinguals to have access to the curriculum and to conceptual development. They do not need activities or approaches that are different from their monolingual peers. The definition of good English teaching which the department aims for is valid for all learners, whether mono- or bilingual. Learning, for all, is most successful where motivation is high and stress low. The method of the classroom, therefore, needs to be one which maintains high expectations of bilingual students and acknowledges their knowledge and experience and which combats racism in organisation, behaviour and resources . . . (Quoted in LINC (unpublished) p. 310)

6.3 Special educational needs

'Special needs' is a broad term including all those children who have needs that require additional thought and attention from the teacher, and provision from the school. The Warnock Report of 1978 accepted the suggestion that one in six children at any one time in their school career will require some form of educational provision. Warnock introduced the concept of special educational needs (S.E.N.), and maintained that the purpose of education is the same for all children: the goals are the same, but the help individual children will need to progress towards them will be different. The 1981 Education Act placed a new focus on the child rather than his or her disability: a child has a learning difficulty if he or she has a significantly greater difficulty in learning than the majority of children of his or her age, and a special educational need if he or she has a learning difficulty, or gift, which calls for special educational provision to be made. The NCC document *Special Needs and the National Curriculum: Opportunity and Challenge* (NCC, March 1993) reported on a review of teacher attitudes, and refers to seven issues that were raised by the teachers consulted. Among these are:

- 'the entitlement of all pupils to have a broad, balanced and relevant curriculum, including the National Curriculum and religious education'.
- a rejection of the 'negative concept of disapplication'.
- for pupils with S.E.N. the 'National Curriculum provides only part of the curriculum. Access to developmental work across the curriculum, personal and social education and enrichment activities in particular, should be given equal status with access to the National Curriculum'.

What is the relationship between S.E.N. and language development?

Language development may be affected in a number of ways, and some of these ways will slow down progress. A child may be experiencing a hearing impairment, or specific learning difficulties. On the other hand (and we should not forget the needs of those who are left-handed), the need may result from a special abilility, sometimes called giftedness, in some or all areas of the curriculum. We should not forget that a learning difficulty may be the consequence of emotional, behavioural, mental, physical or social disadvantage. This may affect or inhibit language development, manifesting itself as continued baby speech, stuttering, a refusal to try, or reflect language deprivation in the social background.

All of these needs require additional support, and although LEAs are losing many of their responsibilities they are to remain responsible for special needs. Presumably schools will have to pay for these services out of their budgets, and it will be interesting to see if the provision for special needs deteriorates over the next few years.

As language leader your main concern will be to ensure that you have an overall awareness of the number and identities of those children who are experiencing serious language difficulties. Are these, as is likely, translating themselves into serious learning difficulties? Is there a case for a statement leading to additional teacher support? The best strategy to follow when such questions arise is to work with the S.E.N. co-ordinator in suggesting appropriate language work for children with learning difficulties.

The key debate over the past twenty years has been about the most effective whole-school strategies to help children with special education needs. In the main this has resulted in a shift away from the concept of remedial education, which involved withdrawal of children into special units, and, its critics allege, an essentially deficit approach to children (the 'What is wrong with them that needs to be put right?' approach). Gipps, Cross and Goldstein (1987) quote a number of researchers who query the effectiveness of a remedial approach to reading, for example. Whilst they accept, *pace* Marie Clay, that remedial action may lead to short-term advances, these soon evaporate, and in the meantime the process of withdrawal itself has sown the seeds of much longer-term problems. Instead, as Young and Tyre (1986) argue, the key to learning is motivation, and this has meant a move towards classroom support within the normal classroom. Successful reading recovery programmes in New Zealand transform reluctant readers into enthusiastic readers, and New Zealand Heads have commented on the remarkable change in children's attitudes to learning. In jargon terms, this has meant a recognition of the importance of seeing the *trait* rather than the *slate*, the habit rather than the shortcoming. As with reading itself, no single approach is likely to be of assistance to all children, but as we shall see at the end of this chapter, the absence of self-esteem often lies at the heart of the problem, and the creation of this self-esteem may help the child much more than the process of being statemented. This is much easier to say than carry out, however.

6.4 Language and gender

Earlier, in the 'Language and Equality' opening to this section, we referred briefly to gender. It is an important subject, deserving a section in its own right.

In the 1980s, perhaps because we had a woman Prime Minister, you would often hear expressed the view that the battle for sex equality had been won. People − not just those sceptics who had always opposed what they saw as 'feminist' agitation, but teenage boys and girls from both privileged and deprived backgrounds, scorned the idea that women were in any way disadvantaged by society's attitude to them. Women could be seen driving buses, reading the news on television, women were doctors − surely this was evidence of a fair and equal society. Gender began to fade as an issue, partly for this reason, and in the field of language in education partly because other issues began to dominate. Yet statistics suggest that the majority of primary teachers are women while the majority of Heads are men, for example. In many schools the dinner helpers are all women, as are the early years teachers. Children pick up messages from this, as they do from the fact that the register may be divided into boys and girls and P.E. may be unmixed. As Hilary Minns (1991) points out in *Language, Literacy and Gender* there are clearly important issues here. To what extent are they issues which are the direct concern of the language leader? Those who have introduced Year 4, 5 or 6 children to Gene Kemps *The Turbulent Term of Tyke Tyler* (1977), and asked them for their reaction when they discover at the end of the book that Tyke is a girl, will know that there are important issues — especially if you ask children why (as is usual) they have assumed Tyke was a boy! Another way of raising awareness through fiction is by using Anthony Browne's excellent *Piggybook* (1986) or Anne Fine's *Bill's New Frock* (1991). So if we accept that gender is an issue, how can we raise our awareness of it? Hilary Minns proposes a number of strategies, ranging from an observation of the way nursery age children talk, play and perceive toys for boys and girls, jobs for boys and girls, and concepts like 'tom boys' — they have already learnt a number of stereotyped attitudes — to invitations to parents to collaborate in a discussion of bias in the materials in school. How do we feel about fairy stories: should they remain untampered with? What about *He-Man* comics — should they be discouraged, ignored, banned? The National Writing Project (1990) suggested asking a number of questions, about school, home and the community. Here are some of them:

School
What messages is the school giving about male and female writing from the materials, displays and books in the schools?
What kinds of writing are favoured by boys/girls? Is one kind given more status than another?
Are pre-writing discussion groups generally mixed or single sex? Does this affect the outcomes?
Do teachers respond differently to girls' writing and to boys' writing?
If older junior girls write fairy stories for younger girls, are their role models significantly different from the role models older boys offer in their fairy stories for younger boys?
Do boys find it more difficult to speak or write in role with the voice of a female character, than girls do to speak or write as a male? If so, why do children think this is?

150

Home
What kind of writing do they see being done at home? Who writes lists, letters, notes for the milk deliverer, absence notes?

Community
What messages about gender do children get from the following:
– writing associated with jobs?
– the media?
– literature?

It may be that as language leader you wish to pursue these questions further, either through research or staff development sessions.

Practical Activity 6.4

Topics for discussion: possible case studies for teachers interested in doing some research.

The Language and Gender Committee of the National Association for the Teaching of English has suggested and carried out seven case studies of classroom work on gender issues. How appropriate are these for your school?

1. Gender and talk: practical problems and solutions.
2. Girls and boys reading choices.
3. Addressing gender issues in the early years classroom.
4. Gender issues in modern 'anti-sexist' fairy stories.
5. Boys' writing.
6. Problems of free choice and stereotyping in pupils' own writing.
7. Gendered language: ideas for pupil action research.

Clearly in some schools it would be counter-productive for the language leader to present this as a manifesto. Rather it could be introduced as a series of topics for enquiry.

It may be useful to do some preparatory research of your own, with children, and possibly with another teacher and her/his class.

Practical Activity 6.5

Surveying children's attitude to gender.

There are a number of ways you can foreground the issue of gender with the children in your class, and you may wish to encourage your colleagues to do the same.

1. With early years children through drawing and labelling pictures called A nurse/A doctor/Hanging out the washing/A secretary/A scientist or inventor, and so on. The idea is to go on to discuss why the children have drawn males or females in particular roles.
2. With children from Years 3, 4 and 5 you could approach the subject through poetry, or fiction like *Bill's New Frock* by Ann Fine, mentioned above.

> 3. With Years 6, 7 and 8 you could use all of these approaches, plus a more analytical look at magazine pictures and television advertisements, examining how men and women are represented.
> 4. With children of any age you could raise awareness through discussion of Anthony Browne's *Piggybook*, also mentioned above.

So what are the practical implications for the language leader in the primary school? Perhaps the best way could be through a check list which you set before the whole staff for either approval or rejection.

Practical Activity 6.6

Working in pairs consider each of the following:

Would you as a class teacher want to:
1. Check books for gender stereotyping?
2. Invite professional women and male nurses into the classroom as part of an overall discussion about gender?
3. Ensure that groups are mixed in gender – always/sometimes?
4. Comment on and make an issue of sexist comments in the classroom/in the school as a whole.

There should be some lively discussion!

Any consideration of gender will need to take account of the representation of men and women in contexts other than books – in pop music, advertisements, cards and clothing for babies, pictures and roles in newspapers, comics and magazines, and in television soaps. For a staff development session it may be more helpful to focus on books which foreground some of the issues, books such as the following:

Ahlberg, A. (1981) *Miss Brick the Builder, Miss Jump the Jockey, Mrs Plug the Plumber*, London, Kestrel.

Briggs, R. (1975) *Father Christmas goes on holiday*, Hamish Hamilton.

Cole, B. (1989) *Princess Smartypants, Prince Cinders*, London, Picture Lions.

Fine, A. (1987) *Jupiter Boots*, London, Banana Books.

Haddon, M. (1987) *A Narrow Escape for Princess Sharon*, London, Banana Books.

Graham, B. (1988) *The Red Woollen Blanket*, London, Walker.

Hussey, J. (1988) *Little Bear's Trousers*, London, Heinemann.

Hughes, S. (1988) *The Big Alfie and Annie Book*, London, Bodley Head.

Keeping, C. (1982) *Charley, Charlotte and the Golden Canary*, London, Burke.

Most of these books make a deliberate attempt to present their characters in non-stereotypical roles, resist the replication of male dominance and present a world of greater sexual equality. As a bridge between the issue of gender and power, which clearly impinge and frequently overlap, it may be helpful to consider some of the issues raised in *Alice in Genderland* (NATE, 1985), which discusses gender and play in the nursery school, sex-stereotyping in the primary school, female roles in reading schemes and an approach to pastoral care. All of these touch on important issues of power, and in schools where this is a sensitive, not to say difficult subject, they need to be introduced with care.

6.5 Language, power and self-esteem

As we said in the introduction, the fury with which the debate about language is sometimes conducted is a sure indication that language issues overlap with issues of power. What and how: these are the issues that divide people. How, as a society, should we respond to the fact that people speak a diversity of languages and dialects? On the one hand there is the argument that we should value and find space in the curriculum for mother tongue languages, dialects as well as Standard English. On the other there is the argument that Standard English should be given priority, either because it is perceived as the shared language, or, more dubiously, because it is the 'correct' form. Each side claims that it is concerned with the self-esteem and achievement of the child: the former on the grounds that its approach is anti-discriminatory, and the latter on the grounds that *its* approach gives children a more practical entitlement. Each side considers that there is a sub-text to the opponent's state position. Those in favour of diversity argue that the emphasis on 'Standard' English is a controlling mechanism to ensure the survival of the privileged status of those holding power, while those who hold power argue that their opponents are actually misleading children and denying them access to power by failing to mould their speech and writing.

Children have entitlements, and if there is a corollary to the theme of equality which links all the issues considered in the middle section of this book, it is the belief that equality means equality of access to the institutions and strategies through which power is exercised, whether this means access to higher education, professional and managerial

153

careers or decision-making through local or national politics and government. But access has to be real and genuine, and not just notional. Currently in Britain, education, like most other sectors of life, is being shaped to respond to the influence of market forces. One problem with this approach, which in the language of the market regards everyone as potential clients or customers — whether they be trained passengers (now customers), children in school or doctors' patients, that some people have more buying power than others. Perhaps that is not such a problem on a train, where everyone ends up at the same destination, even if they have travelled in less comfort. In education we do not all arrive at the same destination, and if we are to work within the ethos of a consumer led society, then it is up to teachers to make children aware of the enormous buying power of language.

This means taking into account the way that social deprivation can lead to a cycle of social disenfranchisement, that racism and sexism operate in ways that threaten to deny power to those who do not have the voice, language and confidence to challenge them, and the way that self-esteem, which is linked to behaviour and achievement, is something that links us all, whether teachers or pupils, special needs or average. If we use language to improve our self-esteem, our achievement will have been considerable.

Summary

In this chapter we have considered the following issues:
- Language and Equality.
- Language and Variety: Bilingualism and Multiculturalism.
- Language and Special Educational Needs.
- Language and Gender.
- Language, power and self-esteem.

(For a fuller discussion of the power strategies operating within the school, see Sylvia Wareham (1993).)

PART FOUR: SCAFFOLDING: PRODUCTIVE SUPPORT

CHAPTER SEVEN

Subject Expertise: Knowledge about Language

Many teachers feel anxious when it comes to the subject of knowledge about language, either because they feel it involves a knowledge of something loosely called 'grammar' which, for quite valid reasons, they were never given, or because it involves a knowledge of linguistics which they have never acquired. The majority of language leaders are more interested in what they see as the active, productive aspects of language – drama, poetry, story-making – than the analytic aspects, whether these are classifications (descriptive grammars) or scientific (psycho-linguistics and socio-linguistics). But it is a shame if these aspects of language are separated in that way, for knowledge always informs and modifies practice, and the language leader will feel more confident if she has some linguistic expertise. A short chapter like this cannot hope to do these subjects justice, but it can suggest ways in which they can be approached.

We should begin by distinguishing the needs of children from the needs of teachers when it comes to knowledge about language. Let us begin by getting one hoary old chestnut out of the way: prescriptive grammar, which people are still fond of recommending in letters to the newspapers. Hardly a month goes by without someone claiming that children would benefit from studying grammar in the way that it was studied in schools in the 1950s – that is, by subjecting sentences to syntactical parsing. This was discontinued because there was no evidence that formal study improves the ability to write. Wilkinson (1971) summarised very clearly the research that deals with this issue, as follows:

i) Training in formal grammar does not improve pupils' composition: shown by Asker (1923), Macaulay (1947) and Robinson (1960).

ii) Ability in grammar is more related to ability in other subjects than to that in English composition: shown by Boraas (1917) but not confirmed by Segal and Barr (1926).

iii) A knowledge of grammar is of no general help in correcting faulty usage: shown by Catherwood (1932) and Benfer (1935).

iv) Does grammar hinder the development of children's English? There is some evidence for this because of the amount of time that has to be spent on grammar. See Macaulay (1947) and Sears and Diebel (1961).

v) Does written work suffer if grammar is dispensed with? In 1962 Heath monitored the progress of one group who were given no formal exercises of any kind alongside the work of another who were. After nine months the 'first group were significantly ahead in their composition work, without loss of accuracy'.

All this research took place some time ago, but the results were convincing enough for that particular concept of grammar teaching to disappear from the curriculum. Another effect was to make teachers wary of the whole notion of linguistic analysis, and sceptical of the relevance of linguistics to teaching. But to look at it another way, and to quote from Bill Mittins (1993) 'As Diack of Nottingham and others have said, Macauley's research merely demonstrated the futility of teaching bad grammar!' No one, from Kingman to the 1993 proposals for a revision to the National Curriculum, propose a return to this archaic form of work.

The Kingman report raised the question of knowledge about language most usefully by emphasising that such knowledge and interest is developed through use rather than analysis. In other words, children need to be given the opportunity to reflect on their own language, and to discuss what language is *for* rather than what language *is*. Teachers, on the other hand, particularly language leaders, may wish to develop their interest in what language is and does. Language is the medium for education — classrooms are language-centred environments — and is the central factor not just in teacher talk and children's dialogue, but in textbooks, work on the chalkboard, displays, and radio and television programmes. If as adults we are more aware of what language is, and what makes the kind of language the child uses as a child and as a pupil distinctive, then we are better able to understand and explain what that language is for.

7.1 Should the language leader be a linguist?

This is a key question that some teachers worry about from time to time and we have left until now an issue which many would wish to have seen at the beginning. The question of how much knowledge of the structural features of language (not just English) a language leader should have is a tricky one. Those who have a linguistic training – and the majority of teachers in primary and middle schools do not – would argue that one of the important roles of the language leader, which we mentioned briefly in chapter 1, is that of expert diagnostician. In the same way that the teacher with responsibility for science can be consulted on matters scientific, so the teacher with responsibility for co-ordinating language should be able to provide not only bright ideas but informed diagnosis.

We don't all have degrees in linguistics

Some may reject the 'linguistic expertise' role on philosophical grounds, because to regard an individual as an expert undermines the cross-curricular and whole-school approach to language, for which we have argued in the early chapters. Others will be uneasy about such a role because they feel they do not have the knowledge – it may have been touched on briefly in their initial teacher training, but since the language in the National Curriculum project was strangled at birth there have been few opportunities to learn more about grammar and linguistics. The very words may send a chill up your spine! So, assuming that you are one of those who feel that some knowledge in this field would be useful, let us take the bull by the horns, and find out about the ways in which knowledge of language can help us and the children we teach. But how do we acquire such knowledge?

We have a considerable amount of knowledge already

As Eve Bearne and Cath Farrow (1992) observe, 'Knowledge about language can be identified not only by an individual's ability to *talk* about language, but also by the ability to *produce* language in different forms, both in speaking and writing.' What applies to children is equally applicable to teachers. Even if you did not study grammar at school, or take a linguistics course as part of your A Level or degree, you will know all of the following:

i) Some words are more common than others.

ii) Words are formed from a number of basic sounds.

iii) Word order is very important in English.

iv) Some words in a sentence can be removed without destroying it.

v) Some people talk more fluently than they write, and some write more fluently than they speak.

vi) Language changes over time.

vii) Language varies according to region, context and purpose.

vii) Language has a history, and English has been enriched by the many languages that have fed into it, from Norman French to Punjabi.

The list could be extended: if as teachers we reflect on the language work we did in primary and secondary school, at A Level and as part of our initial teacher training qualification or first degree, we soon realise that we have amassed a considerable amount of expertise about the way language works, even if we do not have the formal vocabulary to describe the operation of language in schools and books.

Children, too, possess a great deal of intuitive knowledge about language, and the LINC project suggested a number of ways in which this knowledge can be brought to the surface by discussing the actual language they are using at the time — talking about ways in which stories they have written can be improved, differences between the kind of writing they do when producing a story and writing a report. You may wish to discuss with your colleagues whether this language awareness is cultivated more by discussing their own genres, rather than models of genres they are given.

What do we know about language development?

At the beginning of this book we touched briefly on the changing views of language development, from the behaviourist approaches of early psycho-linguists to the socially situated models advanced by socio-linguists. Behaviourist linguists, who modelled their research on work carried out with animals, emphasised the role of positive reinforcement in early language acquisition, and it clearly is an important factor. A child who receives a smile when she says 'mummy' is likely to repeat that sound. But children can also be rewarded with a smile when they make up their own words ('bubbies' for 'puppies', for example) so the behaviourist model is generally regarded as too simplistic.

It was Chomsky who, in the 1950s, attacked behaviourist theory by emphasising the innate and universal features of the human brain. Children invent and produce their own innovative language. They do not just imitate. The nativist approach emphasised what children are born with: this in turn led to a reaction from the cognitive psychologists of the 1970s who felt that Chomsky's stress on the structure of language unhelpfully separated theories of language development from theories of cognitive development of the kind developed by Piaget. Piaget had described the mental schemas that the infant created through interaction with the environment, and had identified what he saw as a series of stages through which the child passed in the first five years. Bruner (1985) and Vygotsky (1967) emphasised the social context of language acquisition and the scaffolding by the supportive adult, a process of social interaction. This in turn has led to the currently favoured functional model of language, in which language is seen as a tool which allows people to carry out certain functions. These functions may range from descriptions to speculations, reporting to persuading. The functional-systemic model of language is most associated with M.A.K. Halliday, who has argued that although children are born with a desire to communicate, in all other respects language is learnt through an *interaction* with those around them.

All of these theories have something to contribute to our understanding, but at the same time they are constantly being challenged by current research. Piaget, whose theories of developmental psychology have been one of the foundations of teacher education for the past thirty years is being challenged by a new nativistic school on the grounds that children *are* born with the capacity to do full scale analogical reasoning. If provided with knowledge that is known to them, some very young children can succeed at tasks that Piaget assumes they are not ready for − or at least that is what Goswami's (1992) research seems to demonstrate.

Research

The power of research and theory should not be underestimated. Released from the straight-jacket of the Piagetian model we have been able to question ideas of reading readiness, and begin introducing children to reading and writing at a much earlier age. Other research has pushed British education in directions not followed by other countries. Research that showed that there was no real correlation between the possession of knowledge of grammar and the ability to write fluently or well, encouraged teachers to eliminate the study of grammar from their English lessons in the secondary school, even though their colleagues in French, German and Spanish lessons continued the practice. More recent research has not modified this finding, although the title of an article in Educational Studies (1992) reveals another aspect of the subject: 'Illuminating English: how explicit language teaching improved public examination results in a comprehensive school'. Two researchers at Skevington School introduced a three-stage programme, the aims of which were to improve children's performance by giving them confidence in their ability to use academic language. The first stage involved introducing topics such as Greek Roots, sentence structure and parts of speech; the second involved the reading of specific academic texts; and the third the production of written academic discourse. The theory behind this is that all children (and this has implications for multicultural education) can adjust to academic language once they are made familiar with it, and since it is the language of textbooks, examinations and the essay form which dominates secondary, further and higher education, it is something they need to learn. Does this have implications for the primary school? The first stage seems rather narrow as described, but the second and third stages could indeed be introduced from Year 5 onwards. Yet the very fact that such questions are being asked reveals the shift towards an acknowledgement that knowledge about language is something that is not to be lightly dismissed. It was to the credit of those involved in the LINC project that such a shift in perception took place at all. So let us ask some of those awkward questions that this kind of talk about language usually generates at the back of our minds.

7.2 What is the difference between knowledge about language, grammar and linguistics?

Linguistics

Linguistics is the organised, scientific study of language, and this means the whole of language, including the study of how children acquire language. It includes all of the following:

PHONETICS – how we make sounds, using our voice-boxes. This includes a study of the way the mouth, tongue, nose, lips and throat allow us to make a variety of sounds, how w stress these sounds, and how we accompany speech with facial expressions that fall under the heading of 'paralinguistics'.

PHONOLOGY – **how we arrange the sounds we make in speech.**
Some children have difficulties with certain sounds, and the expertise
of the Speech Therapist may be called for.

SYNTAX – **how words are formed and arranged.**
English is a language which relies heavily on words being placed in
a certain order, unlike Latin where the word order is less important
because each word's function is signalled by its ending — its inflection.
In English it is the position of the word in a sentence which governs
the meaning: 'The dog bit the girl' is quite different from 'The girl
bit the dog'. By changing the order we change the meaning.

SEMANTICS – **how words carry a meaning which is separate from
their form.** Saussure, the Swiss linguist from the beginning of the
century, described the way that the meaning we give to words or *signs*
is arbitrary, so there is an important distinction to be made between
the signifier (for example, the word 'apple') and *the signified* (the actual
object that is an apple). Making the connection is the challenge that
faces all children!

PRAGMATICS – **how words are used.**
Ferdinand de Saussure is often described as the founding father of
modern structural linguistics because he described language as a
complete system, distinguishing between language as a rule-governed
system (langue) and specific examples of language (parole). He also
distinguished between the synchronic study of language (what is
happening now) and the diachronic (how language has changed over
the centuries). Earlier this century and until relatively recently, the
synchronic was favoured over the diachronic which was associated with
unfashionable pre-Saussurian nineteenth-century approaches.
Linguistics is part of semiotics, the theory of signs, and is itself divided
into semantics, the study of meanings; syntactics, the analysis of the
relationship between words; and pragmatics, the social function of
language, that is the relationship between language and use. Formerly
the study of language was characterised by an analytic approach, which
drew attention to the observable rules and conventions to which a langue
seemed to conform. Latin had lent itself to this form of analysis (because
it is a very regular language which sticks faithfully to a number of basic
rules). It is the influence of Latin that led to the study of grammar in
English schools, even though English refuses to conform to many of
the 'rules'.

'Grammar' is a term used by linguists to identify those features of a language which make it operable and distinctive: the syntax, the phonology and the semantics. In the Middle Ages 'grammar' referred to literacy, to the area of study that involved the art of writing in Latin. Speech, the subject of rhetoric, was ignored, and consequently downgraded. The language of writing was considered superior, more formal and more correct. People from the generation educated in the 1950s or before use the word grammar in a prescriptive sense to mean 'correct' syntax, and the way that the word order can be labelled and classified using terms like noun, adverb, clause, participle, and so on. Linguisticians do not use the word in this sense, and the notion of 'correctness', which suggests a fixed, morally superior language system, is one which no longer has any currency among language specialists. That is not to suggest that certain forms of language are not more acceptable than others: clearly Standard English is the socially acceptable form and the one cherished by many of those who enjoy positions of influence.

Other issues in the discussion of grammar include the search for a universal grammar that underpins all languages, and the attempt to describe a generative (that is rule-based) grammar. In America in the 1970s Noam Chomsky advanced his theory of transformational grammar, which describes the internalised rules that all children seem to have in their minds from birth. This belief in deep structures which can be transformed into surface structures at the point of utterance has been questioned by other linguists, especially socio-linguists.

Socio- and psycho-linguistics

The link between language and external factors, such as social environment, is the province of socio-linguist. Socio-linguists explore the way that even in what we call 'English' there is not one language but many. This leads to a discussion of dialects (a regional variation of a language) and registers (a specialised style, such as *The Sun* headlines, or the language of the courtroom). It also leads to a recognition that children do not acquire language in isolation.

Psycho-linguists are primarily concerned with the relationship between language and thinking. For example, they might ask the question 'How is information about words stored in the memory?' Do we remember all the forms (sleep, slept, sleeping, sleeps, for example) or just the main stem? Caron (1992) concludes that each form of the word is remembered separately, but that polysemic words (words that have more than one meaning, like 'bill') are stored only once. The perennial questions that exercised psycho-linguists were whether thought and language are separable, and whether the capacity for language is innate or acquired. The second is now seen to be a false polarity: both Chomsky (1965) and Wells (1986) argue that we are innately predisposed to learn a language, but whereas Chomsky placed great emphasis on 'Language Acquisition Device', our predisposition toward language, Wells argued that we would not develop this ability if we did not find ourselves in a highly linguistic environment. In summing up the results of the part of the Bristol Language Development Project, which studied 128 children, Wells writes:

> Those [parents] whose children were most successful [in learning to talk] were not concerned to give systematic linguistic instruction but rather to ensure that conversations with their children were mutually rewarding. They assumed that, when their child spoke, he or she had something to communicate, so they tried to work out what it was and, whenever possible, to provide a response that was meaningful and relevant to the child and that invited further contribution. (Wells and Nicholls, 1985, pp. 415-6)

This shift in emphasis and understanding has led to a rapid growth in socio-linguistics, modifying the work of Basil Bernstein and William Labov. The former is most famous (or infamous) for his description of two distinct codes, one which he called 'restricted' and one which he called 'elaborated'. The former is characterised by short sentences and a reliance on immediate context for meaning. The latter is the very opposite. Bernstein linked these codes to social class, and argued that children from working-class backgrounds were handicapped in a school which operated within the framework of the elaborated code. Labov, among others, has rejected this 'language deficit' view, demonstrating that children whose language at school may appear poor actually have a very diverse and rich language environment at home, and that it is more a case of providing suitable contexts which will allow children to develop their natural language. This was in opposition to the view expressed in the consultative document *English 5-16* (1993), which directed teachers to require spoken Standard English, as if it was the same as written Standard English. It isn't and the instruction was subsequently withdrawn.

Knowledge about language differs from grammar and linguistics in that it assumes a more distant overview of the effect of language in action, rather than the detailed analysis of exemplary language. John Richmond (1990), in the opening chapter of the book called *Knowledge about Language* (Carter, (ed.), 1990) does not attempt an explanation of that phrase beyond 'Knowing things about language. Being interested in and informed about language.' He does not say precisely what the things are that we need to know, but in suggesting the following headings for language study he gives us a pretty good idea of the way he interprets the term:

> Variety in and between languages
> History of languages
> Language and power in society
> Acquisition and development of language
> Language as a system shared by its users.

This closely reflects the units in the unpublished LINC materials, which bore the following headings:

> EARLY LANGUAGE (early talk, early reading, early writing)
> THE PROCESS OF READING
> THE READING REPERTOIRE (narrative voice in children's books, reading the language of science, the language of fiction and non-fiction, simplified texts)
> THE PROCESS OF WRITING
> THE WRITING REPERTOIRE (audience, purpose, form, writing to inform, observation and recount genres, writing about what things are like, writing to get things done — instructions and procedures, writing to get things changed — persuasive writing, narrative writing, the language of poetry)
> THE PROCESS OF TALK
> THE TALK REPERTOIRE
> SPOKEN AND WRITTEN LANGUAGE
> ACCENT, DIALECT AND STANDARD ENGLISH
> MULTILINGUALISM
> GRAMMAR IN ACTION

It is quite clear from this list that the approach is more discursive and generic, less scientific and analytical than that of linguistics and grammatology. In this respect if these materials had been made more widely available, and not vetoed by the government of the day, they promised to build bridges between teachers and the scientific study of language; and conversations between classroom practitioners and those with a linguistic expertise would have proved to be of immense value to both and would have broken down many barriers. That this process was arrested is to the eternal shame of those who made the decision not to release the materials.

7.3 How does language work?

When we consider the very earliest stage of language acquisition there are still more questions than answers. How does the very young child pick out particular words from a stream of sound? What use does the infant make of rhythm and stress to separate elements in a flood of speech? Do they use body language — gesture and facial expression — to help them?

In a recent study of early language development Margaret Harris (1992) argues that initially the very young child's development is determined by external factors — how the adult uses a particular word and in what context a word is used. So a word like 'teddy' will have a specific reference for a child because the mother or father uses it in a specific context, whereas a word like 'ball' may have a general significance for a class of objects. Later this process is internally driven, as the child discovers the rule that things have names, and the 'naming explosion' soon follows.

In *Language and Literacy in the Early Years* Marian Whitehead (1990) refutes the notion that 'the study of language as a system [is] too abstract and remote from the concerns of small children in the early years of schooling, and not likely to touch their lives', firstly, on the grounds that very young children are themselves language learners and deeply involved in language matters, and secondly on the grounds that 'professional teachers who work with young children are actually making linguistic decisions throughout the day and these should be educationally as well as linguistically 'good' reasons for intervention in the early years classroom' (p. 77). Clearly the best way that linguistic knowledge can be applied in the classroom is by encouraging children to reflect on their own language, to discuss their own writing with the teacher, and to share as much as possible with the rest of the class.

If we project some of our children's writing onto the screen, and encourage them to talk about the choice of words, the order of words, the sound of words and the purpose of the writing, then we are demonstrating the relevance to the classroom of linguistic knowledge.

Summary

In this chapter we have taken a brief look at the subject of linguistics. As language leader your position will be strengthened if you have some knowledge of theories of language development, of how children acquire spoken language, and learn to read and write. In chapter 2 we touched on the difference between the top-down models of language development that we get from Frank Smith and Kenneth Goodman, and the interactive models that derive from Vygotsky and M. A. K. Halliday. These models are often rooted in research based in linguistics. Although it is possible to be an inspirational language teacher, and dynamic language leader without any experience of formal linguistic study, the ability to diagnose, discuss and make accurate assessments of children's language needs is enhanced by such knowledge. Neither of us have degrees in linguistics, and so we have merely sketched in the field of knowledge about language by considering the following:

- Kingman, knowledge about language and a rejection of formal grammar teaching.
- The case for and against linguistic knowledge for teachers.
- The knowledge about language we already have.
- Should children be taught a metalanguage?
- Language development theories.
- The new grammar.
- The field of linguistics: socio- and psycho-linguistics.
- Questions about teaching language.

During the course of the chapter some technical terms are used, and more of these are likely to be encountered if you investigate the study of linguistics further. Several of these terms are explained in the glossary that appears at the end of the book.

CHAPTER EIGHT

Performance: Media Education, Writers and Performers in School

8.1 Media education

Reflecting on the issues

Much of the reporting of the alleged fall in reading and writing standards compares the present with the past without reference to the world outside the classroom. Yet is is quite apparent to anyone who works with large numbers of children that, once outside the school gates, the majority of the children we teach will have significant and regular contact with language not through reading or being read to, nor even through conversation, letters or phone calls to friends or family, but through a combination of videos, television soaps, the radio, and walkman cassettes. That is what it means to be a child growing up in the West in the 1990s as opposed to the 1950s, the 1920s or the 1890s. It is a markedly different cultural experience, and has enormous implications for the way we define 'text' and approach language.

Whether we love, tolerate or loathe contemporary culture, there it is, and we and our children are exposed to it relentlessly. If there was no other argument for the inclusion of media education in the primary and middle school curriculum this alone would be a powerful one. For just as contemporary children are entitled to learn something about the ingredients of the food they eat (how much sugar there is in tomato ketchup, for example), so children should have opportunities to examine and discuss the way that television programmes, videos and newspapers are assembled, constructed, and edited. The point about knowing the ingredients is not to put us off (most of us like tomato ketchup too much for that) – but to allow informed decisions and choices to be made.

But there is another argument for including media education, and it is that children love the immediacy, relevance and practical nature of it. It is fun! It is enjoyable to make radio and television programmes, to tell stories on film, and to end up with a finished product that a real audience can enjoy. When we look at the 1993 version of *English 5-16* we find this isolated reference to media in the section on 'Rationale and Structure', where the removal of media from English is explained on the grounds of making the curriculum more manageable. Drama and 'aspects of the media' are to be used

> to assist in the teaching of the fundamental objectives of the Order, rather than as distinctive subjects within English. Both these aspects of English remain in place but more tightly focused on the subject itself. (p. 5)

We should not let unimaginative references like this, which sees the media as unproblematic and marginal, deter us from including the media in our classroom work on texts. But how can this be done?

The National Curriculum English document dated June 1989 has a section called 'Planning Schemes of Work for the National Curriculum', and paragraph 4.9 of this section shows how many of the programmes of study for English can be promoted by activities to do with media education. They give several examples, which we will come onto later, but first let us make clear what we mean by the term 'media education'.

As is made clear in *English 5-16* (1989) we are not talking about the kind of explicit instruction that is more appropriate for a media studies GCSE, A Level or Degree course. Instead

> First-hand use of media equipment (eg in making videos) and other technologies (such as desktop publishing) can contribute to children's practical understanding of how meanings are created. (9.2)

So media education aims, through experience of the technology of the mass media, to enlarge children's understanding of how messages are generated:

> Media education . . . seeks to increase children's critical understanding of the media — namely television, film, video, radio, photography, popular music, printed materials, and computer software. How they work, how they produce meaning, how they are organised and how audiences make sense of them, are the issues that media education addresses. [It] aims to develop systematically children's critical and creative powers through analysis and production of media artifacts. This also deepens their understanding of the pleasure and enjoyment provided by the media. Media education aims to create more active and critical media users who will demand, and could contribute to, a greater range and diversity of media products. (Bazalgette (ed.), 1989, p. 3)

Productive leadership

Talk of using video cameras may still deter some (though camcorders have increasingly become household items with which children are familiar) and it may be that the most straightforward way to approach media education is through photography. (A Yeovil School recently did some very interesting work using pinhole cameras as part of a project on life in the nineteenth century. This would be a natural stepping stone for more advanced photographic work using more up-to-date cameras!)

A recent programme in the 'Teaching Today' Series on BBC-1 (*Media Education in the Primary School*, 1992) showed children being introduced to media education concepts through a picture sorting exercise. Children – and they could be any age, from Year 1 to Year 8 – were invited to look at a pile of pictures on a table and then select two which went together in some way. They were then asked where they thought they had come from (newspaper, magazine, someone's home?), feeling the surface texture of the picture as a possible clue. Another picture activity involved making decisions about whether photographs depicted 'real-life' situations or whether they came from films or television programmes. What makes children decide?

Next they were encouraged to take their own photographs, using a polaroid camera, and a cardboard frame to think about the kind of shot they wanted. An extension of this, leading to video-camera work, is to ask children to tell a story on camera, using pictures (either photographs they have taken or collected, or drawings and paintings they have made) displayed on a board illustrating the stages of the story. This can be done in the corner of the room, with groups of three or four at a time.

A more ambitious project is to make a video programme in the classroom – perhaps an enactment of a scene from a story, or a news or magazine-type programme. The children interviewed said that it did not matter that their programmes did not have the polish of the programmes you see on television – it was the process of learning how to do it that really mattered (yes, they actually said this!). Anyway, they got a great buzz from seeing themselves on the screen!

In approaching all these media education activities it is useful to have a number of questions in mind. The following headings were used in the programme:

CATEGORY (or genre) What is the product?
LANGUAGE What does it mean?

AGENCY Who made it?
TECHNOLOGY What technology was used in its making?
AUDIENCE Who is, or was, it intended for?
REPRESENTATION Who is in it (or who is absent from it)? What is its message?

Another relatively simple way into media education is via radio, as the following activity shows.

Practical Activity 8.1 Making a radio programme

The whole thing can be done in one afternoon, with one tape-recorder, although the finished product is likely to be better if some preparation has been done the day before.
Task: to record a fifteen minute programme called 'Good Afternoon Springtown' (Replace Springtown with the name of your local community.)
The following are required (you will probably want to put this down on a series of worksheets):

2 programme producers (to supervise the two halves of the programme)
1 linking presenter (to speak between items)
1 local news presenter (to read the local news)
4 local news reporters (to collect local news and write scripts)
2 local news editors (to edit and collate the scripts)
1 weather presenter (to read the local weather)
4 weather researchers (to gather data and write weather scripts)
2 weather producers (to edit the weather scripts)
1 interviewer (to ask prepared questions)
1 interviewee (somone with an interesting background, to answer questions)
1 interview producer (to ensure that the interview is rehearsed)
1 local feature presenter (to read from a script about local items of interest)
4 local feature researchers (to gather material on items of local interest)
2 local feature producers (to edit and collate the feature scripts)
1 technical operator
1 traffic news presenter
2 traffic news researchers
1 traffic news producer

The two programme producers have the responsibility for the running order and the timing of each item. They should produce a script which looks something like this:

3.30 Good Afternoon Springtown presenter
3.32 Local news
3.35 Programme presenter
3.36 Feature: e.g. Should the high street be pedestrianised?
3.40 Presenter . . . 3.40.15 Traffic news
3.42 Presenter . . . 3.42.15 Interview
3.44 Weather
3.44.30 Traffic
3.45 Presenter: close

The tape-recorder should be placed centrally, and each part of the programme recorded separately, with presenters coming to the table, overseen by producers, who have a copy of the complete script for their item.

The researchers have to find out the information: using local papers, or phoning the A.A. for traffic news, for example. The interview could be with someone in the class who has done something interesting recently, or with another adult who is willing to come into the classroom. The programme presenter links the separate items by introducing them and commenting on them when they are finished. Sometimes the links will last only a few seconds but the children will see how important the timing is.

If it all appears a bit rushed it could be expanded into a half hour programme, particularly with the inclusion of records. Fifteen minutes is about right for a short activity like this, however.

Everyone has a job: there are 30 in all: add to or subtract from the number of researchers or reporters, according to the size of your class.

If possible follow up with a visit from a local radio presenter, who may invite you to visit an empty studio if you are lucky!

This is clearly an activity for Year 5, 6 or 7 children (or above). With early years, Years 1 and 2, or Years 3 and 4, you could still do a radio programme, but this time focussing on a story. Children could make sounds to accompany the story, or review books in the manner of 'Treasure Island' or 'Bookshelf', working in pairs so that one responds to the two prepared questions that the other asks. For example, 'Rachel's book is called *Give A Dog a Name* by Barrie Wade. What happens in it, Rachel?', and 'What did you like best about the book?'

Practical Activity 8.2 Coca Cola can

This is an activity that can be undertaken with children from Year 1 to Year 10. (As it involves a commercial product at some point you will want to contextualise the activity in terms of the pros and cons of multinational manufacturers and their products. This could be either a simple statement or series of questions, or a full-blown debate – depending on the age and ability of the children.)

The purpose of the activity is to look carefully at the language and graphic imagery on a Coke Can. Collect enough empty cans so that each child has one each and then:

1. Look at the brand names: the different lettering styles (fonts) of *Coca-Cola* and *Coke*. Which do they prefer? How many times do these words appear on the can? Why have two names for one product? Why do they each appear in very large form, accompanied by the other in small form? If you have a computer you could produce different examples of different fonts (the children could write their names, or words like TIME in different fonts). Which do they prefer?

2. The 'Wave' trademark: Why is it there? Cover it with your fingers. Does

172

it make much difference? What is meant by a REGISTERED TRADE MARK?
3. What other symbols are there on the can? In 1992 the can had a recyclable
symbol (show symbol of three arrows) and this symbol of a person next to
a basket (show symbol). What do they mean? Are they still there? It also had
an Olympic Games symbol with the words OFFICIAL WORLDWIDE OLYMPIC
SPONSOR. Why was that there and what did it mean?
4. What other words are on the can. What information do they give?
5. Finish by considering the shape and colour of the can. Why the diagonal
stripes? Why red with white lettering (with a stripe of grey in the wave)?

Children could then design their own cans for milk, or lime, cut them out,
and wrap them round the Coke can.
Other can designs could be considered: children could be asked to bring in
an empty can for the next session. Or the work be followed up in a number
of different directions: recycling, health, advertising, sponsorship , and so on.

Teachers are likely to follow this up with letters to the Coca Cola
Company, and for background reading (to counter any marketing hype)
a book like *For God, Country and Coca-Cola: The Unauthorised History
of the World's Most Popular Soft Drink* (Prendergast, 1993).

Words and pictures

In most media education activities words and pictures will be considered
as they appear alongside each other, from picture books to
advertisements, from television programmes to films.

In *Picture Stories* (1986) Yvonne Davies shows clearly how the books
in the classroom can be the starting point for media education in the
primary school. Books like Anthony Browne's *The Tunnel* and Hiawyn
Oram and Satoshi Kitamura's *Ned and the Joybaloo* are ideal starting
points. Older children will enjoy these as they work on so many different
levels (for an interesting discussion of the ideology of *The Tunnel* see
Language and Ideology in Children's Fiction (John Stephens, 1992).
Children in Years 6, 7 and 8 will also enjoy constructing narratives
for comic books, now a serious genre. A recent Englishtime programme
(BBC 15 November 1992) showed a twelve-year-old boy constructing
and revising a futuristic story for *2000 AD*. It was finally accepted,
and along the way he and we learnt much about point of view, narrative
structure, positioning and characterisation, as well as gender and art.
The boy could draw well, but this kind of activity can work just as
well with stick figures and speech bubbles.

Such work would inevitably lead to a consideration of how television
programmes videos and films are constructed. Both the B.F.I. and Film
Education (addresses at the back) produce good resource packs,

information sheets and other useful materials for primary and middle schools. Also, commercial film companies sometimes produce their own media education videos to promote their own films. The Shell sponsored 'The Making of Freddy the Frog' video is a good example.

Practical Activity 8.3 News at Ten

For older children the running order of the news can be an interesting topic. You will need a free lunchtime so that you can record the 1 o'clock news on the BBC and ITV (if that's too long try the 2 o'clock). Note the running order, for example, six items, train crash first on both channels, and note any differences in order. That afternoon give the children the essence of the six stories (in random order) ask them to write and record the news for a two-minute Radio One bulletin, and then show them the order in which they actually went out. Discuss why that order was the one that the news editors decided on.

Title sequences

One last activity, mentioned in the 'Teaching Today' programme, we have left until the end because, for it to work best, you need clips of programmes from other countries, and that may be difficult to organise. Show children a variety of title sequences, preferably for programmes they are not familiar with (this is where South American soaps, and Italian News Programmes are useful) and ask them to guess the kind of programme that is being introduced. What gave them the clues? The pictures, the music, the style of the lettering, the abstract symbols? This is particularly interesting if the language is unfamiliar to children: an excellent opportunity for some multi-cultural work using Welsh or Bengali Language programmes.

Media education is an important part of the curriculum, and involves aspects of art, geography, history and technology, as well as English. Although we have concentrated on photography, videos, television and radio programmes, a great deal of exciting work can be done with comics (narrative sequencing, stereotypes, audience, plot, words and pictures) ranging from *The Beano* to any comic or magazines that the children are willing to bring in. In encouraging children to think more about the way that the images and words which they encounter every day through the media are constructed and mediated, we are helping them become more critical consumers, and in some cases we may be planting the seeds that turn them into informed producers. The goal here is no different from the other aspects of language work explored in this book.

174

8.2 Writers and performers in schools

Having someone in school to do some work with children can take
a bit of organising, but nine times out of ten the spin offs fully justify
the effort. A good mid-term session with a theatre-in-education group
or recognised writer who is known to work well with children, can
help focus ideas for the first half of the term, and can generate ideas
for the second. Experience suggests that it is wise to choose carefully,
however. Quite fortuitously our chosen title points to an important
distinction — some recognised writers are actually not very good
performers, and it is fatal to assume that the bright voice and manner
that informs the novel or poem will be manifest in the flesh. Others,
like Ann Fine and Michael Rosen, Michael Morpurgo and Adele Geras,
Amryl Johnston and Antony Browne are just the kind of people who
can inspire an audience, young or old. Nationally known figures have
to be booked up a year or so in advance, and it may be that the best
things to do is to join with other schools in the area and arrange a
'Writers in Schools Week', sharing costs and sharing writers. Consult
the Writers in Schools booklet, usually available from your local arts
centre or library. Alternatively you may wish to work with a local
bookshop, or in some cases the author's publisher will pay for them
to visit if some evening sessions at local colleges or arts centres are
also arranged. Inevitably this involves an element of book promotion,
so you have to be careful how this is handled.

With both writers and theatre-in-education groups it is a good idea
to establish the following before the visit is made:

Check to see if you have similar ideas about:
1. The length of the session.
2. The number and age of children attending.
3. The likely format of the session (interactive? participative? or a
reading/performance?)
4. The topic.

Sometimes a local performer or a theatre-in-education group has a good
reputation, and then you don't have the problem of travelling expenses,
wondering if the person is going to turn up, and wondering if the person
will be a success. If you want to do something on a small scale, either
by yourself or with one of your colleagues, this can be a good way
forward. One word of advice from many teachers we have spoken to:
you may want to work alone, but there are reasons why you should

not — it can create a sense of separateness and isolation when you are trying to establish an ethos of co-operation, and it may even cause unnecessary resentment. Include others wherever possible, and let everyone own the writer or theatre-in-education group.

Practical Activity 8.4

The teacher as performer: production in and out of school

In the Bay Area Project of the 1970s teachers were encouraged to write and to consider themselves as writers. Many teachers would say that they do not have enough time to develop their own talents, even though they would like to. However, many in-service sessions encourage teachers to write poems, stories or scripts, to perform scenes or present poems, to produce magazines or make short films or radio programmes. In a pair activity in a staff development session ask colleagues to find out from a chosen partner if she/he:

— keeps a journal.
— writes for any kind of publication — local newspaper (letters?), church magazine, club or society.
— takes part in amateur dramatics or any kind of theatrical production (front or backstage).
— plays music or sings.
— reads poetry for pleasure.
— would be prepared to talk about three favourite childhood books to another class.
— has had good experiences of performances, either at school or during an in-service session.

Should teachers be writers and or/performers? If so, how about producing a joint collection of teachers' and pupils' writings, and publishing it in the school? Or planning a theatre-in-education visit, or a writer-in-school workshop, with which everyone, pupils and teachers alike, become involved?

Summary

In this chapter we have considered ways in which children and teachers can be encouraged to 'read' and respond to performance, whether it is conveyed through visual media, radio or live presence in the classroom or hall. The performance of others should act as a springboard for children to produce their own performance, whether through film, radio, poetry presentations or drama. In our brief discussion of performance we have considered the following:

● Media education in the primary classroom.
● Working with photographs.

176

- Making a short video narrative.
- Making a radio programme.
- The semiotics of the Coca Cola can.
- Analysing news programmes and the opening credits for Soaps.
- Writers in schools.
- Theatre-in-education in schools.
- Activity: teachers as producers.

CHAPTER NINE

Recording and Assessment

Why do we have records and assessments? This is a question worth asking, because unless we agree what something is for, then it is difficult to determine the form the record or assessment should take. Perhaps we should begin by distinguishing between assessment and testing. Teachers are conducting assessment all the time. It determines the way we organise our classroom, the kind of work we offer children, the way that we decide that different levels of work need to be offered to cater for the wide range of ability in the primary classroom. All of these decisions follow naturally from assessment being made by the teacher. These impressions, based on the evidence of children's achievement, form the basis for teacher assessment.

Frequently an assessment is supported by evidence that comes from a test, but tests only have a value if they serve a precise purpose. The driving test in England is a simple example: we know that it is intended to be a measure of our competence as drivers on the public road. Since it has not changed much over the last thirty years, it seems to be pretty good at doing the job for which it is intended. Yet if we look at education over the past thirty years various forms of testing have come and gone: 11 +, IQ tests, certain forms of reading tests, O levels, comprehension tests, parts of speech tests. Are tests intended to assess children's ability measuring one against the other (summative tests) or are they intended to help the teacher and child discover what the child needs more help with (formative tests)? Unless they provide information that could not be obtained by any other means there is little point in having them.

Teacher observation and teacher assessment needs to be recorded so that evidence is available should a teachers' judgement be called into question, or so that a teacher can see whether her intuitive assessment is reflected in performance. If there is a mismatch, which is wrong? For it is possible that our record keeping methods, or our assessment arrangements do not give us the information we need, or that they try and do too many things at once, measuring child, teacher and school all at once!

The language leader has a role to play in the discussion of the assessment and record-keeping procedures adopted by the school. She will wish to ensure that the language record-keeping policy is agreed by the whole staff, and that consideration is given to ways in which time can be set aside for record keeping in class, although this will be difficult. Ideally units of work should be planned and prepared with assessment procedures in mind so that they can be written into the programme. Teachers would love to have the time to carry out such detailed, individual support and monitoring of children, but the current overload makes this unrealistic. It is to be hoped that in England the Dearing proposals to slim down the National Curriculum will be followed by an integrated approach to assessment.

9.1 Questions about assessment and record keeping

It may be useful to begin a discussion of assessment and record keeping by asking a few key questions: What do you want to assess? Why assess it? What is the purpose of asssessment? What form of assessment and record keeping is appropriate for this task? In the light of the answers to such questions we can then take a look at the traditional forms of assessment and record keeping in the primary school. We shall not try to cover the specific demands of Key Stage assessments in England and Wales, as these are currently under review and revision.

Forms of assessment and record keeping

In *Assessment and the Management of Learning* (Ghaye, Johnstone and Jones, 1992) the authors list what they rather chillingly describe as the 'instruments of assessment':

MARK BOOK TESTS OBSERVATION RECORDS/REPORTS OTHER
To each of these they invite us to put the following questions:
DOES IT PROVIDE INFORMATION FOR OTHERS? HOW?
DOES IT PROVIDE EVALUATION OF TEACHING PROGRAMMES?
HOW?
DOES IT SUPPORT THE LEARNING SITUATION? HOW?

In addition to these forms of recording, the children's own work, whether it is in the form of a reading log (with older children) or a reading record (with younger children), serves as a record which can be used as the basis for discussion.

Purpose of asssessment

The purpose of the assessment determines the description of the assessment, as follows:

FORM OF ASSESSMENT	PURPOSE
Summative	To record overall achievement
Formative	To provide information which can be used by teacher and children to monitor the extent of progress and achievement. This information then influences the form of the future learning programme.
Criterion-referenced	Either of the above, when the assessment is based on a set of criteria, or statements such as those in the National Curriculum.
Norm-referenced	Assessment, usually in the form of a test, designed to plot achievement against the average for the group being assessed.
Diagnostic	To identify the strengths and weaknesses of an individual child, so that decisions about appropriate support can be made.

9.2 Types of assessment

One kind of diagnostic assessment: miscue analysis or running records

A miscue is when what a reader says is written on a page differs from what is actually printed. A 'good' miscue fits in with the meaning of the text, while a 'bad' miscue does not and results in loss of meaning.

We do a miscue analysis on the assumption that the miscues which readers make are not random. They reveal something about the nature and process of reading, and how readers make sense of texts. The kind of running records required in the early Key Stage 1 and 2 SATS are very simplified versions of miscue analysis. The full procedure has been described by the Macarthur Reading Team (see Sawyer and Watson, 1989), and involves the following steps:

1. An initial interview to determine the child's interests and attitudes to reading, the background influences on reading behaviour and a broad insight into general reading competence.
2. The selection of a range of suitable reading materials on which to sample the child's reading.
3. Tape recording the child's oral reading and retelling of the text.
4. Teacher marking of the child's miscues on a copy of the text.
5. Teacher classification of the miscues according to their semantic and syntactic acceptability.

180

6. An assessment of the accuracy and completeness of the child's retelling.
7. An interpretation of the miscue pattern in relation to the retelling.
8. Preparation of a profile of reader strengths and weaknesses.

Miscues occurring in the first few lines are not recorded, and there must be at least twenty-five miscues for an analysis to have any meaning.

Self assessment

At the beginning of this book we proposed the model of the reflective learner, a model that applied to both children and teachers. One way of encouraging children to reflect on their own learning is to encourage the process of self assessment. This can be done by means of conferencing, by encouraging children to set goals for their own writing, or issuing evaluation sheets which will include a range of precise questions such as 'What was I trying to achieve in this piece of writing?' With the use of the tape recorder children can be encouraged to reflect on their own achievements as talkers and readers. Self assessment and peer assessment takes some time to set up, but once in place it can be a valuable educational tool, especially where the criteria for assessment are made explicit, and perhaps negotiated. Self assessment could form the subject for a staff development session, in which case it may be useful to read Brian Johnston's *Assessing English: Helping Students to Reflect on their work* (1987) first. Although this was written with secondary schools in mind, there are examples of self assessment and reflective learning which which could easily be adapted to primary and middle school use.

9.3 Keeping records

Records of achievement

Some schools keep primary records of achievement, starting with school entry information sheets (completed by parents, teacher and child). This form of record, often called baseline assessment, records such details as dominant hand, whether the child can hold scissors or recognise its name, listen to stories or draw patterns. As the child gets older she or he plays an increasing part in the drawing up of the record of achievement, and assumes ownership, taking the record with her to the next school.

Who will want to see a teacher's records?

Although there is a requirement for teachers to keep a record of National Curriculum achievements, generally teachers' records are kept for their own use. It may be that the Headteacher, the Adviser or an Inspector asks to see them, in which case they would have to be produced. Of course if there is the practice of conferencing, or negotiating with children in developing pupil profiles, then they will be seen by pupils. They will also form the basis for the written report which is sent home to parents. Unless the teaching team has agreed to bring along their language records to a discussion session, the language leader will not normally see them.

Primary Language Records, county records, wheels and bar charts

There are a number of published record-keeping systems, ranging from the detailed and valuable Primary Language Record devised by the Inner London Education Authority, to the tick boxes or colour-shading bar charts produced by some local authorities, which serve simply as a summative record of work done. Each school will have its own system, but there may be an opportunity to adapt or replace the system if people are generally unhappy with it or feel it is not meeting the needs of the school and its pupils. The Dearing Report signalled the end of tick boxes and the reduction of record keeping in primary schools.

9.4 Gathering evidence

Standardised Reading Tests, 11+ tests, Standard Assessment Tests

Despite the fact that these tests are sometimes inconsistent with the theory that informs contemporary views of learning they are unlikely to disappear. What the reading aspects of these tests have in common is a view of learning as a series of separate skills, rather than a holistic process. This leads to the belief that it is possible to form an impression of a child's language ability by assessing certain aspects of language usage through standardised tests. If the results of the SRTs and SATs are used to support teacher assessment, then the limited information they provide can serve a useful purpose. Ros Fisher (1992, p. 118) summarises the strengths and weaknesses of Standardised Reading Tests, particularly with early years children in mind:

182

These tests give informatioin about how the child performed in relation to his/her peers, but do not give diagnostic information. Most teachers do not need to be told that a certain child is performing below average at reading; they have already come to that conclusion. Teachers will often mistrust information from tests that does not match their own perception. For example, if a child who was reading quite well in the classroom was found to have a below-average reading age, this result would be put down to test conditions rather than misjudgement on the part of the teacher. This is not to say that norm reference tests do not serve some purpose; teachers like to know how their group of learners compare to a national norm, especially in small schools where there is little opportunity for comparison. However, for the classroom teacher, assessment that gives indication for further teaching is more useful and effective.

Using the results to modify programmes

It is important to remember that assessment is an integral part of good teaching, and not something bolted on to the end. In the primary school its purpose is to help children, teachers and parents. Parents are likely to be very interested in their child's writing and reading, and so the language leader will not need to tell staff about the importance of having detailed information and evidence about all aspects of language to pass on to parents should they ask for it. Teachers, too, will want to make use of the assessment. Having conducted the various forms of assessment and kept a variety of records it is important to reflect on their significance, to evaluate the results and to consider whether the teaching programme needs to be changed in any way. We need to keep reminding ourselves that assessments, reports and records are tools, and not ends in themselves.

9.5 Sir Ron Dearing and Assessment

In 1993, Sir Ron Dearing, in an interim report to the DfE, recommended a reduction in the amount of administration that was being imposed on teachers. We shall end this section by quoting from the School Assessment Folder (SCAA, 1993) for Key Stage 1 which was sent to all schools:

What teacher assessment records and evidence should be kept?

How teachers record their children's progress is a professional matter entirely for schools to decide. However, it should be emphasised strongly that it is not intended or desirable to record everything a child does in relation to every statement of attainment. Different schools will have used a variety of approaches both before and after the introduction of the National Curriculum. Notes of observations, transcripts of questioning or discussion with children, photographs of work in progress, completed samples of work in written, diagrammatic, and visual forms and other teacher's records have always played an important part in tracking children's progress and can all support teacher assessment. Whichever approach is taken, recording should not get in the way of teaching and learning.

Summary

In this chapter we have considered each of the following:
- Purpose of assessment.
- Forms of assessment.
- Miscue Analysis and Running Records.
- Self Assessment.
- Records of achievement.
- Standardised tests and forms of record keeping.
- Using the evidence.
- How much to keep.

CHAPTER TEN

Resources

In the survey that appeared in chapter 1 'deciding between available resources' was one of the duties ticked by every one of the subject co-ordinators consulted. Resourcing a subject area is time consuming enough, but when the responsibility is for such a broadly-based area such as 'language' the task can assume the proportions of a full-time job. The majority of language leaders will have a teaching timetable, and to make the job manageable will need to draw on the time of classroom assistants and on the skills of outside experts such as area librarians.

10.1 In-school resources

Children's knowledge and experience

Although it is true and worth repeating, we will not begin with the cliche about the biggest resource in a school being the children themselves. At least, we will not say it in an obvious way. For we all know it. Yet even the most experienced teacher is frequently surprised by the sometimes hidden, secret world of children's knowledge and experience. In Barry Hine's *A Kestrel for a Knave* the scene where Billy Casper talks in an English lesson about his secret passion for hawks, has the ring of truth about it: we have all taught children with extraordinary hobbies, or who have parents with unusual jobs, or who come from families with rich family histories. One child we taught was an excellent baton twirler and gave a remarkable demonstration to the whole class (the ceiling was a bit low for her at times). Another had a mother who spent much of her life travelling throughout Europe as a trapeze artist with a circus.

The same is true of teachers. We have met or worked with male teachers who have been police officers and female teachers who have been rangers in Central African Game Reservations.

Staff's knowledge and experience

We can learn a great deal from the records and files about the children in the class we inherit. For the language leader to know more about the other members of staff takes time and tact, but given the right ethos it may be possible to carry out the following practical activity:

Practical Activity 10.1

'Ourselves'
This is the title often given to a term's work with children. It is possible that the staff in a school may benefit by extending it to themselves, seeing its relevance to the idea of 'sharing resources'.
Working with a partner you feel comfortable with, spend ten minutes writing down what you are happy to reveal under the following headings:
1. Childhood home   2. Other town lived in   3. Other job   4. Best two or three holidays   5. Leisure interest

For example: Mary Bell
1. Morpeth, Northumberland   2. Grantham, Lincolnshire   3. Time and motion study for electricity meter readers   4. Canal holiday near Stafford, Washington State and Yellowstone Park   5. British cinema of the 1940s and 1950s.

Robin Peel
1. Oxted, Surrey   2. Bingham, Nottinghamshire   3. Pea-freezing   4. Coast-to-coast greyhound bus journey across the United States, Prague   5. Cricket, and The Titanic.

In pairs discuss which of these items you would be prepared to talk to a group of children about, and how something your partner has recorded might be relevant to the work the children in your class are doing.
The reporting back to the whole-group session involves each person reading from the list, and commenting on whether or not the item led to discussion (some items, for example, cricket (above) may not appear to lead anywhere – but others will).
At least you will all have got to know each other better by the end of this activity.

There could be a problem with the above activity, namely that people consider their past private and confidential. That is a shame, but if you sense that a number of your colleagues would be unhappy with this kind of thing, do not attempt it. If there is only one, then you could perhaps wait until you know him or her better, and then make a decision about how to proceed.

Materials: reprographics

One of the most scandalous features of many primary schools is the condition or accessibility of the photocopier. This machine has been with us in education for nearly fifteen years, and in colleges of further education and in universities the photocopier is the *sine qua non*. Yet there are hosts of primary and middle schools, perhaps the majority, that are making do with substandard machines or Headteacher-controlled ones.

Good photocopied materials are an invaluable stimulus and whether through cutting and pasting or using the desktop facilities in a computer teachers produce a whole variety of interesting resources. The language leader can encourage the circulation of materials, or suggest that single, tacky-backed copies are kept as a central resource. This can be difficult — in schools where there is a very individualistic culture, teachers may not be in the habit of sharing, and sometimes are wary about showing to their colleagues worksheets which they would have improved if they had more time. This takes us back to chapter 1, and the importance of working towards working together. One tactful way to approach sharing is by suggesting that you have a collaborative session to discuss ways in which individual worksheets can be tailored for the needs of others in the school. But they must be done on a photocopier, a good photocopier.

If the school authorities are worried about the cost implications of letting everyone loose on the machine, persuade them to adopt a copy card or key number system.

Other materials

Books are obviously the most expensive resource, but you will want to have a good range of attractive fiction and non-fiction books in your classroom, with a number on display. It maybe that you are responsible for ordering books for the library as well, and, to keep in touch with what is currently on offer, try to have regular contact with the schools section of a nearby library, with reviews of the kind you get in NATE News, with primary language groups, and language and literature conferences at which there is likely to be a book display. Two useful publications are:

The Good Book Guide to Children's Books New editions are published by Penguin Books, and Braithwaite and Taylor Ltd each year.

Books for Keeps Published by The School Bookshop Association, 1 Effingham Road, Lee, London SE12 8NZ.

As for your own school stationery and library furniture, it is probably monitored and ordered by a colleague. Most people like orders well in advance, and you are more likely to get what you want if you can quote prices and catalogue numbers. Some stock controllers are even quite happy for you to fill in the official order yourself, as long as their controlling signature appears at the bottom!

If you are fairly well established it is always worth having a good rake around the school to see what all those old cupboards, lofts and storage areas contain. Finds have included a pair of pre-war scales for weighing babies (restored to their former glory by a Year 6 pupil, and consequently featuring in a fortnight's work on health and autobiographies) and a gas mask — both of these from the sealed-up air raid shelter in the playground. Other discoveries have been the punishment book from the 1920s and a set of reproductions of famous paintings. The former fed nicely into a 'How We used to Live' session, while the paintings, enough for one between four, led to discussion work, imaginative writing, painting in the style of, and research into the life and times of the painter, climaxing in group presentations.

Organising and supervising the school library

In Australia and North America the primary school library is often housed in its own room and run by a specially-appointed teacher-librarian who comes in for at least two days a week and does not have a responsibility for a class of children. In the U.K. the library is quite often the responsibility of the language leader who has her own class, no extra time is given, and the library itself may be located in a corridor or corner of a hall (unless it is a community school). If the library is in need of a thorough overhaul, help and advice is available from a number of quarters. The most obvious is the Schools Library Service, assuming that your school buys in to it, which can give advice on layout, display posters, borrowing systems and book-buying policy. The physical environment of the library is very important as the HMI Report *Better Libraries* (1989) emphasised:

Some schools have enlivened their libraries by arranging bright displays of pictures, posters, mobiles, friezes, book jackets and displays of writing and pictures about books which customers have read for pleasure as part of their school work. They have made their libraries more homely and

188

welcoming with informal furniture such as easy chairs, low tables, bean bags and scatter cushions. (p. 8)

Decisions need to be made about such issues as the teaching of library skills (how can children improve their information retrieval abilities?), the classification of books (by theme or 'Dewey'?) and the function and availability of computers in the library area (for writing, for book searches, or for both?) Books like *Hooked on Books* (Lutrario, 1990), and *Book Policy in the Primary School* (Essex, 1991) are useful here, as are some of the lists produced by *Books for Keeps*. Before ordering books it is wise to have a book selection policy, and this could form the subject of a staff development session. This could consider each of the following:

Literary qualities: how vital and engaging is the language?
Appearance of the book: how attractive are the jacket and the illustrations?
Use of book: how will it be used, for what purpose will it be used, how does it relate to the curriculum, is the language level appropriate for the ability range in the class?
Cultural and Social qualities: does the book avoid stereotyping, and will it improve the self image of children and adults from a range of cultures and social backgrounds?

For advice on practical matters (vitally important!) such as shelving, bookends, labels and guiding, consult your local library.

10.2 Out of School

Parents' knowledge and experience

As we suggested earlier, teachers who inherit new classes tend to know something about parents before the first meeting, from conversations with the previous teacher. Knowledge will be increased following the first parents evening, and little hints dropped by the children as they talk and write. This is a sensitive area because teachers and schools, whilst finding it extremely useful to know as much as possible about parents must make sure that there can be no suggestion of prying. In areas of high unemployment there is a particular need for care and sensitivity.

Yet what can be better than a parent talking about what her grandmother told her about her schooldays, with photographs and items of clothing, or a mother showing children how to build a brick wall, or a father showing how a telephone works?

Practical Activity 10.2

What has this to do with language work? Everything! At a recent NATE conference, Amryl Johnson talked about how the subject 'Walls' was a good one to inspire the writing of poetry, and afterwards we all wrote poems and put together an anthology. What was noticeable was that everyone had interpreted the word 'walls' in a different way. For some it simply triggered the thought of actual physical walls, in a house that was being converted, or between gardens. For others it was metaphorical, the barriers between people. With a demonstration of brick-laying (using those reusable bricks and mortar that they use in brick-laying departments in Colleges of Further Education) as a starting point, the technology of brick-laying could lead to a discussion of the walls of castles, the walls of houses, famous walls like Hadrian's Wall, the Great Wall of China and the Berlin Wall, and then the Wall in the Pyramus and Thisbe scene in *A Midsummer Night's Dream*. But first of all find your parent who knows how to lay bricks.

Other Adults: the local community

Practical Activity 10.3

Early years teachers quite often take their children out to the High Street on a language spotting expedition. One class was taken to a cafe where the owner explained all the things he has to do involving language: the menu, the bills, the food ordering, the open and closed sign, the price list. The children were then able to incorporate this into their activity in the home corner, which for this purpose was converted into a cafe with signs, opening times, and pads for orders to be placed.

Practical Activity 10.4

It may be that a letter to the local post office manager, followed by a personal visit, could lead to a tour behind the scenes for children from Years 2 to 7. The visit could lead to lots of follow-up work, and a greater understanding of how letters are sorted and delivered, and the use of the computer in the modern post office.

People in the local business community are often quite happy to receive visits from children as long as the whole class does not come at once, as long as the visit seems structured and purposeful, and as long as the initial letter has made the right impression. Given the last fact, it could be useful to get the children themselves to draft their own versions of the letter they would write, and to foreground the need for certain information being included, the right tone being achieved, and Standard English, correctly spelt throughout!

Finally, it is worth remembering that there is one group of adults who in some ways are more able to visit schools during the day. Retired people — whether living in their own flats or houses or in Senior Citizens' homes may be willing to come in. Of course preparatory contact has to be made: it may mean a visit to a home, and asking someone there if she or he knows if any of the residents served in the Second World War, for example, and whether they would be prepared to come and talk. A meeting could be arranged, and you could take it from there. It may be that it is better for a group of children to go to the home, rather than the other way round, depending on mobility.

There is one other group of people who are neither in or out of school. Students on school practice may have their own contacts. One student in a Torquay school had a father who taught English to groups of Japanese, and he arranged for a group of Japanese women to come into school where they showed children their traditional costumes which they had brought with them. It was a wonderful, unforgettable sight.

Materials from museums, libraries and other collections

This section could just as well have gone under the previous heading, because sometimes the best resource that the local library or museum has to offer is the person or people that run it. The school that we just mentioned is lucky to be in a town with an excellent Schools Library Service, run by really dedicated and helpful personnel, and Torbay also has an excellent Schools Resource Centre (ironically under threat) which will loan out anything from a skull to a set of slides on traditional farming methods. They also have videos, maps, charts, posters, models and a host of other useful resources. It is well worth asking for some non-teaching day time to be set aside so that you can research the resources on offer in your nearest town, and this may include collections held privately. Exeter has a good museum collection, and one of us was to be seen walking down the street carrying an enormous rusty mantrap into the classroom!

INFORMATION CENTRES AND LOCAL SHOPS
These have to be treated with care. Instead of sending thirty children into your local tourist information centre, or British Rail Travel Centre,

or Travel Agents, to strip the place, go in yourself, take a few brochures, maps and timetables or whatever is on offer. It may be that you can speak to the manager: information that may be out of date for them, and about to be thrown out, could be still very up to date. Last year's travel brochures can be used as a resource for reading, writing, talk, as well as maths, geography and media education. Why not make a poster or video selling the merits of your local community? Or ask the children to write two accounts: one for a guidebook saying all the good things about the place, another for a newspaper article exposing all the bad!

LOCAL INDUSTRIES AND BUSINESSES
Again these have to be approached with care. Sometimes they can be helpful, sometimes not. A personal contact is always useful. Do the children have parents or neighbours who work there?

Here are a few examples of resources provided free by local firms. A company which specialises in bathroom design had examples of marble: just right for the Roman day that the teacher had organised. Language work? The class (and teacher and all visitors, including me) had to dress in togas (made from sheets provided by the parents) for the open air playground Senate meeting, at which issues were debated. The children sat in a circle wearing their togas, and in turn rose to deliver short prepared speeches on issues they felt strongly about. Questions and answers followed in full Senatorial fashion. Later that day there was the retelling of myths (from characters inside the story) and Roman food prepared by another parent. A tremendous amount of resources for one day, but the day was memorable, once again providing a tremendous focus for the term.

COMPUTER PROGRAMS AND I.T. RESOURCES
This is a specialised area and teachers have said that they find it very difficult to keep up to date. Many rely on some or all of the following:

a) The I.T. post-holder, who should be able to give advice on programs and explain the potential of Electronic Mail and CD Roms.
b) The I.T. support team in the nearest University Faculty of Education, or in some cases College of Further Education or Secondary School.
c) The LEA I.T. Consultant (primary) if there is one.

Students on school practice may be knowledgeable, and it is worth picking their brains and inviting them to recommend programs they have used. Finally, there is the excellent National Council for Educational Technology, the address of which is given at the end of the book.

10.3 Financial: Handling the budget

This is an important responsibility, for in an increasing number of schools with devolved budgets, individuals such as language leaders are being given responsibility for handling substantial amounts of money. The curriculum post-holder will need to be involved in discussions regarding the Management Development Plan, and decisions about priorities, including the future of particular 'subject areas' within the school. As we have seen, there is likely to be a responsibility for the library, and the cost of books and equipment will have to be carefully monitored and accounted for. The library budget is likely to be cross-curricular, representing a percentage of the other subject budgets. In fact it is the cross-curricular nature of language that makes it essential for a team approach to be developed, for the language leader may well be responsible for keeping a record of textbooks ordered, performances arranged, expenditure on drama, not to mention all the other books for class libraries or central resource.

Conclusion: towards the collegial school

We began chapter 1 by emphasising how the detail of leadership needed to be considered in the context of co-operation. Everything we have seen in schools, everything we have heard from teachers, everything that language leaders, consultants or curriculum co-ordinators have reported confirms that children, education and successful language work is likely to flourish in schools where people are used to collaborating, and where there is a common unit of purpose. To call a school a community of learners may sound rather idealistic, and in the end it may be better just to think in terms of friendship: getting on with the children, getting on with the staff, getting on with the parents and wider community. If the simple factor of friendship is there, then great things are possible. If it is less developed, and we all know schools where this is so, then the language leader's job will be that much harder. Yet, if at the end of the year you can look back and say 'Yes, this has been achieved', then you will have achieved success of a significant kind. If this book has offered recognition that much of what you do already is evidence of that success, then it will have served its purpose.

REFERENCE SECTION

1. Useful addresses for keeping up to date

Primary and middle schools have become increasingly bombarded by directives, circulars, advice, policy statements, revisions to the curriculum and assessment regulations. The feeling that we are not only in the middle of a blizzard, but actually being buried alive, is a common one in many schools. Make efforts to keep up to date! Rather than asking for another lorry load of snow the language leader might protest that all he or she wants is to drill a hole to the surface and gulp in some fresh air. In the current climate this is an understandable reaction. Yet if we view the process of 'keeping up to date' as a way of getting hold of some snow clearing equipment, some salt and a warming electric fire, then the effort is clearly worth it! There is only space here to give the names and addresses of a dozen supportive organisations: for a more comprehensive list consult an education diary: your LEA, Union or Professional Association may be able to provide you with one.

(i) Subject teaching and related associations

National Association for the
Teaching of English
50 Broadfield Road
Broadfield Business Centre
Sheffield
S8 0XJ

National Association for Special
Educational Needs (NASEN)
York House
Exhall Grange
Wheelwright Lane
Coventry
CV7 9HP   Tel: 0203 362414

Bilingual Family Newsletter
Multilingual Matters
Clevedon Hall
Victoria Road
Clevedon Avon
BS21 7SJ

United Kingdom Reading
Association
The Membership Secretary
c/o Edge Hill College of
Higher Education
St Helens Road
Ormskirk
Lancs

(ii) Film and media education

Film Education
37-39 Oxford Street
London W1R 1RE

B.F.I. Education
British Film Institute
21 Stephen Street
London W1P 1PL

Educational Media
Film and Video Ltd.
235 Imperial Drive
Rayners Lane
Harrow
Middlesex HA2 7HE   Tel: 081 868 1908

(iii) Educational Broadcasting

For Channel 4 and BBC Schools Broadcasting addresses, consult posters
for the current year's programmes.

(iv) English and Information Technology

National Council for
Education Technology
Sir Williams Lyon Road
Science Park
Coventry CV4 7EZ
Tel: 0203 416944

Micros and Primary
Education (MAPE)
Newman College
Genners Lane
Bartley Green
Birmingham B32 3NT
Tel: 021 476 1181

(v) Educational Publishers

For an up to date listing, see *The Writers and Artists Year Book* held
in all reference libraries.

The other ways of keeping up to date — scanning the INSET and
Professional Development courses offered by the LEA and local
university Schools of Education, reading publications such as *Reading*
and *The Times Educational Supplement*, and joining regional networks
which focus on anything from Children's Literature to Language and
I.T. — will vary according to interest and locality. But there's nothing
like a well-organised two or three day residential course (such as the
NATE National Conference) to make you realise that there is an exciting
life beyond the Attainment Targets.

2. Glossary of language terms

The following terms either appear in the text, or are ones likely to be encountered in your reading and inservice activities.

Academic Councils: in England these are representative groups which discuss academic issues relevant for their group of schools.

Accent: the pronunciation of spoken language, something often determined by geographical and/or social factors.

Acrostic: in poetry a poem that is formed using the initial letters of a word, e.g.   Lordly creature
Irritable when tired
Occasionally roaring
Nocturnal terrible warnings.

Adjective: class of words whose function is to add information, and sometimes describe, e.g. *heavy* trunk, the bag was *light*, the *weightiest* matters.

Adverbs: words which modify verbs (drinks *slowly*), other adverbs (drinks *very* slowly) or adjectives (the bag was *very* light).

Anaphoric: backward referencing function of words like pronouns, e.g. the dog barked when *it* saw the hedgehog.

'Breakthrough to Literacy': a language experience approach which used materials such as sentence makers.

Cataphoric (opposite of anaphoric): where the pronoun precedes the word or noun and is a forward acting reference, e.g. she hated being called Elizabeth.

Chronological writing: writing which is concerned with a sequence of events in a certain time order.

Cloze: exercises in which elements are left out of texts so that children can replace them.

Cohesion: the means by which a series of statements are seen to be linked, e.g. by using personal pronouns such as she, it, they, or by using cohesive ties such as and, but, then, therefore (conjunctions).

Cohesive ties: see above.

Conferences: meetings and discussions between teacher and child or children, or among groups of children themselves to assist the development of reading and writing.

Conjunctions: connecting words, like 'because', 'and', and 'so'.

Constructivism: view of language, associated with Piaget, which suggests that children construct a view of the world in line with their concept development.

Conversational turn taking: the social convention of speaking, then listening, then speaking again in a way that shows a response to what others have said.

Criterion-referenced tests: tests assessed according to a set of previously agreed criteria

Cues: signs or clues that help us recognise meaning and make texts meaningful.

Cursive handwriting: handwriting which uses joined letters.

DARTS: Directed Activities Relating to TextS.

Developmental models: show how language is acquired, and how this is not a linear process as we might suppose.

Dewey: The most well-known system for classifying books with a number, e.g. 832.2 which corresponds to a subject heading.

Dewey Decimal System: classifies books according to numbers so that books on language and literacy in the primary school are likely to be found at 374.42, or thereabouts.

Diachronic analysis: studying how language uses change across time. In the last century this kind of analysis was called Philology.

Dialect: a regional variation of the language, with its own words.

Diegesis: term (used by Plato) to describe situation in which poet/writer speaks directly to the audience in his or her own voice. Most children's picture books are examples of the opposite which is Mimesis, in which the writer is concealed from the narrative (e.g. Anthony Browne *tells* us about Gorilla, but does not speak to us directly).

Discourse: any pattern of speech that arises from our ability to put thoughts into words in a coherent way. Sometimes used in contrast to written *text*, but sometimes used to describe any passage of language.

Discourse analysis: studies these patterns of speech in context. Classroom discourse analysis, for example, has shown how much teacher talk tends to dominate the classroom, and teachers are often unaware of this.

Ellipsis: leaving out words to improve the cohesion, e.g. She walked into the lobby, up the stairs and into the dining room (avoids repetition of 'she walked').

Emergent writing: very young children like to imitate writers, even before they can 'write'. The imitation marks they make on the page, and the way that they set out their marks, is known as emergent writing, and it is a way of encouraging children to become writers.

Expertise: everything you know that enables you to operate as a teacher.

Functional model: a model which considers the ways in which language helps people do things, and serves certain functions. These may be to describe, report or imagine, for example.

Genre: a form of text that conforms to certain conventions. Science fiction is a genre, as is the Western. Yet genres can blend together, as in the film *Star Wars* which contained elements of both science fiction and the western.

Grammar: the conventions and rules which characterise the way a language is used.

Haiku: usually understood to be a three line poem of seventeen syllables with the pattern 5-7-12, corresponding to the Japanese form. Variations are possible, however.

Hypercard: a mass of information already stored on a disc or progamme by the manufacturer.

Idiolect: your (or one's) personal way of speaking.

Improvisation: in drama, the freedom to develop a series of movements, a scene or a sketch drawing on the inventiveness of the participants rather than the demands of a script.

Interactive: anything which allows children to intervene and make decisions in the learning process.

Interactive Computer Programs: as above. The hypercard *Storymaker*, available from N.C.E.T. (see list of useful addresses), is a good example, as it enables children to make their own stories using words, pictures and sounds.

Interactive Video: allows children to influence the narrative or information provision by making choices by pressing certain keys or buttons.

Language Experience: an approach to language which emphasised the social and active nature of learning by introducing Big Books and sentence makers to the classroom.

Lexis: all the elements which make up language.

Metalanguage: a language about a language, e.g. terms like phrase, phoneme.

Miscue analysis: examining a record of a child's reading, to see if the occasions when the child reads variations of the words printed on the page form any kind of pattern.

Modelling: process whereby the teacher or a child gives a demonstration of talking, writing or reading.

Modelling: the idea that the teacher offers a model, and therefore should read and write alongside the children at appropriate moments.

Morpheme: the basic unit of grammar, or language seen as a functioning system. 'Window' has one morpheme whereas 'windows' has two: window + s. The 's' makes it plural, and therefore different grammatically. 'She' is one morpheme, but so is 'Mississippi', so length of word, or number of syllables is no guide.

Narrative: stories, involving events and sequencing.

Norm-referenced tests: tests in which results are measured against the average or norm.

Phoneme: a sound, e.g. 'd', 'i', 'b'. They need to be put together to make sense: b i d.

Phonetics: the study of human speech sounds and how they are made in the mouth, e.g. we use our lips to make a 'p'. Phonetics comes under the umbrella of linguistics.

Phonics: breaking words down into their sounds, and then building words from these sounds.

Pragmatics: the study of language in use and how it is used. This is the focus of the Kingman report and socio-linguistics. Saussure began this interest by distinguishing between *parole* (speech acts in use within a language) and *langue* (a language, like English itself). Before Saussure the study of language had focussed mainly on the history of language. See Synchronic and Diachronic.

Proactive: a term from management theory suggesting action which initiates developments rather than responding to them.

Reactive: the opposite. In its worst form it is characterised by crisis

198

management.

Readers' Theatre: a term from Australia which emerged from the belief that careful reading is fostered by encouraging performance and production. In reader's theatre non-fiction, poetry and prose can be performed by individuals, pairs or groups of children.

Reading Recovery: a system of concentrated one-to-one support for those experiencing reading difficulties, following a programme divised by Marie Clay.

Real books: books which are not part of reading schemes.

Received Pronunciation (R.P.): accent formerly known as BBC English, and one which can provoke discussion of issues such as power and privilege.

Register: a variation in language according to use ('goodbye' at the end of an interview, as opposed to less formal 'cheers, then').

Response partners: pairs of children who will read and comment on each other's work.

Semantics: what signs, particularly word signs, are presumed to *mean*.

Semiotics: the study of the theory of signs, including both pictures and words. The broad field includes pragmatics, semantics and syntactics.

Sentence makers: banks of words on card, which can be slotted onto a display ledge to form a sentence.

Social constructivism: view of language, associated with Bruner and Vygotsky, which emphasises that language development is closely linked with social interaction. In the words of Gordon Wells, children take and *make meaning* from their surrounding world, as they interact with adults and with their peers.

Synchronic analysis: studying the way language is used at one particular time (like now!).

Syntactical Parsing (and analysis): examining the word order in writing and the relationship between words. Syntactics looks at signs and the relationship between signs in the abstract, and contrasts with pragmatics.

Systemic Functional Linguistics: model of language which emphasises the purpose or function that particular pieces of language serve. Theory developed by M. Halliday.

Whole language: the approach to language which treats it as something unified, so that the elements which we call talk, drama, reading, listening, writing, and so on, are all interrelated and inseparable.

Writing corners: places in primary schools, particularly early years classrooms, in which children have all the resources for writing activities.

3. Bibliography:

Adams, C. *et al.* (1976) *The Gender Trap* (London: Virago).

Alexander, R., Rose, Woodhead, C. (1992) *Curriculum Organisation and Classroom Practice in Primary Schools* (London: DfE).

Alexander, R. (1992) *Policy and Practice in Primary Education* (London: Routledge).

Alexander, R., Willcocks, J. and Kinder, S. M. (1989) *Changing Primary Practice* (London: Falmer Press).

Andrews, R., Costello, P., Clarke, S. (1993) *Improving the Quality of Argument* (Hull: University of Hull).

Arnold, R. (1991) *Writing Development* (Milton Keynes: Open University Press).

Askew, S. and Ross, C. (1988) *Boys don't cry: boys and sexism in education* (Milton Keynes: Open University Press).

Baalaam, J. and Merrick, B. (1987) *Exploring Poetry 5-8* (Sheffield: NATE).

Barthes, R. (1953) *Writing Degree Zero* (Translated and published in Britain, 1967) (London: Cape).

Bazalgette, Cary, (ed.) (1989) *Primary Media Education: A Curriculum Statement* (London: B.F.I. Education Department).

Bearne, E. and Farrow, C. (1992) *Writing Policy in Action: the middle years* (Milton Keynes: Open University Press).

Bentley, D. and Rowe, A. (1991) *Group Readings in the Primary School* (Reading: University of Reading).

Benton, M. (1988) *Young Readers Responding to Poems* (London: Routledge).

Bereiter, C. (1980) 'Development in Writing' in L. W. Gregg and E. R. Steinberg (eds.) *Cognitive Processes in Writing* (Hillsdale NJ: Lawrence Erlbaun Associates).

Bereiter, C. and Scardamalia, M. (1987) *The Psychology of Composition* (Hillsdale, N.J: Lawrence Erlbaun Associates).

Bernstein, B. (1964) 'Elaborated and Restricted Codes: their origins and some consequences' in *Ethnography of Speech*, a monograph issue of *American Anthropologist* (March 1964).

Board of Studies (1992) *English K−6: Syllabus and Support Document* (Sydney: New South Wales Board of Studies).

Borba, M. and C. (1982) *Self Esteem: A Classroom affair Volume 2* (London: Winston).

Bottery, M. (1990) 'The Ethics of Participation' in *Curriculum* 11 (1).

Brice Heath, S. (1986) 'Separating "Things of the Imagination" from Life: Learning to Read and Write' in Teale and Sulzby (eds.) (1986) *Emergent Literacy: Writing and Reading* (New Jersey: Ablex Publishing Corporation).

Britton, J.N. (1975a) 'What's the Use?' in A. Wilkinson, *Language and Education* (Oxford: Oxford University Press).

Britton, J. N. *et al.* (1975b) *The Development of Writing Abilities 11−18*, (London: Macmillan).

Britton, J. N. (1978) with Bars, M. and Burgess, T. 'No, No, Jeanette'.

Brooks, G. (1992) 'The Development of Talk from Five to Eleven' in Norman, K. (ed.) (1992)

Browne, A. (1986) *Piggybook* (London: Julia MacRae Books).

Brownjohn, S. (1980) *Does it have to rhyme?* (London: Hodder and Stoughton).

Brownjohn, S. (1982) *What Rhymes with Secret?* (London: Hodder and Stoughton).

Brownjohn, S. (1989) *The Ability to Name Cats* (London: Hodder and Stoughton).

Bruner, J. S. (1985) 'Vygotsky: a historical and conceptual perspective' in J. V. Wertsch, (ed.) (1985) *Culture, Communication and Cognition: Vygotskyan Perspectives* (Cambridge: Cambridge University Press).

Bruner, J. S. (1986) *Actual Minds, Possible Worlds* (Sussex: Harvester Press).

Bruner, J. S. and Haste, H. (eds.) (1987) *Making Sense: The Child's Construction of the World* (London: Methuen).

Bunting, R. and Robinson, R. (1992) *Linc broadsheets: some approaches to talking, writing and reading in Primary Classrooms* (London: Orangebox Editions).

Burgess, A. (1992) *A Mouthful of Air: Language and Languages, especially English* (London: Hutchinson).

Bush, T. (1989) 'School Management Structures — Theory and Practice' in *Educational Management and Administration* **17**.

Calthrop, K. L. and Ede, J. (1984) *Not Daffodils Again — Teaching Poetry 9-13* (York: Longman).

Campbell, R. J. (1985) *Developing the Primary School Curriculum* (London: Holt, Rinehart and Winston).

Campbell, R. J. (1991) 'Curriculum Co-ordinators and the National Curriculum' in Sullivan, M. *Supporting Change and Development in the Primary School* (Harlow: Longman).

Campbell, R. J. (ed.) (1993) *Breadth and Balance in the Primary Curriculum* (London: Falmer Press).

Carlin, E. (1986). 'Writing Development — theory and practice' in Wilkinson, A. (ed.) *The Writing of Writing* (Milton Keynes: Open University Press).

Caron, J. (1992) *An introduction to psycholinguistics* (Sussex: Harvester Wheatsheaf).

Carter, R. (ed.) (1990) *Knowledge about language and the Curriculum* (London: Hodder and Stoughton).

Cato, V., Fernanded, C., Gorman, T., Kispal, A., White, J. (1992) *The Teaching of Initial Literacy* National Foundation for Educational Research.

Cazden, C. B. (1992) *Whole Language Plus* (New York: Teachers College Press).

Chomsky, N. (1959) 'Review of *Verbal Behaviour* by B. F. Skinner' in Language **35**, 26-28.

Chomsky, N. (1965) *Aspects of the Theory of Syntax* (Cambridge, MA: M.I.T. Press).

Clark, J. (1993) *Management in Education.*

Clay, M. (1979) *Reading: the Patterning of Complex Behaviour* (London: Heinemann).

Collins (1988) *No More Butts: Tobacco and Smoking* (London: Collins).

Cook, G. (1989) *Discourse* (Oxford: Oxford University Press).

Corson, D. (1990) *Language Policy Across the Curriculum* (Clevedon: Multilingual Matters).

Crystal, D. (1987) *The Cambridge Encyclopaedia of Language* (Cambridge: Cambridge University Press).

Czerniewska, P. (1992) *Learning about Writing* (Oxford: Blackwell).

Davies, Y. (1986) *Picture Stories* (London: British Film Institute).

Day, C. Whitaker, P. and Johnston, D. (1990) *Managing Primary Schools in the 1990's* (London: Paul Chapman Publishing).

Dearing, R. (1993) *The National Curriculum and its Assessment* (London: SCAA).

Delamont, S. (1990) *Sex Roles and the School* (London: Routledge).

DES (1975) *A Language for Life* (London: HMSO).

DES (1978) Primary Education in England: A Survey by HM Inspectors of Schools (London: HMSO).

DES (1988) *Report of the Committee of Enquiry into the teaching of English*, (London: HMSO).

DES (1989a) *English For Ages 5 to 16*, (London: HMSO).

DES (1989b) 'Non-statutory guidance: Translating Planning into Practice' in *English in The National Curriculum* (London: Central Office of Information).

DES (1990) *Aspects of Primary Education: The Teaching and Learning of Language and Literacy* (London: HMSO).

Dewey, J. (1933) *How We Think: A Restatement of the Relation of Reflective Thinking to the Educative Process*

Dixon, J. (1967) *Growth through English* (Oxford: Oxford University Press).

Dixon, J. (1987) 'The Question of Genres' in Reid, I. (ed.), 1987 *The Place of Genre in Learning* (Australia: Centre for Studies in Literacy Education, Deakin University).

Doughty, P. (1971) *Language in Use* (London: London University Press).

Dougill, P. and Knott, R. (1988) *The Primary Language Book* (Milton Keynes: Open University Press).

Durkin, K. (ed.) (1986) *Language Development in the School Years* (London: Croom Helm).

Edmonds, W. (1992) *The Puffin Book of Spelling Puzzles* (London: Penguin).

Elkin, S. (1992) 'Borrowed from a giant book' *The Independent*, 19 November 1992.

Essex Education and Library Service (1991) *Book Policy in the Primary School* (Essex: Longman).

Falkner, K. (1991) *Emergent Writing; how do children learn?* (unpublished school-linked study, Rolle Faculty of Education Polytechnic South West, 1991).

Fine, A. (1991) *Bill's New Frock* (Harmondsworth: Penguin).

Fisher, R. (1992) *Early Literacy and the Teacher* (London: Hodder and Stoughton).

Flender, M. G. (1985) 'Children's Literature' in *Education* **16** (2).

Fox, C. (1983) 'Talking like a book': Young children's oral monologues' in Meek, M. (ed). *Opening Moves: Work in progress in the study of Children's Language*

202

Development (Bedford Way Papers, 17, London: University of London Institute of Education).

Fox, C. (1984) 'Learning from children learning from home' *Language Matters 2* (London: Centre for Language Primary Education, ILEA).

Fox, C. (1988) "Poppies will make them grant" in Meek and Mills (eds.) (1988) *Language and Literacy in the Primary Years* (Lewes: Falmer Press).

Fox, G. and Merrick, B. (1981) 'Thirty-six things to do with a Poem' *The Times Education Supplement* (20 February 1981).

Galloway, D. (1985) *Schools, Pupils and Special Educational Needs* (London: Croom Helm).

Galton, M. (1989) *Teaching in the Primary School* (London: David Fulton).

Garton, A., and Pratt, C. (1989) *Learning to be Literate: The Development of Spoken and Written Language* (Oxford: Blackwell).

Gawith, G. (1990) *Reading Alive* (London: A and C Black).

Gentry, J. R. (1987) *Spel....... is a four letter word* (London: Heinemann).

Ghaye, T. Johnstone, E. and Jones, J. (1992) *Assessment and the Management of Learning* (Leamington Spa: Scholastic).

Gipps, C., Gross, H. and Goldstein, H. (1987) *Warnock's Eighteen Percent Children with Special Needs in the Primary School*

Goodman, K. (1986) *What's Whole in Whole Language?* (Portsmouth, NH: Heinemann Educational Books).

Gorman, T. *et al.* (1988) *Language Performances in Schools: Review of APU Language Monitoring 1979-1983* (London: HMSO).

Goswami, U. (1992) *Analogical Reasoning in Children* (London: Lawrence Erlbaum).

Graves, D. H. (1983) *Writing: Teachers and Children at Work* (London: Heinemann Educational Books).

Gurney, P. W. (1988) *Self-Esteem in children with Special Educational Needs* (London: Routledge).

Hackman, S. *et al.* (1993) 'Strategies for supporting bilingual learning' in *NATE News* (Spring).

Hall, N. (1987) *The Emergence of Literacy* (London: Hodder and Stoughton).

Halliday, M. A. K. (1973) *Explorations in the Functions of Language* (London: Edward Arnold).

Halliday, M. A. K. (1975) *Learning How to Mean* (London: Edward Arnold).

Halliday, M. (1989) *Spoken and Written Language* (Oxford: Oxford University Press).

Halstead, M. (1991) 'Individual Rights and the Common Good: Some Dilemmas for Policy-makers in Multi-lingual Britain', Paper presented at Seminar on Multi-lingual Teaching, Moscow.

Harris, M. (1992) *Language Experience and Early Language Development: from input to uptake* (London: Lawrence Erlbaum).

Howe, A. and Johnson, J. (1992) *Common Bonds: Storyteling in the Classroom* (London: Hodder and Stoughton).

Johnston, B. (1987) *Assessing English: Helping students to Reflect on their Work* (Buckingham: Open University Press).

203

Jones, K. (1992) *English in the National Curriculum* (London: Bedford Way Papers, University of London Institute of Education)

Kelly, A. V. (1990) *The National Curriculum: A Critical Review* (London: Paul Chapman).

Kemp, G. (1977) *The Turbulent Term of Tyke Tyler* (London: Faber and Faber).

Kolb, D. A., Rubin, I. M. and McIntyre (1979) *Organisational Psychology: an experiential approach* (Eaglewood Cliffs, NJ: Prentice Hall).

Kroll, B. M. and Wells, C. G. (1983) *Explorations in the Development of Writing* (Chichester: John Wiley).

Lane, S. M. and Kemp, M. (1967) *An Approach to Creative Writing in the Primary School* (London: Blackie).

Language and Gender Working Party (1985) *Alice in Genderland* (Sheffield: NATE).

Laverty, M. (1986) 'Are You a Draft Dodger' *Gnosis* March 1986

Leavis, F. R. and Thompson, D. (1933) *Culture and Environment.*

LINC (unpublished) *Language in the National Curriculum: Materials for Professional Development.*

Linguistic Minorities Project (1985) *The Other Languages of England* (London: Routledge and Kegan Paul).

Lodge, S. (unpublished) *The Practicality of Simulation computer programs as valid educational tools, with specific regard to productive group work* (1992 dissertation, Rolle Faculty of Education, University of Plymouth).

Lutrario, C. (1990) *Hooked on books* (London: Harcourt Brace Jovanovich).

Maclure, M. (1992) 'The First Five Years' in Norman, K. (ed.) (1992).

Macnamara, J. (1972) 'Cognitive basis of language learning in infants' *Psychological Review*, 79, 1-13.

Mallett, M. (1992) *Making Facts Matter: Reading Non-Fiction 5-11* (London: Paul Chapman Ltd).

Martin, J. R., Christie, F. and Rothery J. (1987) *Social Processes in Education: A reply to Sawyer and Watson (and others)* in Reid, I. (ed.) *The Place of Genre in Learning* (Australia: Centre for Studies in Literary Education, Deakin University).

Mason, H. and Mudd, S. (1992) 'Fact on Fiction' in *Junior Focus*, 65 (London: Scholastic Publications).

Mason, M., Mason, R. and Quayle, A. (1992) 'Illuminating English: how explicit language teaching improved public examination results in a comprehensive school', *Educational Studies*, 18, (3).

Meek, M. (1991) 'The Child, the Book and Television: Television and Early Literacy' in *Books for Your Children*, 26, (3).

Meek, M. and Mills, C. (eds.) (1988) *Language and Literacy in the Primary Years* (Lewes: Falmer Press).

Merrick, B. (1991) *Exploring Poetry 8-13* (Sheffield: NATE).

Minns, H. (1991) *Language, Literacy and Gender* (London: Hodder and Stoughton).

Mittins, B. (1991a) 'Does Spelling Matter?' in NATE News Spring 1991.

Mittins, B. (1991b) *Language Awareness for Teachers* (Buckingham: Open

204

University Press).

Mittins, B. (1993) *Letter to the authors* 9 5 93.

Moffett, J. (1968) *Teaching the Universe of Discourse* (New York: Houghton Mifflin).

Moon, C. (1988) 'Reading: Where are We Now?' in Meek and Mills.

Moon, C. (1992) *Feelings* (Reading: Reading and Language Information Centre).

Moore, P., and Tweddle, S. (1992) *The integrated classroom: language, learning and I.T.* (London: Hodder and Stoughton).

Moyles, J. R. (1991) *Organizing for Learning in the Primary Classroom: a balanced approach to classroom management* (Buckingham: Open University Press).

National Writing Project (1989) *Becoming a Writer* (London: Nelson).

National Writing Project (1990a) *A Rich Resource: Writing and Language Diversity* (London: Nelson).

National Writing Project (1990b) *Ways of Looking: Issues Arising from the National Writing Project* (London: Nelson).

National Writing Project (1990c) *What are Writers Made Of? Issues of gender and Writing* (London: Nelson).

NCC (1990) *Curriculum Guidance 3: The Whole Curriculum* (York: NCC).

NCC (1993a) *Consultation report: English in the National Curriculum* (York: NCC).

NCC (1993b) *'Special Needs and the National Curriculum: Opportunity and Challenge'* (York: NCC).

Nene College of Higher Education (1991) *Equal Opportunities Policy Statement* (Nene: Northampton).

Neville, M. (1988) *Assessing and Teaching Language: Literacy and Oracy in Schools* (Basingstoke: Macmillan).

Nias, J. (1989a) *Primary Teachers Talking* (London: Routledge).

Nias, J., Southworth, G. and Yeomans, R. (1989b) *Staff Relationships in the Primary School* (London: Cassell).

Nias, J., Southworth, G. and Campbell, P. (1992) *Whole School Curriculum Development in the Primary School* (London: Falmer Press).

Norman, K. (ed.) 1992 *Thinking Voices* (London: Hodder and Stoughton).

Packwood, T. (1989) 'Return to the Hierarchy' in *Education Management and Administration*, **17** (British Educational and Management Society).

Payton, S. (1984) 'Developing Awareness of Print: a young child's first steps towards literacy' in *Education Review Offset Publication*, **2** (Birmingham: University of Birmingham).

Peel, R. W. (1992) 'Reading and Writing the SATS' in *Reading*, **26**, (2).

Pendergast, M. (1993) *For God, country and Coca-Cola: The Unauthorised History of the World's Most Popular Soft Drink* (Weidenfeld and Nicholson).

Perera, K. (1984) *Children's Reading and Writing* (Oxford: Blackwell).

Perera, K. (1990) 'Grammatical Differentiation between Speech and Writing in Children aged 8 to 12' in Carter, R. (1990) *Knowledge about Language*

and the Curriculum: The LINC Reader (London: Hodder and Stoughton).
Piaget, J. (1926) The Language and Thought of the Child (New York: Basic Books).
Piaget, J. (1953) The Origins of Intelligence in the Child (London: Routledge Kegan Paul).
Pollard, A. and Tann, S. (1987) Reflective Teaching in the Primary School (London: Cassell).
Redfern, A. (1992) 'Spelling it Out' The Times Educational Supplement (12 June 1992).
Redfern, A. and Edwards, V. (1992) How Schools Teach Reading (Reading: Reading and Language Information Centre).
Richmond, J. (1990) 'What do we mean by knowledge about language?' in The North Circular: the Magazine of the North London Consortium (London: Language in the National Curriculum Project).
Rosen, M. (1989) Did I Hear You Write? (London: Andre Deutsch).
Rosenblatt, L. (1978) The Reader, the Text, the Poem: the transactional theory of the literary work (Carbondale: South Illinois University Press).
Sawyer, W. and Watson, K. (1989) English Teaching from A-Z (Buckingham: Open University Press).
S.C.A.A. (1993), School Assessment Folder: Key Stage 1 (London: HMSO).
Schein, E. H. (1985) Organizational Culture and Leadership (San Francisco: Jossey-Bass).
Schon, D. A. (1983) The Reflective Practitioner (London: Temple Smith).
S.E.A.C. (1992) Children's Work Assessed (London: Central Office of Information/HMSO).
Smith, F. (1982) Writing and the Writer (London: Heinemann).
Somekh, B. (1991) 'Learning Autonomy' in Electronics Education (Spring).
Southgate, V. et al. (1991) Extending Beginning Reading (London: Heinemann).
Spencer, M. (1986) 'Emergent Literacies: a site for analysis' in Language Arts, 63 (5).
Stephens, J. (1992) Language and Ideology in Children's Fiction (London: Longman).
Straker, A. (1989) Children Using Computers (Oxford: Blackwell).
Stratta, Dixon and Wilkinson (1974) Patterns of Language
Strickland, S. (1992) 'Holiday reading attracts children back to the classroom' The Independent, 19 August 1992.
Styles, M. (ed.) (1989) Collaboration and Writing (Milton Keynes: Open University Press).
Swann Report (1985) Education for all (London: HMSO).
Tabor, D. C. (1991) Curriculum Continuity in English and the National Curriculum (London: Falmer Press).
Tabor, D. (1992) 'Bridging the Dividing Line' in Junior Education, 16 (6).
Tann, S. (1991) Developing Language in the Primary Classroom (London: Cassell).
Tizard, B. and Hughes, M. (1984) Young Children Learning (London: Fontana).

206

Turner, M. (1990) *Sponsored Reading Failure* (Warlingham, Surrey: IPSET Education Unit).

Vygotsky, L. (1962) *Thought and Language* (Cambridge, MA: MIT Press).

Vygotsky, L. S. (1967) *Thought and Language* (Cambridge, MA: MIT Press).

Walker, S. (1992) *How it Looks* (Reading: Reading and Language Information Centre).

Warham, S. (1993), *Primary Teaching and the Negotiation of Power* (London: Paul Chapman).

Washtell, A. (unpublished) 'Reading in the Early Years' Talk given at Mary Ward House, Tavistock Place, London, 7 February 1991.

Wells, G. (1985a) *Language, Learning and Education* (Windsor: NFER Nelson).

Wells, G. (1985b) *Language Development in the Pre School Years* (Cambridge: Cambridge University Press).

Wells, G. (1986) *The Meaning Makers* (Sevenoaks: Hodder and Stoughton).

Wells, G. and Nicholls J. (eds.) (1985) *Language and Learning: an interactional perspective* (London: Falmer Press).

Wells, G., and Gen Ling Chang (1986) 'From Speech to Writing: some evidence on the relationship between oracy and writing' in Wilkinson (1986).

Whitehead, M. R. (1990) *Language and Literacy in the Early Years* (London: Paul Chapman).

Whyte, J. (1983) *Beyond the Wendy House: sex role stereotyping in Primary Schools* (London: Longman).

Wilkinson, A. *et al.* (1980) *Assessing Language Development* (Oxford: Oxford University Press).

Wilkinson, A. *et al.* (1980) 'The Development of Writing' in *English in Education*, **14** (3).

Wilkinson, A. (ed.) (1986) *The Writing of Writing* (Milton Keynes: Open University Press).

Wilkinson, A. (1971) *The Foundations of Language: Talking and Reading in Young Children* (Oxford: Oxford University Press).

Wilson, C. (1980) *The Language Abilities Test* (Melbourne: Heinemann).

Wilson, J. H. (unpublished) 'A Study of the Use of Computer Assisted Learning with Children with Severe Learning Difficulties (School-linked Study, Rolle Faculty of Education, University of Plymouth).

Wray, D. (ed.) (1988) *Developing Children's Writing* (Leamington Spa: Scholastic Publications).

Wray, D. and Gallimore, J. (1986) 'Drafting in the Classroom' in *Primary Teaching Studies*, **1**, (3).

Wray, D. and Medwell, J. (1991) *Literacy and Language in the Primary Years* (London: Routledge).

Young, P. and Tyre, C. (1986) *Dyslexia or Illiteracy* (Milton Keynes: Open University Press).

INDEX

adult learning, 11
Ahlberg, J. and A., 74
Alexander, R., xi, 15, 20
Andrews, R., 77
argument, 77
assessments
− purpose of, 179
Bakhtin, M., vii
Bazalgette, C., 168
beginner readers, 89
Bernstein, B., 75, 76
Big Books, 92
bilingualism, 141
− support for, 142
Bottery, M., 27
Brice Heath, S., 89
Britton, J., 33
Browne, A., 114
Bruner, J., x
budget handling, 184
Bullock Report, 3
Campbell, R., 15, 23
Carlin, E., 115
Cazden, C., x, 20
change
− management of, 59
Chomsky, N., 69, 159, 162, 163
circle activities, 51
Clay, M., 97, 148
codes and registers, 75
collaborative talk, 76
community involvement, 55
conferencing, 63
Cox Report, vi, 64
cross curricular language, 33
cross phase language, 54
dance − drama, 52
Derrida, J., 33
Dewey, J., xiii
Dixon, J., 109
drama
− policy, 49
− and role-play, 47

emergent literacy, 85
emergent writing, 113−121
equality
− assurance in English, 137
Fine, A., 149
flash cards, 93
Foucault, M., vii
freeze frame, 52
gender and language, 148
genre/context in writing, 128
Goodman, K., 32
grammar, 162
Graves, D., 32
Halliday, M., 33
Halstead, M., 139−141
handwriting, 121−124
information books, 99
information technology and
    language, 35−47
− special needs, 46
− gender & bilingualism, 45
− resources, 191
Kingman Report, 32
knowledge about language, 164
language
− and power, 152
− development, 158
language leader
− changing role, 27
− role of, 15−16
language research, 159
language terms, 195
leadership −
across the phases, 30
− check list, 17−18
− planning across the curriculum, 30
− working together, 7
− reflection and analysis, 1−2
library
− school, 186−7
LINC, 2, 158
linguistic diversity, 139−141
linguistics, 156−160

literacy, 85
management
– of the National Curriculum, x–xiii
– and the team, 8
– and yourself, 8
media education, 167
Michael, I., 85
miscue analysis, 179
Mittins, B., 121
models of English, vi
Moffatt, J., x
Moon, C., 85
multilingualism, 141, 143, 144
NATE, 186
National Oracy Project, 64
National Writing Project, 107, 108, 110, 128
Newbolt Report, 3
Nias, J., 23, 24
parental involvement, 55
parental liaison, 17
Payton, K., 85
pedagogy and language, vii–x
Perera, K., 111
performances in school, 174
phonics, 93
Piaget, J., x, xiii, 159
planning, 9
Plowden Report, 3
poetry, 130–133
print awareness, 90
psycholinguistics, 167
reading
– advanced skills, 100
– intervention, 89
– learning to, 85–87
– listening to, 95
– recovery, 96, 97
– schemes, 81, 94
record keeping, 177–178
records of achievement, 180
reference section, 193
registers and codes, 75
reprographics, 186
revised orders, 144, 145
Richmond, J., 164

Rosen, H., 106
Rosen, M., 114
Rosenblatt, L., 97
running record, 179
scaffolding, viii, ix
Schon, D. A., viii
self assessment, 180
shared reading, 91
Sidney, Sir Philip, 130
skills – co-ordination, 12
Smith, F., 32
sociologists, 162
speaking and writing, 78
special educational needs, 146–148
specific learning difficulties, 97
spelling
– strategies, 124–127
– tests, 127
standardised tests, 181
story-telling, 73–74
study skills, 101
Swann Report, 142
tableaux and freeze frame, 52
Tabor, D., 57
talk
– early years, 66–68
– policy on, 79
– stages of, 65
television and reading, 84
Turner, M., 93
Vonnegut, K., 64
Vygotsky, L., x, 65
Warnock Report, 146
Wells, G., 163
Whitehead, M., 166
whole language, 81
working together
– whole school, 22–25
writers
– in school, 174
– reluctant, 121
writing
– advanced skills, 133
– audience, 109–111
– developmental stages, 113–117
– purpose of, 103–109